D0213607

*Decolonization and the Evolution
of International Human Rights*

Pennsylvania Studies in Human Rights

Bert B. Lockwood, Jr., Series Editor

A complete list of books in the series is available from the publisher.

Decolonization

and the Evolution
of International Human Rights

Roland Burke

PENN

UNIVERSITY OF PENNSYLVANIA PRESS

PHILADELPHIA

Copyright © 2010 University of Pennsylvania Press

All rights reserved. Except for brief quotations used for purposes of review or scholarly citation, none of this book may be reproduced in any form by any means without written permission from the publisher.

Published by
University of Pennsylvania Press
Philadelphia, Pennsylvania 19104-4112

Printed in the United States of America on acid-free paper
10 9 8 7 6 5 4 3 2 1

Library of Congress Cataloging-in-Publication Data
Burke, Roland.
  Decolonization and the evolution of international human rights / Roland Burke.
    p.   cm. — (Pennsylvania studies in human rights)
    ISBN 978-0-8122-4219-5 (alk. paper)
    Includes bibliographical references and index.
    1. Human rights. 2. Decolonization. I. Title.
JC571.B85   2010
323—dc22   2009029042

Contents

Introduction
The Politics of Decolonization and the Evolution of the International Human Rights Project

the "backward" countries are in revolt! . . . [Eleanor Roosevelt] thinks that it is
a revolt of the dark skinned people against the white. It is more than that.
                        —*John Humphrey, Director of the Human Rights Division,*
                        7 and 24 November 1950

On 10 December 1948, an overwhelming majority of states adopted
the Universal Declaration of Human Rights in a momentous night session of the United Nations General Assembly. It was the culmination
of nearly three years of intensive debate, negotiation, and far-reaching
philosophical inquiry. The final text drew on more than fifty constitutions, countless written submissions, and the religious and moral traditions of every major belief system in existence. Among the delegations
that delivered their assent were those from Afghanistan, Egypt, Taiwan,
India, Pakistan, Liberia, Lebanon, Thailand, and the Philippines. Only
the communist bloc, apartheid South Africa, and Saudi Arabia with-
held their endorsement. Not without reason did the UN proclaim the
declaration "a common standard of achievement for all peoples and all
nations." For the fifty-eight-member General Assembly, it was an auspicious beginning to its mission to promote human rights around the
globe.

This is the story of what happened after the passage of the Universal
Declaration, as those fifty-eight members were joined by another fifty-
eight, and then almost fifty-eight again, becoming a truly global General
Assembly. Between 1950 and 1979, the process of decolonization trans-
formed the UN and the shape of human rights discourse. The Asian,
African, and Arab states that coalesced into the self-conscious "Third
World" brought a powerful new set of voices to those of 1948. These
Third World diplomats made pivotal contributions to some of the most

significant events in the UN human rights project. Their arguments shifted debates that determined the universality of rights. Their votes shaped the two most authoritative instruments of human rights law, the International Covenants. Their activism led to individuals from across the world having petitions heard by a UN that once filed them away in secret. Above all, their very presence was an essential prerequisite to any genuine claim of legislating on behalf of all peoples and all nations, as the assembly had so famously done in the Universal Declaration.

This study seeks to add another dimension to the history of the international struggle for human rights. Through each of these landmarks in the evolution of the UN, I will argue for the central importance of Arab, Asian, and African participation. The impact of these states in the development of the rights program was at least as important as that of the Western democracies, the Soviet bloc, and the ever-growing constellation of NGOs. While the effects of the Cold War and the rise of international civil society have been documented by an impressive array of scholars, the revolutionary influence of decolonization has yet to be fully explored in human rights history.

Yet the importance of the nascent Third World was striking from the earliest moments of UN activity. Less than two years after the 1948 vote, John Humphrey, the first director of the Human Rights Division, was expressing alarm at the rise of a confident group of Arab and Asian delegates. "The 'backward' countries are in revolt!" he declared in his diary in November 1950.[1] Eleanor Roosevelt and Charles Malik, major figures in the creation of the Universal Declaration, observed the same phenomenon. Well before the high point of decolonization, the emerging Third World voice had already begun to transform the human rights project.

Within academic literature, a number of scholars have recovered the role of Arab and Asian diplomats in these foundational years. Mary Ann Glendon, Susan Waltz, Paul Gordon Lauren, and Kenneth Cmiel have illuminated the work of key Third World figures in the UN human rights program in the late 1940s and early 1950s.[2] Most of these studies terminate in the immediate aftermath of the Universal Declaration, long before decolonization's impact was fully apparent. They cover a small chronological range that predates the principal era of Third World activism and so deal with only the earliest period of Third World participation. The years in which decolonization virtually remade the UN, between the late 1950s and mid-1970s, have paradoxically received the least attention.

This study will shed light on those vital years and forgotten voices that have been missing from human rights historiography. It is the first historical account of the influence of decolonization on the UN human rights program, and surveys the three decades in which the anticolonial movement radically altered the human rights agenda. Through its expansive chronological scope, it seeks to show the outcomes of Third World participation, and how Arab, Asian, and African approaches to international human rights changed over time. Using UN transcripts, archives, and the personal papers of key historical actors, it provides a detailed narrative of decolonization's effects on thirty years of UN human rights debates, and a dedicated analysis of the Third World's crucial position in human rights diplomacy.

The first chapter investigates the place of human rights at the founding moment of the Third World, at the 1955 Asian-African Conference in Bandung. It explores the relationship between anticolonial nationalism and individual rights, and the enthusiasm with which the decolonized states embraced the concept of universality. At Bandung, human rights were both a central feature of the political vocabulary and the source of serious debate. When communist China challenged the legitimacy of the Universal Declaration, it was forced into an embarrassing retreat by the smaller Arab, Asian, and African states present, which demanded the declaration's recognition by the conference Final Communiqué.

In Chapter 2, rights and nationalism are discussed in relation to the campaign for a right to self-determination. The self-determination debates reveal the competing tendencies within anticolonialism, and the tension between the struggle for sovereignty and the struggle for rights. The right to self-determination campaign began with two strands, one that exalted sovereignty for its own sake, and one that claimed it as a means to individual freedom. For a decade, these two antagonistic facets of anticolonialism coexisted, until gradually one began to take precedence over the other, consuming it entirely in the 1960s.

Chapters 3 and 4 assess the stunning political shifts of the 1960s, which followed African decolonization and the proliferation of authoritarian regimes across both Asia and Africa. The impact of these changes on one of the most important UN debates, that on the right to petition, is the focus of Chapter 3. Beginning in the late 1940s, Arab and Asian delegates were among the most passionate advocates of a right for victims of human rights abuses to petition the UN. Their campaign failed, obstructed by both the Soviet bloc and the Western states. Ironically, the struggle for the right to petition met with much greater success in the 1960s, when the majority of Third World states were ruled by authoritarian regimes that jealously guarded their sovereignty.

Chapter 4 measures the cumulative effects of decolonization, as exemplified by the First World Conference on Human Rights, held in Tehran in April 1968. Two decades after the adoption of the Universal Declaration, the political rights once embraced by anticolonial nationalists at

Bandung were subject to unprecedented attack. Development, modernization, and armed liberation struggle were elevated as the tenets of a
disturbing new human rights platform. A confident Afro-Asian majority
dominated the proceedings, and sidelined the two superpowers in the
process. In response to the Third World assault on traditional human
rights, the Western democracies reacted defensively and abandoned
promotion of ideas that supposedly defined their political systems.

Chapter 5 traces the provenance of cultural relativist claims in UN
discourse, and the rise of this relativist ideology in the rhetoric of Third
World diplomacy in the 1970s. During the late 1940s and throughout the 1950s, Afro-Asian delegates were the most vocal champions
of universality. They made strident demands for universal application
of rights a key plank in the attack on colonialism, while the colonial
powers responded with well-crafted arguments about the essential cultural differences of their overseas territories. Yet in the late 1960s this
universalist position began a precipitous reversal, coincident with the
spread of authoritarian governments in Asia and Africa. The 1970s saw
the virtual abandonment of universality in a profoundly undemocratic
UN. Unlike the first wave of nationalist leaders, these governments denounced human rights as a Western imposition, and emphasized the
need for different rights in Third World countries. The most extreme
among them rejected the very possibility of universal human rights.
Universality, unimpeachably anticolonial in the 1950s, was rendered
deeply suspect by the 1980s.

Three main arguments run through this book. First, it argues for
the primacy of decolonization as a political force in the evolution of the
UN human rights agenda, refuting the assertion that rights were formulated exclusively by the West. Second, it elucidates the multidimensional
nature of anticolonialism and its relationship to individual rights, con-
testing the claim that human rights were little more than a rhetorical
weapon for lambasting the Western democracies. Finally, it challenges
orthodox assumptions about the overall outcome of decolonization for
the human rights program, which have been polarized between those
who laud the Third World contribution and those who perceive it as
highly detrimental or even disastrous.

Academic experts and East Asian political leaders alike have questioned the very existence of a Third World role in the human rights
program. Politicians such as former Singaporean Senior Minister Lee
Kuan Yew and former Malaysian Prime Minister Mahathir Mohamed
have dismissed human rights law as dominated by the West. In July 1997,
Mahathir demanded a review of the Universal Declaration, dismissing it
as the product of negotiation between "superpowers which did not understand the needs of poor countries."[3] Kenyan human rights commen-

tator Makau Mutua has written that "the levers of power at the United Nations and other international lawmaking forums" were "out of the reach of the Third World."[4]

Contrary to Mutua's lamentation and the polemics of Mahathir and Lee, I contend that Third World actors were principal arbiters of power in the human rights program almost from its inception. This was not just a corollary of numerical superiority; the power of Third World diplomats was manifest well before decolonization had made their ranks a majority. For almost three decades, the situation in the UN was precisely the opposite of that claimed by Mutua. The levers of power were frequently operated by Arab, Asian, and African delegations. Assertions of Third World impotence would come as a surprise to both Western and Soviet foreign service officers who spent much of their time reacting to Afro-Asian bloc initiatives, and to members of the UN Secretariat, who spent their careers resigned to Third World dominance.

Among scholars of both imperialism and human rights, the status of anticolonialism as a human rights cause has also been sharply criticized. Brian Simpson, in his impressive history of human rights and the end of the British Empire, has argued that "the anti-colonial movement was not in essence a human rights movement" because "its primary aim was not to reduce the power of the state over the individual," that being the defining characteristic of all human rights activism.[5] This view has been amplified by Reza Afshari in a groundbreaking article that proposes a radical revision of the canonical set of human rights campaigns, with anticolonialism a prominent deletion from the list.[6]

These critiques are properly skeptical of colonial nationalist invocations of human rights, but they are too dismissive of the genuine optimism with which Third World diplomats approached the human rights question, especially in the 1950s. The relationship of rights and anticolonialism combined both political self-interest and natural ideological affinity. Instrumental use of human rights in anticolonial politics was certainly a feature of UN debates, as exemplified by some of the unlikely proponents of universality during the drafting of the two covenants. Equally, there were representatives like Hansa Mehta (India) and Salvador López (Philippines) who were at least as consistent as their Western counterparts. These figures were no more cynical in their use of human rights than the great Western icons of the early UN program.

Most fundamentally of all, scholarship on the role of the Third World is divided between those who view decolonization as generally beneficial to the development of international human rights and those highly critical of its results. Among the leading proponents of the more positive view is Paul Gordon Lauren. Lauren has extolled the commitment to human rights that supposedly characterized the foreign policy of African, Asian, and Arab states, which ensured that human rights was elevated "high on the global agenda" after World War II.[7] By contrast, eminent international law expert Louis Henkin has described the politics of decolonization as nothing short of a disaster for human rights. "The struggle to end colonialism," he has asserted, "also swallowed up the original purpose of cooperation for promotion of human rights."[8]

Neither of these positions has fully captured the complex and contradictory constellation of outcomes that followed decolonization. The politics of anticolonialism both advanced and obstructed the progress of international human rights. In some areas, the Third World's role was undoubtedly positive. It confronted European colonialism and Western racism and demanded the recognition of universal human rights. In others, such as the right of petition, the results were less clear. A number of Arab, Asian, and African diplomats pioneered efforts to recognize individual petitions, while others worked tirelessly to prevent them. Given the diversity of the Afro-Asian bloc and the changing political complexion of the states that constituted it, the consequences of decolonization were inevitably complicated and unpredictable. Their significance, however, was unmistakable.

Explaining the Influence of the Third World in the Human Rights Program

Decolonization's impact on the UN human rights program was disproportionately great compared to other areas of the organization. The UN Third Committee, which dealt with human rights, was viewed as an environment where Third World states could vote as they pleased, without significant consequences for their security or that of the Western democracies. Heavy criticism of the Western powers was permissible, even desirable, in human rights debates, while far less dissent was possible in those involving traditional Cold War politics and security concerns. Negative Western attitudes regarding the status and value of the human rights program greatly magnified the influence of the Third World delegations.

Robert Quentin-Baxter, who represented New Zealand in both the General Assembly and the Commission on Human Rights, has argued that the Third Committee was a forum that afforded much greater independence to the smaller countries outside the political West. In the security and political organs, the West had allies. But as Baxter observed, "in the Third Committee the situation was different."[9]

This Committee was, after all, dealing with the realm of theory and there were seldom any immediate practical consequences of decisions taken. Therefore it was much easier for Asian and Latin American countries, in particular, to express their own fervent dislike of colonialism and their strong identification with anti-colonialist forces.

For many Western policy makers and diplomats, Quentin-Baxter observed, "the only comfort was a shallow belief that things decided in the Third Committee did not really matter."[10]

John Humphrey, director of the Human Rights Division, attributed the chaotic nature of the Third Committee to the unique opportunity it presented to smaller, non-Western states. Writing in January 1952 after another frustrating series of deliberations on the human rights covenants, Humphrey reflected on the emerging dynamics of the Third Committee. The special influence accorded to the small states was, he argued, a major factor in why human rights debates were "so hard to conduct."[11]

It is easier for small delegations to play an important role in a committee which is not ostensibly dealing with the great issues that divide the communist and non-communist world. In the First and Ad Hoc committees the small countries must be kept in line, in the Third all inhibitions disappear.

Human rights were one of the only topics on which the Third World diplomats could express an independent opinion, with little fear of Western or Soviet pressure. It was an opportunity that many embraced.

Western states were content to cede leadership in the human rights program in exchange for solidarity in Cold War security matters elsewhere in the UN, which were accorded much greater priority. Human rights debates were perceived as superfluous to real international diplomacy. Defeats in the Third Committee and Commission on Human Rights were to be taken with equanimity. After all, these losses on human rights issues facilitated victories in the more important political and security bodies, according to the State Department report on the 1952 session of the Third Committee:

The determination of the Arab-Asian and Latin American groups to write their aspirations and grievances into resolutions, and, more important, into treaties will create even greater difficulties next year. It seems likely that, for the foreseeable future, our delegation will continue to be in the minority on many important issues in this Committee. In view of the overriding need of keeping the delegations of the free world united so far as possible in the Political Committees, the Delegation will have to be content to take occasional defeats in the Third Committee, and take them as graciously as possible.[12]

The Third Committee, argued the 1952 report, operated primarily "as a safety valve by which the representatives of the smaller countries, which follow the United States in the two Political Committees, let off steam."[13] It advised that the U.S. should remain quiescent in human rights debates, which were both peripheral and futile. It was "essential" to "avoid undue pressure in trying to sell our causes, especially our lost causes."[14]

As early as 1950, Asian, Arab, and Latin American states had seized the initiative on human rights matters, capitalizing on the policy of neglect pursued by the Western powers. Even before African decolonization, when the influx of new states made Third World dominance almost inevitable, the Western states pursued a strategy that cultivated Arab and Asian assertiveness. According to Humphrey, the emergence of Third World leadership was predicated on carefully studied inaction on the part of the West. "Because they have not been willing to accept their responsibility," Humphrey wrote in his diary, "the logical leaders in the U.N. battle for human rights have lost leadership in the Third Committee to certain demagogic forces."[15] By December 1951, he feared that "the whole human rights program" had been jeopardized, with the Western democratic countries "themselves largely to blame for what has happened."[16] According to Humphrey, if the West had "provided some really dynamic leadership there would have been no vacuum which the little demagogues rushed to fill."

Charles Malik, the Lebanese philosopher who had played a central role in the success of the Universal Declaration, also lamented the absence of Western leadership. In June 1949, after the defeat of a proposal to study allegations of human rights abuse, Malik questioned why Britain and the U.S. had failed to take a "bolder lead."[17] Malik was wrong. They had, in fact, led the opposition, along with the Soviet Union. By May 1950, his public criticisms were considerably harsher. Interviewed on radio with Eleanor Roosevelt, he urged the West to take a more positive approach to the UN program. He gently rebuked Roosevelt's intonations for caution, "to go slowly and to be careful" because of the special needs of the "great powers." Unimpressed by caution, he pressed for Western leadership. "You've got to move faster," Malik declared, "you've got to lead the rest of the field more than you have been doing so far."[18] More ominously, he highlighted the consequences of continued somnolence on the part of the great Western democracies. "If you don't lead the rest of the world, there are others who will lead it."[19]

During the pivotal decade of the 1950s, when the two human rights covenants were being drafted, diplomats from the most powerful Western democracy sat in silence while the debate proceeded around them. Conceived as the successors to the 1948 Universal Declaration, the covenants dominated the human rights agenda for more than fifteen years.

Yet following the campaign of U.S. Senator John Bricker, who sought an amendment to restrict the president's treaty making powers, Secretary of State John Foster Dulles withdrew American support from the covenants in 1953. Dulles then instructed the State Department not to participate in covenant debates. The consequences were predictably corrosive for American influence in the human rights program. In its report from the 1957 General Assembly, four years after Dulles's decision was put into effect, the U.S. delegation complained that their instructions demanded a "position [that] is defensive or passive" for "almost two-thirds of the time of the Committee."[20] Under orders not to participate, the U.S. representation mournfully "sits in silence for approximately half the Committee session and raises its hand only to abstain when votes are taken."[21]

As they witnessed their growing irrelevance, these U.S. diplomats pleaded for a change in instructions relating to the covenants, which were alienating friends and compromising any future U.S. influence. Every time the U.S. refused to offer an opinion, its status among the other delegates was diminished. Friendly regimes, like those from Pakistan, Iran, the Philippines, Liberia, and Canada, time and again fruitlessly sought out the opinions and leadership of the United States. Frustrated by inaction, these states complained to their American counterparts "that our silence might be misinterpreted as a lack of interest."[22] Given the situation, that was an altogether explicable "misinterpretation" for them to make.

Such pious non-intervention was not a policy that could be reversed at the State Department's convenience—when the U.S. chose to speak again, it was questionable whether anyone would be interested in hearing what it had to say. One day, the delegation wrote, there would be human rights questions that simply required U.S. participation. Prevailing on these "vital points," the report advised, "will be difficult if we have remained silent during all the rest of the debate."[23] When the covenants were finally finished, the damage would persist. The delegation warned that "We will have lost the momentum of our leadership."

"Little Demagogues" Versus Flourmill Heiresses: The Nature of Third World Diplomacy

The relative priorities accorded to the human rights program were reflected in the quality of personnel sent by the West and the Third World. Apart from towering figures like René Cassin and Eleanor Roosevelt, for almost two decades between 1950 and 1970 the general performance of Western diplomats was typically weaker than that of their non-Western counterparts. Humphrey complained in 1954 that governments had "gotten into the habit" of employing the Third Committee "as a berth for politically important people who they want to honor with the experience of having sat in a U.N. Committee."[24] This practice seems to have been more common among the Western democracies—which sent mistresses and election fundraisers to represent them in the human rights program. It was not the most impressive demonstration of national will.

Mary Lord, Eisenhower's representative to the Commission on Human Rights, embodied the perils of rewarding political allies with a UN appointment. Heiress to the Pillsbury flour fortune, Lord had been heavily involved in Eisenhower's electoral fundraising.[25] She had very little knowledge of human rights, and still less diplomatic experience. Although Lord gradually grew into a reasonably capable representative, her early years were marked by gaffes. Before she took up the post, she mistakenly announced that the U.S. had not signed the Universal Declaration because it was too communistic. Even U.S. allies were appalled at her proposals to the 1953 Commission on Human Rights, though admittedly she had been given remarkably bad instructions.[26] By the time she had become proficient in the work of the commission, she was rapidly approaching replacement by the appointee of a new administration.

A decade after Lord's departure, Ambassador Daniel Patrick Moynihan castigated the continuing weakness of U.S. diplomats involved in the UN program, and the mindset of the State Department that had appointed them. His opinion was encapsulated in an infamous August 1972 cable to Secretary of State Kissinger.

One plump-minded American official after another had silently or enthusiastically assented to a prolonged slander on American democracy, a sustained advocacy of totalitarian dictatorship. You know why? Because we sent stupid men and worse women to those conferences. And why did we do this? Because the hard-nose Cold Warriors on the Sixth Floor think such things don't matter.[27]

Moynihan, who viewed human rights as the central struggle of the Cold War, introduced a vastly more assertive style of diplomacy into the General Assembly, and repudiated the traditional policy of neglect and defeatism. Yet his appearance came after nearly twenty years of relatively ineffective U.S. human rights diplomacy in the UN, and it was difficult indeed to prove that the State Department was now serious about human rights, particularly when much of it was not.

When compared to their Third World counterparts, both Western and Soviet diplomats were often at a marked disadvantage by the very existence of their detailed instructions. Monitored and assisted by large foreign service bureaucracies, delegates from the West had only modest scope for initiative, and were accordingly less effective at getting things done in the committee and the Commission on Human Rights.

Quentin-Baxter, the veteran New Zealand delegate, observed that in "the great debates . . . people who had to rely on speeches written for them, or on detailed instructions from their governments, were like the crossbowmen at Crecy—absolutely outmaneuvered by the more mobile opponents."[28] A similar analysis of Western failure was noted by Humphrey in a 1954 diary entry: "In most cases these people can do little more than read out a statement prepared by someone else."[29] Because of this lack of autonomy, "a half dozen capable people are able by their maneuvering to control the committee in their own interest." More often than not these "capable people" were from the Arab and Asian group, including the one Humphrey identified as most capable of all, Jamil Baroody, who represented Saudi Arabia.[30]

Baroody exemplified the impact that a confident, autonomous, and agile delegate could have on the course of human rights debate. In addition to being among the most intellectual and energetic members of the UN, Baroody was granted virtually unprecedented leeway by King Faisal.[31] One of Baroody's loudest critics, U.S. Ambassador William F. Buckley, observed that this maneuverability was a central reason for his effectiveness. Unlike his peers, Baroody was "not afraid of anybody" or operating "under any restraint."[32] This stemmed from the trust Faisal had in Baroody. Buckley argued that it was "not conceivable that King Faisal would reproach him on account of anything he said." Without rigid instructions, Baroody was vastly more influential, and often more principled.

By contrast, autonomy and flexibility were actively punished when practiced by Western delegates. In one prominent example, Mary Lord's successor, Marietta Tree, almost lost her job after adding a single word to a draft declaration on racial discrimination in 1964.[33] Tree was one of Ambassador Adlai Stevenson's mistresses, and had been an important supporter of his presidential campaign.[34] This did not save her from the wrath of the State Department, however, which on learning of her initiative promptly advised her that a repeat occurrence would see her recalled and sacked the next morning. Tree's future efforts appear to have been uneventfully consonant with State Department wishes.[35] Paradoxically, the greater the level of government instruction, the less able a delegate was of actually getting something done in the peculiar and dynamic atmosphere of the Third Committee.[36]

The "little demagogues" derided by Humphrey embody the contradictory and multifaceted nature of Third World human rights diplomacy. Figures like Bedia Afnan, Charles Malik, Carlos Romulo, and Jamil Baroody resist easy generalizations. Iraqi delegate Afnan insured the inclusion of equal rights for women in the human rights covenants and denounced cultural relativism, but he fought relentlessly against

the proposed High Commissioner for Human Rights. Malik was arguably more committed to anti-communism than was Dulles, but he voted
with the Soviet Union to ensure that colonies received equal rights. Romulo was bitterly anticolonial, yet he castigated the hypocrisy of Soviet
anticolonialism, and thus alienated a potent ally in the fight against
European colonialism. Baroody had been among the eight delegates
who abstained on the Universal Declaration, yet in conjunction with
Humphrey he developed a serious proposal for studying individual complaints from the victims of human rights violations. This book documents the impact of these complex figures, and countless others, who
came to shape the human rights project just as much as the celebrated
Western heroes of human rights. It is the story of those who challenged
Roosevelt and Cassin, and rapidly drove John Humphrey to despair.

These figures, and those who joined them in the following decades,
made the debate on human rights a global one, for good and ill. At crucial points, they tipped the balance in favor of universality and cleared
away the objections of a defensive imperialism. In subsequent years,
Asian and African diplomats repudiated that universal vision with even
greater force. The evolution of UN human rights activity registers, with
great precision, a parallel evolution that occurred in the Third World
itself. The human rights agenda advanced in the era of the Bandung
Conference was sharply distinct from that which emerged later. Decolonization initiated a global human rights debate, but the fault lines of
that debate often cut across a changing anticolonial movement.

Recognition of this complexity is crucial for understanding the state
of the modern UN rights system. The UN Human Rights Council of the
early twenty-first century rehearses many of the same arguments that
were popularized in the 1970s, when confident dictatorships dominated
the General Assembly and the "North-South" divide hardened into a
seldom-bridged antagonism on human rights questions. This study
charts the changing character of that seemingly crystalline "South"
from the moment of its official birth in 1955, and the myriad ways in
which it transformed the first thirty years of UN human rights promotion. Historical exploration problematizes the easy oversimplifications
that are so often made about the role of the Asian, African, and Arab
states. Decolonization's impact on the human rights enterprise cannot be captured in a single historical moment, or defined solely by the
claims of its most prolific ideologues. The Third World of 1950s spoke
with just as much legitimacy as that of the 1970s, and what it said then
was much less amenable to the defenders of authoritarianism.

Chapter 1
Human Rights and the Birth of the Third World: The Bandung Conference

At Bandung something unexpected happened. The voices of freedom spoke
clearly and decisively.
—*Carlos Peña Romulo, Philippine delegate, 1956*

I understand the chief objective of this Conference is to promote neighborly
amity and mutual understanding among the peoples of the Asian-African
region. . . . This objective tallies exactly with the aim of the Universal
Declaration of Human Rights calculated to preserve peace, freedom and
justice. It will, I trust, appeal to all men and women who have at their hearts
the progress of mankind.
—*Tasunosuke Takosake, Japanese delegate, address to the opening
session of the Asian-African Conference, April 1955*

The 1955 Asian-African Conference in Bandung, Indonesia was a landmark in the emergence of the non-aligned movement and the birth of
the Third World.[1] Celebrated as a turning point in international affairs,
its participants included the six independent states of Africa, along with
virtually all of Asia. The meeting at Bandung, which was so vital to the
later development of ideas of non-alignment and Afro-Asian solidarity,
also served as a key point of origin for the human rights agenda that
would be pursued by the decolonized states in the General Assembly.
Just as importantly, its proceedings revealed the prevailing attitude
toward human rights amongst the leaders of the nascent Third World.
Their speeches at Bandung marked out many of the basic contours
that came to define key UN human rights battles, such as that on self-
determination.

While the implications of the Asian-African Conference for international relations have been widely acknowledged, little scholarship has
been devoted to conference's significance for human rights. Given the

considerable prominence of human rights at the conference, its virtual absence from most accounts is surprising. Mary Ann Glendon, in her pioneering history of the founding years of the UN human rights regime, has offered a brief, generally negative assessment. Glendon argued that the conference's significance lay predominantly in its latent anti-Western dimension. The conference "signaled trouble ahead," despite the affirmation of universality contained in the Final Communiqué.[2] Initial opposition to the recognition of the Universal Declaration by the Chinese presaged future struggles over the universality of human rights.[3] Unity at Bandung was achieved, in Glendon's view, "through shared resentment of the dominance of a few rich and powerful countries."[4] This anti-Western "mood" at Bandung very quickly found expression "in characterizations of the Declaration as an instrument of neocolonialism and in attacks on its universality in the name of cultural integrity, self-determination of peoples, or national sovereignty."[5]

Paul Gordon Lauren, another leading historian on the early foundations of the human rights movement, has presented a more positive interpretation, but has simplified the dynamics of the conference debate.[6] According to his account, the conference provided "unparalleled inspiration and self-confidence for Asians and Africans," an outlet for "pent-up frustrations," and "release from the psychological chains of presumed inferiority."[7] Its significance was, for Lauren, primarily in its effects on the shape of the international system and the mindset of colonial peoples. In particular, he lauds the recognition of the Universal Declaration by the delegates.[8] However, he is too sanguine on the role played by Chinese Premier Zhou Enlai, and neglects to mention the divide between communist China and the smaller states on the question of human rights. Closer examination of the conference record reveals that Zhou was certainly not among the gallery of Third World heroes Lauren has praised for "advancing the cause of international human rights" at Bandung.[9]

Contrary to the accounts of both Glendon and Lauren, this chapter argues that the legacy of the Bandung Conference contained a distinctive mixture of both positive and negative possibilities for the evolution of the international human rights project at the UN. It will show that while the human rights objectives of anticolonialism and antiracism, so energetically pursued by the Afro-Asian states in the 1960s and 1970s, were indeed established as priority concerns at Bandung, they coexisted with a more general concern for civil and political rights, one that extended to situations all over the world. Anticolonialism was in part conceived of as a struggle for human rights, the two concepts proceeding together in the campaign for freedom and independence. The conference marked a high point in support for the universality of human rights among the Third World states. On the Bandung agenda, support for rights was balanced, albeit precariously, with the intense desire for national liberation. That fragile arrangement would later collapse, but it had yet to do so when the conference opened in April 1955.

Bandung as History: Assembling the Third World, April 1955

The Bandung Conference was held at a moment when the Cold War had become an established feature in the world system. Collective defense arrangements continued to proliferate throughout the world, ossifying power alignments and formalizing the polarization between East and West. This geographical extension of the Cold War was symbolized by the Baghdad Pact (later CENTO), which was agreed only months before the conference opened. Hostilities appeared possible in North Asia, the Korean War had ended in a precarious armistice, and negotiations for a permanent settlement had failed in Geneva in 1954. There was escalating tension over Formosa, which became a major discussion point for the delegates at Bandung. Most of Asia was now independent, but the decolonization process had yet to transform the African colonies, with only Ghana and Sudan close to achieving full sovereignty. Armed campaigns for independence continued in Tunisia, Morocco, Algeria, and Kenya. The ANC was resurgent in South Africa, pushed by the more activist leadership of the Youth League.

At the United Nations, the human rights project had entered a transitional phase, with the West ceding its early dominance. States that had been independent for less than a decade, like the Philippines and India, were beginning to play a major role in the absence of U.S. leadership. During the 1955 session of the Commission on Human Rights at the UN, the few Third World delegates present were some of the most active and committed. John Humphrey, first director of the UN Human Rights Division, would later comment that "the delegations with the strongest positive convictions were now without any doubt those which represented the Third World" and observed "the growing importance of issues like the self-determination of peoples and racial discrimination" in the Commission.[10] These topics would only gain momentum in the wake of the conference, becoming nothing less than the annual mainstays of the UN agenda.

Bandung assembled the most influential anticolonial politicians of the era. One of the principal organizers, Jawaharlal Nehru, the first prime minister of India, had been imprisoned seven times by the British in his agitation for independence. Nehru was an unyielding defender of human rights and democratic society, having endorsed the Sankey Declaration of Human Rights of 1940. He had framed much of his opposition to British rule in democratic terms. Nehru would become the leading exponent of non-alignment as a political philosophy, an idea that developed into a formal coalition of states in 1961.

Co-founder of the non-aligned movement Gamal Abdel Nasser was another prominent nationalist figure at Bandung. Nasser established the modern, independent Egyptian republic, leading the Free Officers movement that deposed King Farouk in July 1952. A strong opponent of colonialism, Nasser had successfully negotiated an agreement with the British in October 1954 that removed British troops from Egypt, ending a seventy-two-year presence. Ever confident, charismatic, and aggressive, Nasser advocated pan-Arab unity as the solution to both conventional imperialist domination and the plight of the Palestinian people.[11] An iconic figure for much of the Arab world, he would become the most durable leader of the region, his appeal surviving the disastrous Six Day War of 1967 and years of domestic authoritarianism.

While markedly different from these nationalist heroes, Chinese Premier Zhou Enlai was nonetheless one of the most outspoken critics of colonialism, having witnessed the effects of imperial power both in his homeland and during his travels in colonial Asia. He elevated anticolonialism and Afro-Asian friendship to major objectives of China's foreign policy, and in December 1963 would embark on a tour of thirteen Asian and African countries, attempting to rally support for a second Asian-African Conference. Like Nehru and Nasser, Zhou stood out as an impressive and threatening new voice from a region that had finally begun to find self-expression.

Despite attracting a diverse range of states, including many with conflicting ideological positions, few at Bandung were in doubt of the meeting's historic character. Communist and non-aligned leaders were enthusiastic about the prospect of a new and independent bloc reshaping the international system. Communist Zhou nominated it an event of "important historic significance," one that had "inspired all oppressed peoples and nations."[12] Chief exponent of non-alignment, Nehru, claimed that Bandung marked "the political emergence in world affairs of over half the world's population . . . a great movement in human history."[13] Nehru's neutralist counterpart, Indonesian President Ahmed Sukarno, announced that it was "a new departure in the history of the world," with the African and Asian leaders meeting for the first time as the representatives of "free, sovereign and independent" peoples.[14]

Leaders from the pro-Western contingent of states were similarly convinced of the conference's importance. Philippine delegate Carlos Peña Romulo, already a stand-out figure in both the Commission on Human Rights and the General Assembly, described his delegation and Nehru as being on "opposite sides of the fence."[15] He nevertheless celebrated the gathering in Bandung as "the coming of age of Asia and Africa" and a moment of "historical exuberance."[16] Ceylonese Prime Minister Sir John Kotelawala, who launched a scathing attack on 'communist colonialism' at the conference, nominated it as a "critical juncture . . . not only in the history of the Asian-African region but in the history of mankind."[17] Charles Malik, part of the Lebanese delegation and a major contributor to the Universal Declaration of Human Rights, was another fierce opponent of both communist totalitarianism and the neutralist doctrine. Yet he was equally effusive on the significance of the conference, noting that while "the word 'historic' is often used about all sorts of things . . . in the case of the Bandung Conference, it is fully justified."[18]

The enthusiasm across Asia and Africa was matched with an equivalent alarm in Western political circles, which anticipated the birth of an anti-Western bloc.[19] U.S. Secretary of State John Foster Dulles warned that the conference would diminish Western influence in the former colonies and encourage "communist engulfment" of the emerging post-colonial world. This would, he feared, lead to the creation of "a very solid block of anti-Western votes in the United Nations" as the new states were progressively admitted to the international body.[20] Dulles argued that if the Bandung Conference could be stopped "without strong-arm methods" the "US would welcome such [an] outcome," though open opposition was not advisable because such a course "would probably bring a bad reaction" from the countries involved.[21] European colonial powers such as the Netherlands, Britain, and France were concerned about the evolution of a communist-backed "antiwhite" coalition of Afro-Asian states united by racial solidarity and anticolonialism.[22] Much of this anxious speculation would later seem prescient, though the immediate outcomes of the conference bore only vague resemblance to the prophecies of Dulles and his European counterparts. Preoccupied with near tectonic realignments in international relations, few of the Western policy makers devoted much space to pondering the question of what Bandung would mean for human rights. For the participants themselves, though, human rights were not pushed aside by the exuberance of national liberation.

Human Rights at Bandung: From Absolute Monarchies to Arab Nationalisms

Even before the conference began, human rights were highlighted as a central issue for discussion in an appeal from Mahmoud Aboul Fath, an Egyptian senator who was living in exile after his newspaper had been suppressed by Nasser.[23] In his letter to the Bandung delegates, Fath exhorted the conference not to ignore human rights in the clamor to condemn colonialism:

How can you ask colonialist and imperialist countries to put an end to the ruthless methods they employ in Africa and Asia, to restore freedoms and human rights to peoples under their influence when some of you treat their [your] own peoples in a worse way? Such a call will sound weak and lack some sincerity unless your courage will know no bounds or limits when conditions represented in your own congress are concerned. . . . The violation of human rights is certainly bad and intolerable when committed by imperialists against peoples on whom they force their authority but it is also worse and more obnoxious [when] committed by a few nationals against their own people.[24]

The extent to which the conference truly lived up to Fath's ambitious standard is open to debate. Few of the states represented at Bandung could plausibly claim to have impeccable human rights records. However, human rights were central to the political debate at Bandung, and provided much of the lexicon for the articulation of grievances and aspirations by the assembled nationalist leaders. Militant anticolonialists were comfortable with professing their support for a set of universal claims.

Interest in human rights was a distinctive feature of the optimistic atmosphere that characterized the dawn of the postcolonial era. Rights were incessantly invoked in speeches to the conference, with only the related but more immediate preoccupations of racism and colonialism featuring more prominently. The president of the Conference, Indonesian Prime Minister Ali Sastroamidjojo, lamented in his opening speech that the world was "still a long way off" from both racial equality and "respect for human rights."[25] Of the twenty-five delegates who gave addresses in the opening session on 18 April 1955, no fewer than eleven invoked human rights. The speeches came from an extraordinarily diverse collection of states, and encompassed the full spectrum of political systems in attendance. The speakers ranged from His Royal Highness, Foreign Minister Sardar Mohammed Naim of Afghanistan, an absolute monarchy, to Prime Minister Zhou Enlai of communist China, and included such ideologically disparate regimes as Egypt, Iran, Japan, Jordan, Lebanon, Thailand, Turkey, South Vietnam, and Yemen.[26]

Human rights were again a major feature of the closing session, when four delegations nominated their recognition as one of the achievements of the conference. Afghan representative Sardar praised the conference for proving "that all of us, from different parts of Asia and Africa, have felt and acted as one, for the achievement of our common desire . . . the protection of human rights."[27] Nasser of Egypt endorsed it as "a tremendous success," not least because of the "deep concern and

full support which all the Asiatic and African countries have shown with
regard to questions of human rights."[28] His views were echoed by Prime
Minister Mohammed Ali, head of the Pakistani delegation, who extolled
human rights as one of the core beliefs that defined the Asian-African
attitude toward world affairs. Ali pronounced that, among other things,
"the peoples of Asia and Africa . . . stand for the fundamental principles
of human rights and self-determination."[29]

Eloquent endorsements for universality rang out alongside the abun-
dant rhetoric on Afro-Asian distinctiveness. Speakers embraced both
the Universal Declaration and the Draft Covenants on Human Rights,
weaving universality with national and cultural particularity. Prince Wan
of Thailand, for instance, asserted a common basis for rights. Western
and Eastern religions, he argued, "all teach the same lesson—the dignity and worth of man, faith in fundamental human rights, and respect
for fundamental freedom for all without distinction as to creed, color
or race."[30] Given the bitter debates of the 1990s on cultural specificity
and "Asian Values," the language of the Final Communiqué of the conference, which declared "full support" for the "fundamental principles
of Human Rights," is stunning. The Bandung states, a number of which
would go on to lead the "Asian Values" crusade, recognized the Universal
Declaration as "a common standard of achievement for all peoples and all
nations" just as the General Assembly had done seven years previously.[31]
Endorsement of the Universal Declaration as a valid normative standard
for all was perhaps the most promising development for human rights at
Ban-dung. At least in principle, the delegates agreed that human rights
were universal. This was not the case two decades later.

Philippine representative Romulo, who had been heavily involved in
the drafting of the Universal Declaration, described the Bandung Conference as a major victory for human rights and the democratic system,
representing a serious commitment to these concepts on the part of
the decolonized regimes. In his 1956 assessment, Romulo exalted the
triumph of Bandung for democracy and individual rights.

Democracy had its day in court at Bandung and emerged with flying colors.
It was upheld by most of the delegates, because the peoples they represented
had cast their lot with freedom. They did not take that position because they
were pro-American or pro-West. In fact, they are placed on the defensive in
their respective countries when they are referred to by the American press as
pro-American or pro-West. That the position of these delegates happens to be
that of the United States or of most of the Western countries is only because the
ideals of freedom . . . are universal.[32]

These "ideals of freedom" had been "enshrined in the Magna Carta of
England, the Declaration of the Rights of Man by France, the Declara-

tion of Independence of the United States, and the Universal Declaration of Human Rights."[33] Romulo hoped that the meeting at Bandung would add another ringing declaration to the list, and was contemptuous of the idea that Asian people could only speak of freedom and human rights as "tape recordings from Washington or London"[34] He identified this as a prejudice shared by both the former colonial political elite and communist China. When the delegates at Bandung spoke "clearly and decisively" for human rights and democracy, it was "something unexpected" for both parties.[35] The reflexive anticolonialism of the new regimes was not so strong as to make the delegates "turn away from the universal ideas of human decency, of democracy, and of true freedom." If anything, anticolonialism had probably turned them toward those ideas.

The Human Rights Debate in the Political Committee: Chinese Obstructionism, Third World Enthusiasm

The triumph of universality at Bandung was far from pre-ordained. As Charles Malik explained in 1955, human rights were a major point of contention, dividing communist China from many of the other Asian and African states, especially those sympathetic to the West.

One of the basic issues on which we were sharply divided . . . was the question of Human Rights. What are the ultimate fundamental Human Rights? For the Communists these rights are for the most part social and economic rights; but for some of the rest of us the ultimate human rights that should now be guaranteed by the world and by the diverse nations are the personal, legal, political rights to freedom—to freedom of thought, to freedom of expression, and certainly of free elections. So on this issue too, of the concept of human rights, we were sharply divided. . . . [Liberation] To the Communists, in the present context of this Conference meant the liberation of the various nations and peoples of Asia and Africa from foreign Western rule. But to some of us—while this certainly belongs to the notion of freedom, freedom was much larger and deeper than liberation from foreign rule. To us freedom meant freedom of mind, freedom of thought, freedom of press, freedom to criticise, to judge for yourself—freedom, in short, to be the full human being. And in these respects the Communists could not possibly agree with some of the rest of us.[36]

For some of the delegates, the struggle against colonialism was an aspect of the struggle for human rights. China asserted that anticolonialism was solely concerned with the elimination of foreign domination and the attainment of sovereignty. These conflicting notions of freedom would erupt into an acrimonious debate when the conference attempted to define colonialism in its Final Communiqué.

The conference's Political Committee, and later its special eight-member drafting sub-committee, spent most of Wednesday, 20 April, the first day allotted to working on the communiqué, discussing human rights.[37] In two long meetings, the delegations debated the inclusion of human rights in the official Asian-African platform. Early in the first meeting, Malik put forward a proposal for the conference to recognize the 1948 Universal Declaration. His initiative won backing from Ceylon, Iran, Iraq, Japan, Pakistan, Thailand, Turkey, and South Vietnam. It was opposed by China, India, Indonesia, and North Vietnam, with Zhou Enlai the opposition leader.[38] While all agreed in principle that the conference should endorse human rights in some form, the specifics of the question were bitterly contested, with Zhou reluctant to offer any affirmation of the Universal Declaration, as the Chinese regime had not contributed to its drafting. The Indian and Indonesian objections were more a show of support for Zhou than any substantive rejection of the 1948 text. India had played an integral role in its preparation in the UN Commission on Human Rights, through the work of their representative, Hansa Mehta. The rights section of the 1950 Indonesian constitution was drawn from the Universal Declaration.

Recognition of the Universal Declaration was the principal source of conflict, rather than a more fundamental critique of individual rights. Djalal Abdoh, acting head of the Iranian delegation, reported China's efforts to challenge the legitimacy of the 1948 decision. Human rights, he observed, "seemed simple enough to discuss," but there was some controversy over what those rights actually were, that is "whether human rights should be listed again by the Conference" in preference to an endorsement of the Universal Declaration.[39] An unofficial British observer at the conference, Roderick W. Parkes, Counselor to the British Embassy in Jakarta, asserted that there was "at the outset . . . a good deal of rather woolly discussion about a definition of Human Rights," but that the delegates "eventually fell back on the United Nations Charter and Declaration."[40]

Yet Zhou's resistance meant that recognition of the Universal Declaration was far from a foregone conclusion. His basic argument on the need for representation had obvious application to many of the Bandung states, which had been similarly absent from the drafting process. Malik later recounted the incident in detail at a meeting with Australian diplomats. He observed that "the problem of human rights" absorbed "practically the whole of Wednesday."[41] As one of the architects of the Declaration, Malik's ability to explain the text and to persuade the others was critical. On the most elementary level, it was Malik who brought along a printed Universal Declaration to the meeting for circulation among the participants.

Much more vital was the knowledge he held. Along with Romulo,

Malik brought countless hours of experience from the Commission on Human Rights to Bandung. Well aware of his role in the UN process, the other delegates actively sought out Malik's explanations and opinion on the great document. In the Bandung debates, he reported being "asked again and again by members of the conference to tell them about the Declaration," and wryly noted that he had "had something to do with" the finished product.[42] "It took us three years to work it out," Malik warned his Bandung compatriots, who had only days to agree.

After much deliberation and pressure from the smaller states, Zhou relented on a weaker phrasing of acknowledgment. The conference would "take note of" the Universal Declaration. Romulo attributed Zhou's concession to the "strong, spontaneous support in the conference" for the document and its principles.[43] Far from a compromise solution, Romulo praised the Final Communiqué as a document that "fully supported the Universal Declaration of Human Rights," an interpretation that rests on the inclusion of the phrase "a common standard of achievement," which directly reproduces the universalist language approved by the UN. Abdoh thought the agreed resolution "a very simple one expressing the conference's support of the United Nations Declaration of Fundamental Human Rights."[44] By the accounts of these figures, a majority of the delegates at Bandung were prepared to defend the status of the Universal Declaration against the premier of the most populous state in the world.

Although Zhou had cultivated a reputation as a pragmatic moderate, his past actions indicated that he was no supporter of human rights.[45] Nevertheless, he was careful to frame his opposition in a manner that did not suggest a rejection of the principles contained in the Universal Declaration, instead focusing on his regime's exclusion from the body that formulated it. In his discussion of the human rights debate, Romulo reported that Zhou "signified objection to any conference statement predicated on a United Nations precept, principle, or position." He argued that his country's exclusion from the UN had denied it the "opportunity to participate in the formulation" of all of the organization's decisions and declarations.[46] Malik's perception was similar, and he understood the Chinese obstructionism as an attempt to "use every action to impress upon us the fact that they were not present at the United Nations, that therefore they could not be responsible for the decisions of the United Nations."[47]

Chinese hostility to the Universal Declaration made no reference to the substance of the text, and was instead focused on the much broader point of the need for representation. Parkes, the unofficial British observer, remarked that Zhou made "a good propaganda point by asking for an adjournment to study this document, issued by an organization of which he was not a member."[48] Australian Keith Shann, also acting as an unofficial observer, found the Chinese opposition essentially a generic protest against their exclusion from the UN. Shann commented that while "difficulties about the Chinese attitude towards the United Nations first arose in the discussion . . . on Human Rights and Self-Determination . . . it may be assumed that wherever reference to the United Nations occurs these difficulties were also present."[49]

Zhou's evasive tactics testified to the intensity of the other delegates' defense of the Universal Declaration. He had witnessed the apparent enthusiasm with which the Asian and African speakers addressed human rights, evident from the first session of the conference. An outright dismissal would have damaged the Chinese position, and risked alienating the allies it was so assiduously courting. At the same time, Zhou was pursuing international recognition of his regime. Unsurprisingly, he was prepared to exploit every opportunity that presented itself for this purpose. The Political Committee's agenda was most fortuitous for the Chinese premier, allowing him to express his government's entirely reasonable resentment at being outside the UN, while simultaneously avoiding any serious discussion of its position on human rights. Any such debate could have discredited the communist state in the eyes of the smaller African and Asian states, a number of which already viewed communism with some suspicion.

The Chinese stand was not in any meaningful sense a harbinger of the cultural relativist dismissal of universal human rights that would become so prominent later in the century. Although Zhou's own personal conduct and statements demonstrate little sympathy for human rights, he was aware of the sensitivities of the other participants, and this constrained him to a more conservative mode of opposition at the conference. As Romulo noted, widespread support for a reference to human rights persuaded Zhou to accept a positive acknowledgment of the Universal Declaration. Even if he had felt his audience would be receptive to a tirade against human rights, it is much more probable that any such challenge would have been articulated in the terms of his favored political discourse, Marxism-Leninism.

Zhou's reluctance to offer a full endorsement reflected his recognition of the Universal Declaration as a significant and potentially threatening document. According to Malik, the Chinese considered it "an important text," which they could not support without serious deliberation.[50] While Zhou forced a weaker version of the human rights section, the overall phrasing of the Final Communiqué's human rights section was generally regarded as highly promising and perhaps stronger than might have been expected. "We managed at the end to add a phrase which was very satisfactory," noted Malik, who hoped that "the Chinese knew what they were doing when they accepted it."

Malik, who had developed a working relationship with Zhou, was in an excellent position to observe the prime minister's attitude toward the Universal Declaration. In a secret conversation between Malik and Zhou on the morning of 25 April 1955, the subject of human rights was again raised. Zhou cited his initial opposition to any reference to the Universal Declaration as one of the "many mistakes" he had made in the conference, and noted that he "too had to crave the indulgence of the Committee and even later to apologize" for his stance.[51] While the sincerity of his concession and apology is highly suspect, the fact that Zhou was moved to this reversal, and identified his initial opposition as a diplomatic error, further demonstrates the strength of support for human rights among the emerging nations China was attempting to court. Opposing a reference to the Universal Declaration, even for bureaucratic reasons, was a significant tactical misstep. By 1968, it was closer to a tactical necessity, as the current of opinion turned, and exclusion from the debates of 1948 became a rallying cry for a number of Third World dictators and diplomats.

Following the conference, Zhou paid conspicuous lip service to human rights, and cynically professed his government's support for them. He referred to the human rights provision of the Final Communiqué in his assessment of the Asian-African Conference to the Standing Committee of the Chinese National People's Congress. His report of 13 May 1955 noted that the conference "declared its support of the fundamental principles of human rights," and further asserted, with breathtaking hypocrisy, that "respect for fundamental human rights" was one of the principles that the "Chinese people consistently stand for" and one "which China has consistently observed."[52]

China's concession on the status of the Universal Declaration was certainly perceived as noteworthy by other states. Abdoh, acting head of the Iranian delegation, described it as a "somewhat significant" step forward, because it signaled Chinese recognition of the United Nations, but also because it indicated that China "subscribed to acceptance of the principles of human rights."[53] An appraisal of the conference and its outcomes by the National Assembly of the Republic of Korea singled out the Chinese move as one of the chief positive outcomes of the conference, which was "a success for the anti-communist world" because, among other things, "communist China was forced to endorse the Universal Declaration of Human Rights."[54] Australian Foreign Minister Richard Casey highlighted the inclusion of "respect for human rights" in the Final Communiqué as one of the "important additional principles" that made the document more attractive than the original Five

Principles of Co-existence enunciated by Zhou and Nehru, and one of the reasons the communiqué "could be regarded as generally acceptable to the free world."[55]

"Jealous Guardians": Human Rights, National Sovereignty, and Non-Interference

If human rights were a serious issue for the emerging Asian and African leaders at Bandung, non-interference and respect for state sovereignty were almost an obsession. After being subjected to colonial control and domination for such a long period, the newly independent states were naturally preoccupied with defending encroachments on the sovereignty for which they had fought so hard. In many instances, delegates had personally suffered imprisonment or other forms of persecution in the battle to achieve independence, which at least in part explained the sympathy for individual rights. Yet many had a strong reflex to be the masters of their own fate, having been for so long, in President Sukarno's phrase, "the peoples for whom decisions were made by others . . . the tools of others, the playthings of forces they cannot influence."[56] Zhou pointed out that after such a difficult road to independence the African and Asian states "treasure all the more their own national rights," and repeatedly warned against interference in the internal affairs of sovereign states.[57] Speaker after speaker, from all political blocs, reiterated the fact that the states represented at Bandung had control of their own destinies, and would no longer be instructed on how to organize their societies. Economically weak and militarily vulnerable, the representatives of the decolonized peoples at Bandung were fearful of intervention from larger, more powerful countries.

Even the Lebanese delegation, which included Malik, one of the leading human rights advocates in the world, stressed the importance of the rights of nations. "If human rights are sacred," the Lebanese representative declared, then "the right of nations themselves, no matter how small, to the respect of greater nations is at least just as sacred."[58] The resultant emphasis on state sovereignty and non-interference in the Final Communiqué emerged in this context of "national" rights and international "respect." Of the ten principles for the "Promotion of World Peace and Cooperation" enumerated at Bandung, five deal with matters directly related to state sovereignty, while only one directly related to human rights, with one more indirectly related.[59]

The potential antagonism between rights and sovereignty was ignored by most of the speakers, who exalted both with seemingly little awareness of the tension between them. President Gamal Abdel Nasser, who led the Egyptian delegation, was outspoken in his defense of the

rights of small states, but remained an equally enthusiastic advocate of
the primacy of human rights:

No less important as a condition for a world peace is the full respect by all states
of their international obligations. Under the Charter of the United Nations and
the Universal Declaration of Human Rights the treatment by any state of any
national or ethnic group has ceased to be a matter of domestic jurisdiction as
certain states still advocate. It has become a question of international jurisdiction and a matter of world concern.[60]

The competitive nature of sovereignty and the protection of individual rights were conveniently avoided in the Bandung rhetoric, so
deeply removed from the practicalities of securing those rights. Syrian
Foreign Minister Khaled Bey Al Azam lamented the failure of the
United Nations to take effective action against "the flagrant violations"
of the principles of the UN Charter in South Africa, and accused it
of "thereby assuming the role of a debating society."[61] Yet he did not
examine the implications of this line of argument and the challenge
it posed to the newly won sovereignty of the decolonized states—not
least his own.

National rights and human rights were typically presented as parallel
and mutually supportive projects, a proposition that would be advanced
in session after session of the UN in the 1950s. Several speakers simply
conflated the pursuit of self-determination and human rights, making
the struggle for one coterminous with the struggle for the other. "Our
conception of independence is not different in any respect from our
conception of the observance of fundamental human rights, especially
the right of peoples and nations to self-determination," remarked Af-
ghani Foreign Minister Sardar Mohammed Naim in his opening address.[62] Abdoh, the Iranian representative, went farther, invoking the
Draft Covenant on Human Rights, which already contained a provision
for self-determination, forced in no small part by the activism of the
Third World group at the UN:

The conception which lies behind this sacred right has always been defended
in the secular struggle of people for their liberties. National self-determination
might be regarded as implicit in the idea of democracy; for if every man's right
is recognized to be consulted on the affairs of the political unit to which he
belongs, he may be assumed to have an equal right to be consulted about the
form and functioning of the unit.[63]

The problems with this reasoning would be amply revealed as the conference went on, and still further exposed as the right to self-determination evolved in the resolutions and covenants of the 1960s.

Defining "Freedom": Colonialism, Communism, and Indigenous Despotism

Questions about the nature of freedom, and the relationship between national self-determination and individual liberty, emerged in the competing definitions of colonialism, which had been the subject of considerable controversy from the first day of the conference on 18 April 1955. Six of the opening speeches identified communism as a form of colonialism. Iran, Iraq, Libya, Pakistan, Philippines, Turkey, and South Vietnam all warned of the imperialistic aspects of world communism. In addition, Cambodia and Thailand expressed fears about communist China. The speeches ranged from moderate expressions of concern to full-blown denunciations, and foreshadowed the major dispute over the reference to colonialism in the closed sessions of the Political Committee that threatened the success of the conference.[64] The debates on communism and colonialism, while primarily concerned with foreign domination, would raise important issues about how postcolonial regimes would be structured internally, and often deployed the language of rights in their arguments.

The problem of communist subversion was first touched upon in the address delivered by Abdoh, who was also Iran's permanent representative to the UN. Although colonialism in its "nineteenth-century conception" had been defeated, he warned of "new forms" which attempted to subvert the "sovereignty and freedom of peoples."[65] This new colonialism practiced by the "more subtle aggressors of our times" used "various invisible and deceiving weapons" and aimed at "re-inventing colonialism under new forms," while its subversion remained hidden "under ideological disguises." These posed a new challenge, but Abdoh was confident that the decolonized would recognize a threat to their freedom "under any disguise" and resist attacks on their national independence in the course of defending their individual freedom. Concern for personal political and economic liberty would ensure the failure of communist tactics, as it had ensured the demise of the old colonialism.

Mohammed Fadhel Jamali, Iraqi foreign minister, followed with a much more violent anti-communist tirade. Jamali attributed the disruption of global "peace and harmony" to the influence of three pernicious forces, all of them imperialistic. European colonialism and Zionism predictably constituted the first two. Yet he reserved much of his invective for communism, and its international organ, Cominform, which ensured the proliferation of "their activity and subversion" around the world. Communism was a worse form of subjugation than either of the old colonialisms:

The peoples of Asia and Africa who have been struggling for decades to achieve their freedom and independence are liable through Communist machination to jump from the pan into the fire. . . . They confront the world with a new form of colonialism, much deadlier than the old one. Today the Communist world has subjected races in Asia and Eastern Europe on a much larger scale than any old colonial power. . . . Under the old form of colonialism, there is some chance of one hearing the cries of pain of the subjugated peoples. Under Communist domination, however, no such cries are permitted to be heard.[66]

For Jamali, communist colonialism was both more aggressive and more repressive than European imperialisms, and had to be included in the fight for self-determination. Furthermore, it was a grave threat to traditional religions. Libyan representative Mohammed Bey Muntassar amplified Jamali's argument about the greater tyranny of Communist imperialism, which was "more dangerous and of much stronger effect" because it incorporated "all the disadvantages of classical colonialism, and, in addition, intellectual slavery."[67] He went on to pledge his support for a democratic system, though democracy's fate in Libya delivered rather less than Muntassar might have hoped.

Communist attempts to co-opt nationalist sentiments and subvert the self-determination process were denounced by Prime Minister Ali of Pakistan. He called for the delegates at Bandung to expedite conventional decolonization, but urged caution in the process. Colonial peoples had to distinguish between genuine movements for national self-determination and communist front organizations. "We must be very careful," said Ali, "that we are not misled into opening our doors to a new and more insidious form of imperialism that masquerades in the guise of liberation."[68]

These attacks on communism as a type of foreign subjugation were accompanied by condemnations made on the basis of human rights. Fatin Rustu Zorlu, Turkish deputy prime minister, formulated his justification of the North Atlantic Treaty Organization in part as a defense against the communist threat to human rights, as evidenced by Soviet conduct in Europe. He cited the "terrible war [that] had been fought for human rights and the liberation of oppressed peoples" and the disappointment when Eastern Europe's liberators transformed into its oppressors.

Employing "human rights" as an omnibus term for colonial hopes and desires, Zorlu stressed the importance of collective security as a bulwark against the main threat to freedom and independence: communism. He was "fully convinced that colonialism and racialism," already in decline, "should be made to vanish from the earth."[69] To this standard anticolonial line, Zorlu coupled an endorsement of anticommunist security measures.

If we wish to see the realization of these aspirations, in one word, if we wish to see the enjoyment of Human Rights and justice all over the world, our first task should be to remember that we bear the responsibility of safeguarding the independence which we have won, that we must be prepared to undergo sacrifices for it and to provide for our security.

Zorlu understood the resonance of rights language, and readily appropriated it for his advocacy of the North Atlantic Treaty Organization and collective defense arrangements, which were, he argued, "natural and inalienable rights."[70]

Rights discourse was also integral to the South Vietnamese attack on communism, and its communist neighbor, the Democratic Republic of Vietnam. Nguyen Van Thoai, head of the South Vietnamese delegation, argued that a regime respectful of human rights was the best protection against communism. "A regime of true freedom, respecting human personalities and the basic rights of mankind" was, he argued, "the only way to safeguard efficiently the Free World from the menaces of dictatorial Communism."[71] Admittedly, his own government was not particularly scrupulous in implementing such a regime, nor especially well placed to decry foreign interference. He cited the influx of North Vietnamese refugees, and explained their movement as the result of a "dictatorial regime, which completely disregards human values and the basic rights of man."[72] The refugees were "the most eloquent proof of the free and spontaneous will and determination expressed by our people in [their] quest for liberty against dictatorship." He appealed for an extension of the open border that had been temporarily instituted between the two countries in the name of "the most sacred rights of man" and as a "logical concretization of the Universal Declaration of Human Rights."

These arguments over communism, in which human rights and related concerns formed an important part of the vocabulary of political debate, also raised deeper questions about what precisely was at issue in the struggle against colonialism, and what form the postcolonial state should adopt. Such issues were at the heart of Philippine delegate Romulo's speech, which offered a series of powerful observations on individual freedom, independence and economic development. National self-determination and individual human rights were the two goals Romulo had fought for his entire life, and he was unique among the delegates as one of the foremost champions of both causes on the international stage. In 1946, Romulo successfully agitated for the inclusion of provisions for colonial self-determination in the UN Charter, against the wishes of many of the established European powers. In the field of human rights, he had been an important Third World voice in the drafting of the Universal Declaration.

Romulo, with his impeccable anticolonial and human rights credentials, warned of the dangers of national independence, which
could degenerate into "an instrument for a new and different kind of
subjection."[73] Freedom was not won merely by casting-off of alien rule.
Anticolonialism should not seek the transposition of a foreign ruling
elite for an indigenous one, but a complete democratic reformation of
the repressive colonial state:

> Is political freedom achieved when the national banner rises over the seat of
> government, the foreign ruler goes, and power passes into the hands of our own
> leaders? Is the struggle for national independence the struggle to substitute
> a local oligarchy for the foreign oligarchy? Or is it just the beginning of the
> conquest of real freedom by the people of the land? Is there political freedom
> where only one political party may rule? Is there political freedom where dis-
> sent from the policy of the government means imprisonment or worse? It strikes
> me that autocratic rule, control of the press, and the police state are exactly the
> worst features of some colonialist systems against which we have fought all our
> lives and against which so many of us are still fighting. Is this really the model
> of freedom we seek? Or is it the free interplay of contending parties, the open
> competition of ideas and political views in the market place, the freedom of a
> man to speak up as he chooses, be he right or wrong?[74]

He acknowledged that there were "many possible answers to these questions," but argued that the best answer, and the one selected by the Philippines, was a pluralistic, democratic state. Philippine independence
was a means for ensuring the rights of all citizens, not an end in itself,
argued Romulo, and he pledged to construct "a society in which the
freedom of our Republic will truly become the freedom of every one of
its citizens."[75] National rights would enable individual liberties.

Communist preoccupations with economic development and modernization, at the expense of personal freedom, were subjected to a
withering critique from Romulo, who had previously offered a similar
argument against the putatively superior economic performance of the
Philippine colonial administration of General Wood.[76] Authoritarian
modernization programs, of the sort advocated by the communist states,
were a tempting prospect for the underdeveloped colonial countries,
and even Romulo, a passionate supporter of human rights, recognized
the difficult choices faced by postcolonial leaders. Yet he was deeply
skeptical of the authoritarian development path and its consequences:

> There is one road to change which some countries have adopted and which of-
> fers itself to the rest of us as a possible choice. This is the road which proposes
> total change through total power, through avowed dictatorship and the forcible
> manipulation of men and means to achieve certain ends, the rigid control of
> all thought and expression, the ruthless suppression of all opposition, the per-
> vasive control of human life in all spheres by a single, tightly run, self-selected

organization of elite individuals. I know that an elaborate series of phrases and rationalizations are often used to describe this system. But I am concerned not with propaganda myths. I am concerned with realities. I think we all have to be concerned with what the system offers and what it means.[77]

The sacrificing of individual human rights for development was dismissed by Romulo, who claimed that such a choice betrayed the promise of independence. Apart from this, the cannibalization of individual liberty in the name of economic success was not required for development, and was in any event a grossly disproportionate exchange. In phrase reminiscent of Russian radical Alexander Herzen over a century before, he implored the new leaders not to turn their people into the means for securing a future end.

Is it for this that we have in this generation raised our heads and taken up the struggle against foreign tyrannies? Has all the sacrifice, struggle, and devotion, all been, then, for the purpose of replacing foreign tyranny by domestic tyranny? Do we fight to regain our manhood from Western colonial rulers only to surrender it to rulers among ourselves who seize the power to keep us enslaved? . . . Can we really believe that this price will, in some dim and undefined future time, be redeemed by the well-being and freedom of the yet unborn? This road is open before many of us. The gateway to it is strewn with sweet-smelling garlands of phrases and promises and high-sentiment. But once you march through it, the gate clangs behind you. The policeman becomes master and your duty thereafter is forever to say aye.[78]

The people of the Third World, who had struggled for so long against colonial authoritarianism, had not succeeded only to reimpose upon themselves another dictatorial regime, whatever its ideological justification. It was, sadly, a position Romulo himself would drift away from in the late 1960s.

These attacks on communism forced Zhou to supplement his original speech, which had been distributed as a printed text, with a spoken address that tried to assuage the concerns of the numerous small countries which had expressed anxiety or even outright hostility toward international communism, and in particular, the concerns of those who had alluded to China specifically, such as Cambodia and Thailand. This extremely conciliatory speech denied that China intended to interfere in the affairs of other countries, and emphasized the need for coexistence among diverse social and political systems. Yet it was not solely concerned with addressing concerns about the threat China posed to the sovereignty of other states. Given the importance placed upon religion and spirituality by Jamali of Iraq and Prince Wan of Thailand, Zhou gave special attention to the respect for the right to religious freedom in his country.[79] He repeatedly assured the conference that his was "a country where there . . . [was] freedom of religious belief" and that his government would "respect all those who have religious belief."[80]

Despite Zhou's attempts at persuasion, many of the delegates were not convinced, and the offensive against communism continued in the closed sessions of the Political Committee. Communist imperialism, as demonstrated by the Soviet Union's conduct in Eastern Europe, was once again the main point of contention. In the process of this second debate, the questions of human rights, sovereignty and even freedom of expression were all revisited.

During the first two sessions of the Political Committee, on 20 April, the representatives had devoted their deliberations entirely to human rights, leaving the question of self-determination and dependent peoples to the third and fourth sessions, to be held on Thursday, 21 April 1955.[81] Late in the fourth session, after much discussion of traditional colonial situations, Ceylonese Prime Minister Sir John Kotelawala raised the problem of communist colonialism that had become a major theme of the speeches in the open sessions. Kotelawala was concerned about the double-standard exhibited in the Committee's initial discussions, which had focused solely on Western colonialism, and argued that there needed to be greater consistency in the application of the term:

There is another form of colonialism, however, about which many of us represented here are perhaps less clear in our minds and to which some of us would perhaps not agree to apply the term colonialism at all. Think, for example, of those satellite States under Communist domination in Central and Eastern Europe—of Hungary, Rumania, Bulgaria, Albania, Czechoslovakia, Latvia, Lithuania, Estonia, and Poland. Are not these colonies as much as any of the colonial territories in Africa or Asia? And if we are united in our opposition to colonialism, should it not be our duty openly to declare our opposition to Soviet colonialism as much as to Western imperialism?[82]

Pakistan, Turkey, Iraq, and Lebanon all seconded his suggestion, while Zhou reserved his right to reply in the morning.[83] The meeting was then adjourned.

When the issue was raised again in the morning, these discussions prompted questions about the nature of sovereignty and what constituted an independent, and legitimate, regime. Nehru, who had challenged Kotelawala after his speech, denied that the term colonialism applied to the Soviet Union. He spoke out in favor of a traditional, legalistic notion of sovereignty, and asserted that, given the UN had accepted the Eastern European states as independent, it was not the place of the conference to challenge this designation.

There has been talk of a new colonialism. Well, speaking technically, however much we may oppose what has happened to countries in Eastern Europe and elsewhere, it is not colonialism. . . . It seems to me rather extraordinary that we should discuss nations as such whose people we have recognized in the capacity of sovereign nations and then say that they are colonial territories.[84]

If sovereignty was going to be contingent on majority rule, or democracy, or some other set of criteria, argued Nehru, then many of the countries at the conference would find their own legitimacy open to discussion. Defining sovereignty according to internal characteristics was too perilous for the decolonized world.

Nehru urged the delegates to limit their formulation of colonialism to the conventional situations, as a broader interpretation would necessarily entail awkward questions.

If we look at this question in its entirety, as the honourable delegates from Iran and Iraq said, and impartially, and if we examine the state of freedom, the state of individual or national freedom, the state of democratic liberty or democracy itself in the countries represented here, well, I feel many of us are lacking, terribly lacking. . . . If we sit down and discuss these matters in all integrity in its entirety then we shall have to go very far and discuss how far countries represented here fulfil that noble standard which we laid down yesterday in the human rights or even the ordinary tenets of democracy and freedom.[85]

After a further two days of discussion, the conference finally agreed to condemn colonialism "in all its manifestations," with different delegations taking away different meanings from this phrase, which could either include or exclude the communist example. They elected to sidestep the difficult questions raised by Nehru, though they would be reprised in UN debates about the crushing of the Hungarian uprising in November 1956, and episodically in the decade long struggle over the right to self-determination.

Conclusion: The Mixed Legacy of Bandung

Bandung was a pivotal moment in the creation of a Third World identity, marking the foundation of the decolonized states as a major political force in international affairs. Human rights, and attendant issues of individual freedom, religious liberty, and democratic governance, formed a central part of the conference, ultimately consuming more of it than the often mythologized question of non-alignment. The successful defense of the Universal Declaration of Human Rights at Bandung by the small countries of Asia, and to a lesser extent Africa, was a remarkable achievement. It demonstrated the significant engagement many of the new states had with the concept of human rights in the early phase of their independence, and the absence of any prejudice against the principles in the Universal Declaration, despite the Western intellectual provenance of both its form and a considerable number of its provisions. Zhou's argument about representation in the drafting body failed to gain serious traction. For a delegate like Romulo, Bandung was nothing short of a triumph for democratic ideas and human rights, and their acceptance across the Third World. It marked, he claimed, the "ever-growing devotion to the principles of democracy and freedom" embodied in "the statement of the Rights of Man."[86]

Cultural relativist critiques of the Universal Declaration, and the notion that human rights were an expression of imperialism themselves, were not discernible in any of the conference rhetoric. Those at Bandung seemed much more inclined to consider human rights as a weapon for expediting the end of colonialism. Yemeni Prime Minister Emir Seif El Islam Al Hassan expressed disappointment that there were "still many remnants of colonizers, though the United Nations Organization already recognized human rights."[87] Far from rejecting the human rights concept as a foreign imposition, the delegates at Bandung embraced it, and urged its extension to their regions, and its use against enemies. Jordanian Foreign Minister Sayyed Wahid Salah lamented that it was "most regrettable indeed that principles of human rights so widely publicized by the United Nations and its various agencies have been the monopoly of the great powers only, while smaller nations had to face an endless period of struggle and endurance."[88] While their domestic practice inevitably fell far short of the standards they pledged support for, there was no philosophical opposition to human rights at Bandung, something that could not be said even ten years later. For reasons of both political advantage and idealism, the Third World loudly proclaimed support for human rights at the conference, drowning out the objections of China in the process.

Mainstays of the new post-colonial human rights agenda also emerged, most obviously antiracism, self-determination, and the plight of the Palestinian people. Bandung consolidated the division of states into "North" and "South," with many of the participants proclaiming a distinctive Third World identity, which was constructed around the common experience of Western subjection and economic underdevelopment. Above all, it inaugurated an era when debates at the United Nations would no longer be divided along East-West lines, but increasingly along the so-called "North-South" axis. As Malik observed shortly after the conference, "the ultimate question today is not whether and how Communism and the West can 'coexist', but whether and how both of these can 'coexist' with Asia and Africa."[89] With the rapid influx of decolonized states into the UN after Bandung, the "North-South" antagonism would gradually make its existence felt in every area of UN activity, not least the human rights program.

Chapter 2
"Transforming the End into the Means": The Third World and the Right to Self-Determination

Our mistake was not in our demand for freedom; it was in the assumption that freedom—real freedom—would necessarily and with little trouble follow liberation from alien rule.
—*Julius Nyerere, 1976*

When all advocates of the liberation of formerly independent peoples invoke democratic ideals and principles for the attainment of that goal, it would indeed be disgraceful if groups of people in newly established States subsequently exploit the inadequate development of the population to introduce not a democratic rule, but dictatorship.
—*Christiansen (Denmark), Debate on the 1960 Declaration on the Granting of Independence to Colonial Countries and Peoples, 13 December 1960*

Since the closing phases of drafting on the Universal Declaration in 1948, the right to self-determination has been the source of intense political controversy. These debates on self-determination encapsulated the fraught and volatile relationship between anticolonialism, rights, and democracy in Third World diplomacy. Throughout the 1950s, Asian, African, and Arab states advocated a right to self-determination with almost fanatical intensity. Their success was both rapid and significant—with the adoption of a right to self-determination as Article 1 of both human rights covenants, and the passage of the landmark 1960 Declaration on the Granting of Independence to Colonial Countries and Peoples, the most frequently invoked resolution in UN history.[1] At the 1955 Asian-African Conference in Bandung, a right to self-determination formed one of the central articles in the Final Communiqué. Its champions portrayed self-determination as a fundamental precondition for all human rights. Anticolonialism involved rights, and respect for rights necessitated decolonization.

Eminent legal scholars have embraced the special status accorded to self-determination in first articles of the two International Covenants on Human Rights. Antonio Cassese has argued that Article 1, declaring the right of self-determination, "should not be underrated" because it "establishes a permanent link between self-determination and civil and political rights."[2] Thomas Franck, perhaps the most outspoken proponent of the democratic view of self-determination, has identified the right as "the first building block in the creation of a democratic entitlement" pivotal to the revolutionary democratization that followed the end of the Cold War.[3] Human rights and self-determination were, for Cassese and Franck, a natural and logical pairing of immense historic significance.

While these scholars have been sympathetic to the idea of an indissoluble link between individual rights and self-determination, others have expressed profound skepticism. Foremost among them is A. W. Brian Simpson, who has argued that the campaign to achieve recognition of the right to self-determination was driven primarily by the need to mobilize the UN for the purposes of decolonization, rather than the connection between the two concepts.[4] With the adoption of self-determination as a human right, most importantly by Resolution 1514 in 1960, "the program of the anticolonial movement came to be expressed in the language of human rights," even though it was not fundamentally a movement for human rights, defined as the rights of the individual against the state.[5] No less critical is Africa specialist Crawford Young, who has claimed that democracy and rights were little more than an "instrumental norm for the anticolonial movement, a means to the transcendent end of immediate independence."[6] According to Young, "the essential value of these freedoms was their utility in the combat against colonial rule, rather than their intrinsic worth." Most hostile of all to the association of individual rights and self-determination is international law expert Louis Henkin, who nominated self-determination as little more than "an additional weapon against colonialism" added to the "roster of human rights" out of political convenience.[7]

This chapter argues that the Third World's advocacy of a right to self-determination was built upon two competing tendencies within the anticolonial bloc at the UN—one universalist and democratic, the other strictly anticolonial, and altogether indifferent to democracy.[8] The campaign began with arguments premised on the value of individual rights, but it developed into an idea that explicitly disavowed the existence of any constraints on the rights of the state to organize itself in any manner it desired. While the right to self-determination was a constant theme in Afro-Asian human rights rhetoric, its content was not fixed, being highly dynamic and subject to radical re-interpretation over time.

Between the preparation of Article 1 of the human rights covenants in the early 1950s and the climate of 1966, the definition of the right to self-determination underwent a dramatic shift, which mirrored the broader trend away from individual rights, and toward state prerogatives in Afro-Asian bloc policy at the UN. Self-determination's metamorphosis mirrors the broader fate of democracy in the Third World, as the first wave of nationalist governments transformed into antidemocratic regimes.

The right to self-determination constitutes the nexus between decolonization and human rights. With the official acceptance of the right to self-determination, the process of decolonization itself became a human right, and lent the moral legitimacy of human rights to anticolonial struggles in Asia and Africa. Yet this outcome was itself a product of the transformation of the UN wrought by the admission of newly decolonized states. The establishment of the right to self-determination in Article 1 of the covenants was, therefore, one of the first direct consequences of decolonization for the international human rights project, and at the same time a rhetorical and legal synthesis of the two concepts, decolonization and human rights.

Yet the recognition of a right to self-determination was far from inevitable. During the drafting of the Universal Declaration, efforts to include self-determination in the final text were rejected by the then preponderant Western group, and dismissed outright by influential members of the human rights program.[9] In the 1940s and early 1950s, opponents of its recognition as a right cited the example of Hitler, who exploited self-determination as a pretext for his annexation of Eastern and Central Europe. Belgian delegate Fernand Dehousse reminded the Third Committee that "Hitler had invoked the right of self-determination in all the successive stages of his dismemberment of central Europe."[10] Gerard Corley Smith (UK) contended that Article 1 of the covenants held the potential for "tragic consequences" if it were adopted.[11] "There could be no doubt," declared Corley Smith, "that the crimes of the Hitlerite regime would have found their justification in an article such as that which it was being proposed to include in the covenant."

The adversaries of a right to self-determination included René Cassin and John Humphrey, two of the most influential figures in the history of the UN human rights program. Cassin was strongly opposed to any suggestion that self-determination constituted a human right.[12] He accused the proponents of the right to self-determination of "reversing the order of the Charter" and "transforming the end into the means since, according to them, peoples should be granted the right to self-determination in order that they should be enabled to enjoy essential political rights and fundamental freedoms."[13] Humphrey's critique was at the level of political practicality, by contrast to the more philosophical Cassin. Though he supported self-determination as a political principle, he argued that the preoccupation with it had the potential to disrupt the completion of the human rights covenants.[14] By their advocacy of the right to self-determination, the Afro-Asian states made the covenants "a pawn in the fight against colonialism," and threatened their passage and adoption by colonial powers.[15] Humphrey found the new states wholly untroubled by this risk, and argued that they "were intent on scoring an immediate victory" and "quite indifferent to the fate of the covenant[s]."[16] These concerns about the politics of the right to self-determination were hardly misplaced.

Although the self-determination controversy is often recognized as the beginning of the Third World "revolt" against a human rights agenda dominated by the West, a collection of African, Asian, Arab, and Latin American diplomats had already demonstrated their willingness to challenge Western leadership well before that debate began. During the drafting of the Convention on Freedom of Information in 1949, both the West and the Soviet Union had been placed on the defensive by the diverse range of demands from some of the Third World states.[17] Many were not prepared to accept a convention perceived as advantageous to Western media interests. Nor were they enthusiastic about the kind of document proposed by the communist bloc, which placed information entirely under state control. As the conflict over freedom of information developed, these assertive Third World delegations were most heavily engaged in the drafting process, proposing all manner of amendments and revisions.[18] The prospect of global agreement dimmed accordingly.

The proceedings of the faltering Freedom of Information debate exemplified the growing influence wielded by the smaller non-Western states.[19] Humphrey attributed the delays in the Freedom of Information Convention to the newfound strength of the Third World delegations, which were "too successful" in achieving their aims and thereby alienated the "conservative" representatives.[20] The resultant failure to pass the convention was, he argued, "probably the worst set back that the U.N. has had in its human rights program."[21] Apart from its immediate impact, the fate of the convention was also "a bad omen" for the human rights covenant. In February 1952 he wrote in despair of the impact that these "little men puffed up with a sense of their importance" had on the fate of human rights at the UN.[22]

On the eve of the self-determination debate in 1950, control of the human rights agenda was already shifting toward these "puffed up" men. New leaders had emerged from the Middle East and South East Asia. Among the most outspoken were Jamil Baroody, a Lebanese Christian employed to represent Saudi Arabia; Abdul Rahman Pazhwak, a journalist and poet from Afghanistan; and Karim Azkoul, a Lebanese academic.[23] These representatives, along with a number of other Arab and Asian members, would dominate the Third Committee in the early 1950s, much to the irritation of Humphrey.

This new leadership drove the self-determination debate, and was at the same time emblematic of the tensions within the new anticolonial bloc at the UN, between the self-determination secured through "sovereignty" and the self-determination achieved by "democracy." Baroody advanced an argument of self-determination as sovereignty. Individual rights were a secondary priority that followed the achievement of independence, and his variant of the right to self-determination did not presuppose the creation of a democratic postcolonial state. By contrast, proponents of "democracy" self-determination, like Azkoul, typically placed individual rights at the forefront of their case for self-determination. Self-determination and political freedom were mutually dependent. Such differences on the definition of self-determination reflected the respective alignments of the various groups within the broader Arab, Asian, and African bloc. Baroody's purely nationalistic self-determination was consistent with his status as leader of the more uncompromising anti-imperialist Third World delegations; Azkoul represented the moderate group.

Colonialism as a Human Rights Violation: The Genesis of a Right to Self-Determination

In the early 1950s, the dominant tendency was that of "democracy" and self-determination. Although national independence was the highest priority, conventional human rights were almost always the central justification for recognition of a right to self-determination. As the delegates at Bandung had so often claimed, national independence would further individual freedom. Arab, Asian, and Latin American diplomats made arguments that were essentially consonant with American and European liberal nationalist traditions of the previous centuries and Wilsonian ideas about democratic self-government.[24] The high moment of democratic self-determination corresponded to the high point of democratic anticolonial nationalism in countries like Indonesia, India, and Pakistan.

Certainly the attitudes of the European imperial powers made the link between self-determination and human rights more plausible than it might otherwise have been. Proposals for a right to self-determination were provoked by the persistent reluctance of France, the United Kingdom, Belgium, and the Netherlands to guarantee the application of human rights in their colonies. In the debates that immediately preceded the introduction of a resolution on a human right to self-determination in November 1950, European delegations had demonstrated their intention to avoid any human rights promises to those outside the metropole by way of a special colonial exemption clause in the draft human rights covenant.[25] The clause allowed European governments to exclude their colonies from claiming the rights in the covenant.[26]

The notion that self-determination was a prerequisite for the observance of individual rights was lent considerable credibility by the patronizing arguments made by the European delegates in their advocacy of the clause. Speakers from Belgium, France, and Great Britain explained that the "backward" indigenous inhabitants were not ready for "Western" human rights. Even René Cassin, famous co-architect of the Universal Declaration, defended the clause, advising that it was unwise to hold "different peoples to uniform obligations."[27] As the clause debate proceeded, it became apparent that there was no guarantee that human rights would be protected under colonial administrations. Past and contemporary practice further illustrated the precarious and marginal nature of individual rights in many colonial territories.[28]

Serious questions on the compatibility of human rights with colonialism emerged over the prolonged course of the colonial clause debate. The day after Cassin's speech in defense of the clause, Philippine delegate Mauro Méndez made the startling contention that "in order to solve the problem in a coherent and satisfactory manner, it must first of all be considered that, in a century in which the dignity of the individual had been solemnly proclaimed, colonies no longer had a *raison d'être*."[29] Baroody and Pazhwak made claims that led naturally from specific problems of the colonial clause to the broader question of colonialism itself. Pazhwak deemed colonialism "a flagrant violation of the most sacred rights of the individual," and further asserted that "in depriving peoples of their rights to govern themselves, colonial Powers had often violated the right to life and liberty and many other fundamental rights of the individual."[30] He invoked the Universal Declaration as a promise of an international order under which human rights would be universally protected, and implicitly located colonialism as outside such an order.[31]

It was hardly surprising that these arguments caused dismay among the colonial powers. Lord MacDonald (UK) was appalled by the attacks on colonialism in October and November 1950. The debate, which began with consideration of a colonial exemption clause, had rapidly become a de facto trial of human rights under colonial regimes, and presaged the introduction of a self-determination resolution. MacDonald declared that "the question before the Committee was not whether it was right or wrong that a colonial system should still exist in the twentieth century but merely whether, with such a system in existence, a colonial [exemption] clause should be incorporated."[32] An official at the British Colonial Office was scathing in his appraisal of the situation, and in early 1951 described the pursuit of a human right to self-determination as "a mere pretext for attacks on the colonial powers."[33]

The campaign for the inclusion of a right to self-determination in the human rights covenant was launched in the immediate aftermath of the defeat of the colonial clause.[34] The draft resolution on self-determination was formally presented on 9 November 1950, one week after a successful move by the Philippines and Syria to excise the colonial clause from the draft covenant.[35] Although the removal of the clause represented a triumph for the Third World, and a success for human rights more generally, the agenda of many in the Committee had become more radical as the sessions went on. Throughout the sessions in late October and early November, the legitimacy of colonialism had come under intense pressure. Arab, Asian, and Latin American representatives had openly challenged the notion that human rights could be respected under a colonial regime. The evasive answers provided by the administering powers did nothing to assuage their concerns.

Baroody and Pazhwak led the efforts for a right to self-determination. Their resolution instructed the Commission on Human Rights to "study ways and means which ensure the right of peoples and nations to self-determination" and report back to the General Assembly.[36] It attracted virtually unanimous support from the Arab, African, Asian, and communist representatives, as well as some Latin American states. Many of the Arab, Asian, and Latin American delegations emphasized the importance of self-determination for the achievement of other human rights. Bedia Afnan (Iraq), a constant critic of colonialism and a strong supporter of women's rights, proposed self-determination as "the essence of all human rights."[37] Nizar Kayali (Syria) identified it "as the essential prerequisite of all other rights."[38] Protection of all other human rights, he claimed, "would be possible only if the fundamental right to self-determination was recognized first." Despite Western objections, the proposal was passed without amendment on 10 November, only one day after its introduction. It was adopted by the General Assembly on 4 December 1950.[39]

Arab and Asian delegations intensified their calls for a right to self-determination the following year, when it again came up for debate in the Third Committee. Battles over the right to self-determination constituted the bulk of the discussion in the 1951 session. Led by Baroody, Pazhwak, Malik, and Syrian diplomat Jawdat Mufti, the proponents of self-determination demanded its inclusion on the covenants. Almost

every non-Western state represented in the Committee insisted that individual freedom rested on national independence, while the European
delegations regarded it as little more than a device invented for attacking colonial administrations.[40]

During the 1951 session, the democratic argument for self-
determination was more fully developed, chiefly by members of the
Arab group. Malik, who had been so pivotal in the drafting of the Universal Declaration, "emphasized the relation between individual rights
and the collective right of peoples to self-determination."[41] He was convinced that "the further people progressed towards self-determination
the more they would respect human rights and vice versa." Individual
rights and national freedom were interdependent.

Apart from Malik, several other, more ferociously anticolonial figures
made the link between rights and national independence. Syrian delegate
Mufti exalted self-determination as "the corner-stone of the whole edifice
of human rights."[42] In a speech that invoked the 1941 Atlantic Charter at
length, he described the two main aspects of self-determination, the domestic and the international. Domestic self-determination, he explained,
was based on "a people's right to adopt representative institutions and
freely to choose the form of government which it wished to adopt."[43] Responding to claims that a collective right had no place in the covenant,
Atlaf Husain (Pakistan) countered that "the right of peoples to self-determination constituted the very basis of all the individual rights laid down
in articles 1 to 18 of the draft covenant."[44]

Indonesian delegate Nazir Pamontjak argued that self-determination
was valuable precisely because it advanced individual rights. Pamontjak
was a significant figure in Indonesian nationalism, and had been imprisoned by the Dutch colonial authorities in the 1940s. With this in mind,
it was unsurprising that he nominated self-determination as "a *condi-
tio sine qua non* of individual human rights." National liberation "was
not an end in itself," but rather "a means essential, as the experience
of centuries had shown, for ensuring those very human rights with
which the Third Committee was concerned." [45] It was an impressive intervention on the self-determination question, although as the struggles over human rights in the Indonesian Konstituante during the
1950s illustrated, not all in the Indonesian government agreed with
Pamontjak's stance on the relative priority of individual and national
rights.[46]

Further debates in 1952 consolidated the connection between individual human rights and the right to self-determination in anticolonial
rhetoric. In the November and December sessions of the Third Committee, speakers from Afghanistan, Iraq, the Philippines, Mexico, and
Greece all argued for the importance of the relationship between indi-

vidual human rights and a collective human right to self-determination. Most presented this in terms of self-determination being a pre-condition for individual rights, but others argued for the interdependence of the two concepts, or indeed the similarity in some respects. The Mexican delegate insisted that "the right of self-determination of peoples was both the basis of, and derived from, individual human rights."[47] Dmitrios Lambros (Greece), went further, and claimed that the right to self-determination was little more than another name for a democratic state which respected human rights:

> For his part, he could not accept the subtle distinctions drawn by some representatives between individual and collective human rights and between "internal" and "external" self-determination. Ultimately, the subject of any human right was the individual. While that might seem to be a new concept, in reality it stated clearly an old idea. Respect for the rights of the individual was the basis of democracy.... The peoples of the Western democracies, justly proud of their free institutions, should realize that their way of life was still enjoyed by few. Theirs was a democracy of an ivory tower, a democracy for the most fortunate. It would become a democracy for all only when all peoples and all nations were granted the right of self-determination.[48]

Third World and Latin American advocates promoted self-determination as a means of extending the individual rights enjoyed by Europeans to colonial subjects, for spreading democracy from its Western "ivory tower" to the rest of the world. Self-determination was, in the speeches of many delegates, the means for achieving the collection of civil liberties denied to those under colonial administration.

Yet the relationship that was codified in the landmark 1952 resolution on self-determination unequivocally asserted the primacy of self-determination over human rights. The interdependence emphasized in so many of the Asian and Arab justifications of a right to self-determination was replaced with a model that made all individual rights dependent on self-determination. In Baroody's amendment to the text, introduced on 24 November 1952, self-determination had to be achieved before other human rights could be realized: "The right of peoples and nations to self-determination is a prerequisite to the enjoyment of all fundamental human rights."[49] While Baroody later conceded that there were other important pre-conditions, the formulation that was adopted by the Third Committee firmly established the supremacy of national self-determination over individual freedom.[50]

Two years later, during the October 1954 session of the Third Committee, Baroody again provided the most dynamic and aggressive leadership to the anti-imperialist cause, equating national liberation alone with self-determination. In a long and impassioned speech, he assailed the Western countries that made academic and legalistic excuses for rejecting the right to self-determination. Effective enjoyment of human rights, said Baroody, "depended on the exercise of a fundamental right—the right of self-determination of peoples and nations."[51] The formalistic European delegations that "invoked laws and principles" were missing the point.

[Baroody] called upon them to come down from their ivory tower, to face the realities of life and of history, in short, to acknowledge that the current wide- spread bloodshed and revolutions were due to the fact that the fundamental right of the self-determination of peoples was not being respected . . . the ex- ercise of human rights was in the first place dependent upon the liberation of oppressed peoples.

For Baroody, the Western position was conditioned by the comfortable enjoyment of sovereignty, they "had enjoyed freedom for a long time" and "therefore knew nothing about foreign domination, or had forgot- ten what it implied."[52] Article 1, included in both covenants after they were split in 1951, was he argued, "of outstanding importance." Colonial powers persisted in the gravest human rights violations, and there was no prospect of their cessation without independence.

Even the more moderate of the Third World group were inclined to agree. Matthew (India) employed more conciliatory rhetoric, but his po- sition was broadly consistent with Baroody's insistence that national lib- eration was a necessity for individual rights. Rights and sovereignty were "closely linked," and "the individual could not enjoy full rights unless he was a member of a self-determined society."[53] But this close link was not symmetrical, Article 1 was the most fundamental right of all; it was, argued Matthew "the source from which all the other rights proceeded." Self-determination's place as the premier article in the covenants was deeply symbolic—it served as the enabling condition for all the other enumerated freedoms that followed.

Universal Right or Anticolonial Weapon? Defining Self-Determination

Throughout the early 1950s, there was considerable ambiguity about whether the right to self-determination was universal or confined solely to the Arab, Asian, and African territories under colonial rule. Within the small Third World group, there were a variety of positions. The most orthodox view was the narrow interpretation of self-determination as a right to be free of European colonialism—essentially the "sovereignty" self-determination championed by Baroody. Others claimed it was a right to be free of all forms of colonialism, including the "communist imperialism" of the Soviet Union. A significant number of voices, notably the Philippines, also argued that it was a right to be free of all oppression, even that imposed by indigenous despotisms.

Competition between these conflicting definitions occupied much of the next phase of the self-determination debate, which began in April 1955. Both in the Commission on Human Rights and at the Asian-African Conference then in session in Bandung, a series of attempts were made to define colonialism. From the first day of the Bandung conference, African and Asian delegates had drawn clear parallels between Soviet oppression in Eastern Europe and Western colonialism. When it came time to define colonialism for the purposes of the Bandung Final Communiqué, their arguments became more insistent, with many representatives demanding the inclusion of this "new colonialism" in the final text. The most dramatic of these interventions was made by John Kotelawala, Ceylonese prime minister, who contended that there was little difference between Soviet practice in Europe and conventional colonialism. "If we are united in our opposition to colonialism," Kotelawala argued, "should it not be our duty openly to declare our opposition to Soviet colonialism as much as to Western imperialism?"[54] The requirement for consensus resulted in an ambiguous compromise text which denounced colonialism "in all its manifestations," but a willingness to condemn Soviet and European colonialisms equally was evident among a majority of the Bandung delegates.[55]

Bandung had strengthened the link between individual human rights and the right to self-determination. Those who advocated an anticolonialism that sought to advance the rights of the individual, figures like Malik and Romulo, won widespread support. Their success was illustrated by the inclusion of the Universal Declaration in the Final Communiqué. Other speakers reaffirmed the relationship between self-determination and the rights of the individual. This was exemplified by Djalal Abdoh (Iran), who argued that self-determination was justified by the logic of democracy. If people had the right to participate in the operation of the "unit" of the state, Aboh deduced that they held an "equal right to be consulted about the form and functioning of the unit."[56]

At Bandung, many of the Afro-Asian delegates indicated their support for a democratic anticolonialism that advanced the rights of the individual as it advanced the rights of the nation. Human rights and self-determination were combined in Article C of the Final Communiqué. Most references to human rights were followed by references to the right to self-determination.[57] Individual freedom and national independence were rarely separated, and the former was never considered without the latter. Afghan delegate Sardar Naim declared that his government's "conception of independence" was "not different in any respect from

our conception of the observance of fundamental human rights, especially the right of peoples and nations to self-determination."[58] There
could be no respect for human rights under colonialism, according to
the consensus that prevailed among the Asian, Arab, and African delegations at the conference. Bandung's self-determination was closer to
the "democracy" variant than the pure "sovereignty" type, though the
latter had some influential champions, including Nehru.

Asian and African delegates at the Commission on Human Rights
exploited the prestige of the Bandung Conference to lend further
weight to their speeches on self-determination. On 21 and 22 April
1955 in Geneva, a chorus of Third World delegations rejected a U.S.
proposal to study and define the right to self-determination before
actually doing anything about it.[59] The most determined among them
was Rajeshwar Dayal (India), who urged the Commission to forget
about a UN definition of self-determination, and proceed immediately
to granting the right. Colonial peoples "would not wait on definitions,"
a point that was amply demonstrated by the fiery rhetoric emerging
from Bandung.[60]

Salvador López, the Philippine delegate, cited Carlos Romulo's
speech at the Bandung Conference, in which he had warned of the perils of "new imperialism." López spoke of "a new and more terrible form
of imperialism than the world had yet known," and of the dangers posed
by a selective approach to self-determination.[61]

It was not a question of preferring one form of imperialism to another; all such
[forms] were to be condemned. The only valid practical consideration was that
those colonial Powers that had already given up dominion over subject countries, rather than the new gigantic communist imperialism that had ingested
vast territories and hundreds of millions of people without setting free one inch
of land or a single human being, should be trusted to achieve speedier progress
in the field of self-determination.

In a reference to the Soviet address in the previous meeting, which had
seen Soviet delegate Platon Morosov clumsily attempt to exploit the
Bandung deliberations, López advised against "intemperate voices." It
was countries like Pakistan and India that were the authentic champions
of self-determination, not the Soviet bloc. Equally, López was dismissive
of the U.S. suggestion that self-determination be defined and studied
by the Commission on Human Rights. This sort of legalism, he warned,
"was completely outmoded" and "dangerous."[62] Notionally aligned to
the U.S., López charted a skillful course that combined anti-Soviet and
anticolonial elements, and in the process proved that the Philippines
was beholden to no-one.

In the wake of the crushing of the Hungarian uprising in November

1956, and the failure of many major Third World powers to back censure of the Soviet Union, there was a drift away from the notion of a universal right to self-determination. Increasingly, the right to self-determination was being defined as a right to national sovereignty, exercised primarily, or even solely, against European colonialism.[63] It had sharp geographical boundaries, and applied to a very specific set of political situations.

UN resolutions to condemn the Soviet intervention in Hungary in 1956 and 1957 revealed much of this attitude, especially among the ardently non-aligned members of the Afro-Asian bloc. The representative from China (Taiwan) complained about the failure of many Asian, African, and Arab states to apply the principle of self-determination universally, a trend that was self-evidently a worrying sign for his state.

I was sorry and disappointed to see so many abstentions . . . [from] delegations which, ordinarily, are in the forefront as regards all matters concerning human rights and self-determination. . . . I wonder whether these delegations of Asia and Africa mean to tell us that the principles of the Charter are good only for Asia and Africa, and not for Europe. Is our particular support for these great principles to be limited to particular regions and particular conflicts?[64]

India was the most glaring example of the narrow, legalistic "sovereignty" thesis of self-determination with respect to Hungary, presumably mindful of its own liabilities in Kashmir.[65] At the 1956 emergency session, Krishna Menon cautioned that the UN should "not forget the sovereign rights of a sovereign State in the Assembly."[66] Although he deplored the Soviet action, he drew a distinction between "Member States" and colonies, just as Nehru had done a year earlier at Bandung. He warned that "We must not refer to a Member State as though it were struggling for its independence." Nevertheless, a number of Asian, Arab, and African countries backed various UN resolutions on Hungary, including major neutralists such as Indonesia, Burma, and Ceylon.[67]

In the Third Committee in November 1957, Mary Lord (United States) tried to rally support for the universal strand of self-determination, which was seemingly on the wane. It was an approach that the U.S. State Department had embraced since the early 1950s, chiefly for its utility as anti-communist propaganda, but with a vestigial allegiance to the ideas of 1776.[68] "Too often," Lord lamented, "self-determination was confused with anti-colonialism."[69] In clear reference to Hungary, she argued that "while self-determination could be exercised against traditional colonialism, it could also operate against the political subjugation of a weaker neighbour by a powerful State."[70] Similar allusions to the fate of Hungary, and Tibet were made by the Taiwanese delegate, who cautioned of "new-style colonies" where "foreign troops [had] suppressed the aspirations of the peoples."[71]

Yet the universal, democratic approach to the right to self-determination was now facing serious challenge. Most strident of all was Zenon Rossides (Greece and Cyprus), who argued that political freedom and national sovereignty were two very distinct issues that could not be compared. "It was," he said, "perfectly clear" that self-determination "did not go into the question of the political system of a particular State." Rossides refuted the relevance of "internal" governance, "where a people enjoyed national independence, the question of self-determination could not arise."[72] There were many different systems of government, varying from state to state, and across time, but these shifts in the character of the domestic regime did not have "the slightest effect" on the right to self-determination. There must be no confusion between individual and national rights, asserted Rossides. In his view, "the idea of self-determination did not include that of political freedom within an independent State."[73]

Baroody strongly endorsed Rossides's argument on the need to separate national liberation and democracy. Once sovereignty was attained, the right to self-determination was exhausted. "There was no yardstick," Baroody contended, "for measuring the extent to which the right to self-determination was respected in an independent country."[74] It was not possible to evaluate a term as imprecise as self-determination, and there existed no standard upon which to base judgment beyond national independence.

> There was no democracy in the absolute sense of the term; there were malpractices even in the countries closest to ideal democracy, as was inevitable in view of the imperfections and complexity of human nature. Such terms were therefore merely relative.[75]

Only by looking at external sovereignty could a consistent judgment about the exercise of self-determination be made. The characteristics of the regime and political system were irrelevant.

Representatives from Ceylon and Ghana, neither of which had been admitted to the UN at the time of the 1954 debate, adopted Baroody's basic position on self-determination.[76] Adae (Ghana) was confident that independence was the priority, and endorsed the view that a domestic dictatorship was preferable to "enlightened" colonial government. In her response to a rhetorical question from Salvador López (Philippines) on the relative merits of the two options, Adae was convinced that "nothing could equal the feeling of confidence and dignity experienced by a people when it attained independence."[77] López himself was ambivalent.[78]

Ceylonese delegate Mahmud was adamant that individual political rights and self-determination had to be decoupled because one had no bearing on the other. Mahmud thought it "dangerous to confuse political freedom with national independence."[79] He advocated a definition based strictly on the absence of foreign control.

Before attaining complete independence, Ceylon had enjoyed great political freedom, and yet it had not been a sovereign nation, able to decide whether or not it wanted to be independent. Moreover, there were sovereign countries where the people had no political freedom or whose Government was not what most of the people wanted, and yet the principle of self-determination in those countries was not violated. The right of peoples and nations to self-determination was simply their right to establish their own political institutions, to develop their economy and to direct their cultural and social evolution without any foreign intervention.

Mahmud's statement was almost the antithesis of Kotelawala's famous speech at Bandung scarcely two years earlier, where he had urged the redefinition of colonialism to include Soviet communism.[80]

Although the strict anticolonial interpretation of self-determination was gaining adherents, there remained a number of influential Arab, Asian, and Latin American delegates who championed a more universal approach. Foremost among them was López, who exhorted those who had won their freedom for European colonialism to consider the fate of those who suffered under other forms of foreign domination. "It would be unseemly," he said, for delegations from newly decolonized states like Ceylon and Ghana, "to speak lightly of less fortunate peoples whom others had annexed by military force or political trickery."[81] Their claims to self-determination were "no less worthy of attention" from the UN. The notion that self-determination "could be exercised only by peoples under the colonial rule of Western powers," he argued, "could not be maintained."[82]

A similar argument was made by the charismatic Karen Olsen Beck Figueres, First Lady of Costa Rica and newly appointed UN representative. Beck Figueres sought to draw the Third Committee's attention away from a narrow focus on forms of foreign subjugation. The discussion, she argued, "had neglected one of the three aspects of the problem of self-determination."[83] While the delegates had been focused on European and communist colonialisms, they "had not referred to the right to self-determination of peoples living under the yoke of a domestic dictatorship." Figueres reminded her audience of peoples "both in the eastern and in the western hemisphere, which were subjected to regimes of domestic tyranny." She found an ally in Iraqi delegate Bedia Afnan, who claimed that the primary importance of independence was its utility in securing individual rights. Well known for her advocacy of women's equality, Afnan "did not consider the right of self-determination as an end in itself," and argued instead that self-determination "should serve to safeguard individual liberty more fully."[84] However, she rejected the notion of an "enlightened" colonial regime—individual rights could not exist when government was controlled "even in the best possible conditions, by a foreign Power."

Fulfilling the Promise of Bandung: Resolution 1514 and Human Rights

The piecemeal skirmishes of the 1950s culminated in a landmark debate held in the plenary sessions of the General Assembly through November and December 1960, amid optimistic expectations about both democracy and independence in Africa. Following an initiative from Soviet Premier Khrushchev, the UN began to formulate a declaration on decolonization and independence.[85] It came at the end of the so-called Year of Africa, when more than a dozen former French African colonies were admitted to the UN. Imminent liberation of British colonies had also been foreshadowed by Prime Minister Harold Macmillan in his "Wind of Change" speech. Only weeks after the passage of the UN declaration, a group of almost two hundred lawyers from across the continent convened in Lagos and proclaim their faith in democracy, rule of law, and human rights as guiding principles for the nascent independent Africa.[86]

Two competing texts were proposed for the declaration, the first from the Soviet Union, which exemplified narrow, sovereignty-based anticolonialism, and the second from the Afro-Asian bloc, which included extensive reference to human rights. The Soviet draft ignored the links that had been established between human rights and self-determination during the drafting of the human rights covenants in the preceding decade. In the Soviet text, self-determination was based on state sovereignty, non-interference and "international co-operation."[87] By contrast, the Afro-Asian proposal maintained the fraying connection between self-determination and human rights that had been evident since the early 1950s, and articulated in the Bandung Final Communiqué.

The Soviet draft declaration was focused entirely on European colonialism and the achievement of national independence. Its preamble was devoted to attacking the colonial powers, often in highly emotive terms, citing the litany of abuses committed by repressive colonial administrations, and the economic exploitation that underpinned the colonial system:

In these countries, violence and lawlessness reign as before; in these countries the highest law is profit for foreigners. Their interest is all, and the inalienable rights of man and people are nothing. . . . There the swish of the overseer's lash is heard; there heads fall under the executioner's axe.[88]

Apart from this one mention of "the inalienable rights of man," the Soviet draft made no explicit reference to human rights. It endorsed violence as a means of ending colonialism, exhorting the "peace loving nations to render every assistance, moral and material" to those struggling against imperial powers.[89] The main text of the resolution was constructed around the abolition of Western colonial regimes and "the equality and respect for sovereign rights and territorial integrity without exception."[90]

Introduced after the Soviet text, the Afro-Asian Group's draft on colonialism was sponsored by a huge array of Asian, Arab, and African states, eventually comprising almost the entire Afro-Asian group.[91] In this draft, human rights were an important justification for self-determination. Eschewing the one-sided propaganda that characterized the Soviet declaration, the declaration was universal in scope, albeit with vastly greater emphasis on African and Asian colonial territories. Its first article declared "the subjection of peoples to alien subjugation, domination and exploitation constitutes a denial of fundamental human rights."[92] Principles enshrined in the Bandung Final Communiqué were central to the draft, which sought to internationalize the interpretation of self-determination that had been agreed upon at the conference in 1955. Borrowing from the compromise language agreed on at the Bandung Conference, it condemned colonialism "in all its manifestations," and made reference to the Universal Declaration.[93] The final text even included one instance of the phrase "colonialism in all its forms and manifestations," which reproduced the term "forms," which had been considered too provocative for the Bandung Final Communiqué.

The Bandung Conference was invoked as the guiding precedent for the declaration by a multitude of delegates in the 1960 debate.[94] Ato Haddis Alemayehou (Ethiopia) commended the Afro-Asian resolution as "a consolidation of the ideals and principles which the African-Asian countries have proclaimed and supported ever since 1955."[95] A more specific emphasis on the linguistic similarities was made by Rishikesh Shaha (Nepal), who observed that the main articles were "based on the text of the final communiqué of the Asian-African Conference at Bandung."[96] To underscore the similarities, Alex Quaison-Sackey (Ghana), a future president of the General Assembly, read out the relevant provisions of the Bandung Final Communique, and gave special attention to those that dealt with human rights, which were repeated in full.[97]

The Declaration sponsors commended the text as the beginning of a new era in the history of human rights. Mehdi Vakil (Iran) described the decolonizing "wind of change" in Africa as a return to "the great principles born of the French Revolution and of its rights of man and citizen."[98] Mamdou Dia, the Senegalese prime minister, argued that his support for the declaration, and for decolonization, was based on universal concern for democratic values. Decolonization would continue until there was "complete democratization" in every state.[99] According to Dia, the Afro-Asian anticolonial campaign was "not confined to one type" of colonialism but "inspired by the universalist spirit of the pioneers of democracy, whether French or American."[100] Omar (Somalia) exemplified the calls of these sponsor states, which argued that the declaration should be incorporated into the corpus of democratic charters:

This session of the Assembly may well go down in history as the "Assembly of Freedom" and our declaration, as a "Declaration of Freedom," would rank with the great Charters of mankind: the Magna Carta, the Declaration of Independence, the Declaration of the Rights of Man, and the Charter of the United Nations.[101]

Human rights did not feature at all among the arguments of those who advocated the rival Soviet text, which offered little more than a confection of tired anticolonial phrases.

Many of the pro-Western African and Asian states argued for a declaration that promoted liberation for all, rather than the selective condemnation of European colonialism. Although several delegates had expressed gratitude for the Soviet initiative to have colonialism placed on the agenda, many were scathing of the hypocrisy the Soviet draft represented. Vakil immediately reminded the assembly of the "young and virulent" new colonialism that had been condemned at Bandung.[102] His criticisms were amplified by Lorenzo Sumulong (Philippines), who launched a tirade against Soviet efforts to capture the anticolonial mantle:

By adopting the African-Asian draft declaration we shall give proof of our capacity to see through pretence and hypocrisy. We shall proclaim the integrity of our own judgment, uninfluenced by pity or flattery. We shall give notice to the neo-imperialists that we are not prepared to accept any lessons from them in the matter of winning freedom and independence. But should they persist in the attempt we shall be constrained to say unto them: What you now do to destroy the freedom of human beings and the independence of peoples is so loud, so deafening, that we cannot hear what you say.[103]

Such sentiments were re-iterated by delegates from across Asia and Africa, who rejected the Soviet attempt to co-opt their anticolonial campaign and transform it into a cynical propaganda exercise.

South East Asian representatives fearful of communist insurgency denounced the Soviet bloc's loud professions of support for self-determination. Champassak (Laos) castigated Soviet anticolonial posturing.[104] He warned that "anti-colonialism must not blind us to the political designs of any ideological bloc which is trying to capture the new States while they are still weak."[105] Nimnanheminda, representing Thailand, a U.S. ally and SEATO member state, alluded to the Chinese invasion of Tibet. Communism might operate under the pretext of achieving independence, but "when it enters by one door, freedom flies out the other."[106] Soviet anticolonial rhetoric was discredited by repressive and imperialistic practice; "what shall it profit a country," Nimnanheminda declared theatrically, "to gain complete independence only to lose its own soul."[107]

Delegates from both Laos and the Malay Federation argued that the declaration would only have significance if it was applied to all those who had been denied their freedom, including those under communist domination. Champassak dismissed the validity of any exercise that was not based on a common and equal idea of freedom. Debate on self-determination was "pointless" if it was "merely an export for the consumption of the poor and ignorant masses."[108] Kamil (Malay Federation) argued that because freedom was a universal value "any declaration for the cause of freedom and liberty must, as a matter of course, be taken as universal in its application and scope."[109] Only months earlier, in July 1960, the Malayan Emergency had concluded after a decade of British and Commonwealth backed counter-insurgency operations against Malay Communist Party guerrillas.[110]

In a speech that echoed Kotelawala's famous outburst at Bandung, the delegate from one of the newest independent states in the assembly, the Republic of Congo (Brazzaville) demanded an even-handed approach to colonialism. Lheyct-Gaboka, who represented the first post-independence government of pro-Western President Fulbert Youlou, had little experience, but delivered a provocative condemnation of one-sided anticolonialism clearly directed at the Soviet Union.

But if there are still peoples under the colonialist yoke in Africa, it should not be forgotten that there are countries elsewhere in the world which know no freedom either. Even in Europe, which prides itself on its civilization, we can count up the people who, at the present time, certainly envy the lot of the African States which have attained independence. We must not forget those countries whose cries are stifled and hence cannot reach us. What are their colonizers waiting for before decolonizing them?[111]

The type of self-determination proposed in the Afro-Asian draft text was strongly backed by diplomats representing the Latin American countries, many of which presented the issue as an extension of democracy and individual rights.[112] Despite the obvious influence of the U.S. across much of Latin America, such statements also reflected the significant role played by the region on human rights questions, with many Latin American jurists involved in the drafting of the Universal Declaration, the two covenants, and the Bogotá Declaration of Human Rights.[113]

Yet there was also a lone voice among the Third World states who warned against the expectation that individual freedom in the universalist Western tradition would naturally follow the exercise of self-determination. Burmese delegate U Thant, the next secretary-general, cautioned that "it would be a mistake to assume that the political institutions and forms of democracy in most of the newly independent countries will be of the same type as those prevailing in Britain or the United States."[114] According to Thant, there was scant capacity for such systems in the new African states in the near term.

The notion that democracy requires the existence of an organized opposition to the government of the day is not valid. Democracy requires only freedom for such an opposition, not necessarily the existence of it. In many newly independent countries—and I am thinking especially of African countries it is most unlikely that there will be a two party system for some years to come. The nationalist movements are going to be very powerful indeed; they will control the government and organize local development in the economic and social spheres without there being any effective challenge to them from within. And any challenge from outside will only strengthen them. . . . It is worth bearing in mind that the democratic system of government, though most desirable, is at the same time the most difficult form of government to operate.[115]

In the high-moment of post-colonial optimism, Thant's speech was a rare exception to the Afro-Asian argument that individual freedom would follow naturally and inevitably from decolonization.

Others from outside the UN wanted a more emphatic assertion of universality included in the declaration, which did not mention Soviet colonialism by name. The leading human rights NGO of the period, the International League for the Rights of Man, pressed for such changes. Roger Baldwin wrote on behalf of the League to at least one delegation from the Afro-Asian group, with amendments to strengthen the anti-Soviet dimension of the text.[116] It would, he argued, discredit the United Nations to promulgate a declaration which failed to "apply equally and everywhere to all States and all peoples."[117]

As introduced it is open to the interpretation that aims only at the traditional forms of European control over subject peoples. Obviously there are other forms of foreign control under which the peoples have no chance to express themselves in accordance with the principle of self-determination. The resolution can easily be strengthened to make it universal as we venture to suggest on the enclosed memorandum.

Baldwin claimed that the League had "no partisanship between the varied forms of colonialism" being "opposed to them all."

Yet its own internal deliberations on self-determination reflected uncertainty about how anticolonialism could be related to individual rights. A League memorandum circulated around the time of the 1960 vote was instructive as to the tensions within the organization. It was unclear on whether self-determination was actually a right of itself, or simply a condition that was often conductive to the securing of rights. The author, likely Baldwin himself, carefully weighed both options, with little sense of a definitive answer.

Was colonialism nothing more or less than a basic denial of a fundamental human right to self-determination belonging to a people which should be bluntly and flatly opposed as such? Or were there more significant individual human rights, especially of a civil and political nature, which should be the primary focus of a human rights organization? Viewed the latter way, self-determination was an instrumental principle which it might sometimes, but not invariably, be necessary to support in order to obtain these individual rights.[118]

Even for a human rights NGO, with no sovereignty to claim, or colonies to protect, the status of self-determination was far from easy. The League's amendments that strengthened the universality and consistency of the "right," were a step in the right direction, but did not resolve this fundamental philosophical point. In any case, they were never debated by the General Assembly.

Despite the failure of Baldwin's proposals, when the Declaration on the Granting of Independence to Colonial Countries and Peoples was passed on 14 December 1960, it represented the zenith of the universalist, democratic tendency in anticolonialism. Not only was it an official endorsement of the link between rights and national independence embodied by the Bandung Final Communiqué, but it also signaled a dramatic elevation in the status of the right of self-determination and anticolonialism. Passed by a huge majority, with only nine abstentions, all from the West, the declaration on colonialism was comparable only to the Universal Declaration in the level of support it garnered. The very size of the majority was also indicative of the success of self-determination on the ground—unlike the 1955 conference, where a mere four African countries were present; there were now over twenty independent states from the African continent in the UN.

Although the Western states abstained, the declaration on colonialism was viewed with considerable sympathy, not least for its universal approach. Some within the U.S. delegation were appalled by the American abstention on a resolution that rejected one-sided Soviet anticolonialism, and was broadly consistent with a number of traditional Western ideas. James Wadsworth, U.S. ambassador to the General Assembly, expressed his disappointment when instructed not to back the Declaration, after personal intervention from President Eisenhower.[119] "For the record," Wadsworth wrote to the State Department, "I am shocked and disheartened."[120] The Afro-Asian text was, he asserted, "far more moderate and constructive draft than could have been expected, and one which both rejects Soviet approach to [the] subject as well as includes language aimed at Soviet imperialism."[121] Even Secretary of State Christian Herter recommended to President Eisenhower that the U.S. vote for the Declaration. Herter commented that although the draft had "much language with which we disagree," it was balanced by "some good language."[122] It also represented the consensus position of the forty-two members of the Afro-Asian group, which had rejected both Soviet and Western amendments for the sake of even-handedness.[123]

From Means to Ends: The Decline of the Democratic Right to Self-Determination

In the euphoric atmosphere of the 1960 "Year of Africa," the universalist, democratic tendency of self-determination reached its peak, and it diminished steadily thereafter. Less than a year later, in November 1961, the General Assembly passed Resolution 1654, which took a much more selective, sovereignty-based approach to self-determination. Under the terms of Resolution 1654, a Special Committee was created to monitor the progress of the Declaration. Yet it applied solely to European colonial territories, and had no interest in the status of individual rights in states that had gained their sovereignty, or indeed those in Eastern Europe. The Committee demanded no democratic procedures for territories that chose to become independent.[124] As the decade went on, the association between democracy and self-determination rapidly receded.[125] By 1963, it was increasingly apparent that the Declaration was being interpreted as a narrow measure against European colonialism only, with no application beyond the attainment of national independence. The Special Committee did not consider the status of Eastern Europe, or of those living under endogenous undemocratic regimes, despite pleas to do so from Baldwin and other members of the League for Human Rights.[126]

   In the second half of the 1960s, during the debates on UN Declaration on Friendly Relations, the most definitive statement on international law since the UN Charter, a purely sovereignty-based notion of self-determination was evident among representatives from Third World states. At a 1967 meeting of the Friendly Relations drafting committee, the Burmese delegate, representing the military junta, argued against any consideration of democracy in self-determination. The UN, he claimed, "had clearly and incontrovertibly established" that self-determination "was relevant only to colonialism and was to be specifically applied in the promotion of independence of peoples under colonial domination."[127] According to the final terms of the Declaration on Friendly Relations, there was no need for governments to be democratically representative of their peoples; they only had to be of the same racial composition.[128] Western arguments for the inclusion of democratic criteria as part of the definition of self-determination failed.[129]

Under the new interpretation embodied in the Declaration on Friendly Relations, it was not democracy but concepts like non-intervention and sovereign equality that best complemented the right to self-determination. This had been the case since December 1965, with the adoption of the Declaration on the Inadmissibility of Intervention in the Domestic Affairs of States and the Protection of their Independence and Sovereignty. Drafted in response to a Soviet propaganda initiative, this Declaration was effusive on sovereignty but virtually silent on human rights.[130] Individual rights are obscured in the language of the 1965 text, which instead grants rights to the state. "Every state," it affirms, "has an inalienable right to choose its political, economic, social and cultural systems, without interference in any form."[131] There was no demand that these systems represent their people.

The limits of the right to self-determination were brutally illustrated in 1968 by the Biafran conflict and the atrocities of the Nigerian Federal Government. Once European colonialism had departed, the right to self-determination ceased to exist. It was an ominous double standard; human rights abuses practiced by indigenous as opposed to colonial dictatorships were of little concern to most of the Afro-Asian group. One of the few exceptions was Tanzanian President Julius Nyerere, who condemned the hypocrisy on self-determination. He lamented that "we will soon be tolerating fascism in Africa as long as it is practiced by African governments against African peoples."[132] African leaders needed to be held to the same standards as their European colonial counterparts. After all, argued Nyerere, "these [Biafran] people are still dead; the colour of those who killed them is irrelevant."[133]

Pursuit of self-determination also became an excuse for indiscriminate violence. During debates in the Ad Hoc Committee on International Terrorism in 1973, attempts were made by African and Arab states to carve out broad exceptions for terrorism carried out in the name of self-determination.[134] The pretext of self-determination was sufficient to override all other concerns, and according to the Zambian delegate, the Committee had to "refrain from doing anything that would restrict freedom fighters in Africa."[135] Those furthering national liberation "'have the right to use whatever means available' to them in their struggle for self-determination." Subordination of means to ends was complete. Individual rights had to be violated to secure national sovereignty, the opposite of the ideology that had animated the self-determination campaigns of the 1950s.

The dominance of the Third World majority had ensured the inclusion of self-determination in the catalogue of rights, but it had done nothing to ensure its promise was fulfilled. By the mid-1960s, the right to self-determination had become little more than the one-sided anti-colonial weapon that the self-interested European critics had charged it to be. The claims of the colonial powers had been unjust in the 1950s, but when the two human rights covenants were passed in 1966, the rhetoric of independence as the gateway to democracy had begun to look less and less plausible. Postcolonial regimes had proven to be anything but democratic, from "Nkrumahism" in Ghana, to "Guided Democracy" in Indonesia, to "Basic Democracy" in Pakistan. The self-determination of "sovereignty" had consumed its "democratic" sibling.

Chapter 3

Putting the Stamps Back On: Apartheid, Anticolonialism, and the Accidental Birth of a Universal Right to Petition

It should be mentioned that from its inception, this activity of the Human Rights Division has been one of the most abortive in the United Nations . . . the United Nations would be well advised to abolish the Communications Unit. . . . It is not disclosing a secret that many Member States of the United Nations are outright dictatorships.
—*Jamil Baroody, Permanent Representative of Saudi Arabia, Confidential Report on the State of the Human Rights Program to the Secretary-General, May 1971*

Please remind staff not to remove stamps from envelopes concerning human rights destined for division of human rights. . . . Apparently it is the practice of the incoming mail section to cut stamps from some communications, and these stamps are then sold in bags at Christmas time . . . it might be a source of the problems mentioned.
—*Exchange of correspondence regarding the fate of human rights complaints within the UN Secretariat, conducted in December 1974*

The Third World's pivotal role in the expansion of the UN human rights powers is one of the greatest paradoxes in the history of the organization. For more than twenty years, diplomats from the Afro-Asian bloc were the most potent force for change in the interpretation of Article 2(7) in the UN Charter, which prohibited intervention in domestic affairs. Yet for much of that time, as the course of the self-determination debates demonstrated, they were also among the most protective of their own state sovereignty. Decolonization transformed the UN into a body with unprecedented willingness to question state sovereignty, yet Third World diplomats often stipulated exceedingly narrow limits for when sovereignty could be breached, and a slender selection of states which were subject to such procedures.

The shift from state sovereignty to individual rights culminated in the recognition of petitions from the victims of human rights abuse as a legitimate object of study for UN human rights bodies. Since the foundation of the UNO in 1945, pleas for help had poured in from across the world. These letters, bureaucratically termed "petitions" or "individual communications," were a mixture of vexatious or frankly irrelevant claims, worthy but unreasonable aspirations, and genuine accounts of flagrant human rights violations. More than any other facet of the human rights enterprise, the letters, or petitions, engaged with the reality of human rights on the ground. They revealed the miserable gap between the grand abstractions that the world body was so good at drafting, and the desperate situation of the people who wanted those promises made good. The letters held the potential to connect the UN program to the streets, prisons, and homes where the rights struggle would be won or lost.

These petitions languished until the 1960s, when they began to be used to advance the struggle against *apartheid*, European colonialism, and racial discrimination. Bodies like the Special Committee of 24, the Special Committee on *Apartheid*, and the Committee on the Elimination of Racial Discrimination all made extensive use of petitions in their operation. This was a stunning departure from the attitude of the Commission on Human Rights, which had expressly denied itself the power to study any individual petitions in 1947. For two decades, the Commission scrupulously avoided any serious consideration of the countless letters it had accumulated, and only began to reverse its position in the late 1960s, several years after the pioneering decisions of the various anti-*apartheid* and decolonization committees.[1]

The fundamental importance of decolonization for the fate of individual petitions has often been observed. In his major monograph on the history of human rights, Paul Gordon Lauren singles out the crucial role of the Third World in finally securing a process for dealing with the letters. The struggle against *apartheid* provoked "the new and determined majority" of African and Asian states to pioneer much more aggressive methods in the pursuit of human rights goals, epitomized by the acceptance of petitions as evidence of racial discrimination in Southern Africa.[2] Their measures here "opened a critical door that had been slammed shut from the beginning, and thereby made possible many other efforts that went far beyond *apartheid*." These innovations, he asserts, "in turn, prompted a number of Western members . . . to take the initiative" and develop a proper mechanism for the investigation of allegations of human rights abuses, efforts that lead to the establishment of a universal right to petition in the late 1960s.[3]

Yet the Third World's role in the evolution of the petition process was considerably more complicated and ambiguous. It was not the initiative of a virtuous clique of Western members that decided the fate of individual petition. Throughout the immensely complex series of resolutions and rhetorical battles that ultimately resulted in the petitions procedure, Third World diplomats were the most significant actors, both in advancing and obstructing progress. These Arab, Asian, and African delegates were not confined to one-sided activism on *apartheid* and colonialism, and were instead active and influential participants in every major phase of the debate. Although Western representatives did make important contributions to the evolution of petition in the late 1960s, their interventions were often reactive, premised on trying to appease and harness the Afro-Asian majority. A meaningful system for the study of petitions emerged from the unpredictable and volatile interaction between insistent Third World demands and defensive Western responses.

This chapter is focused on the influence of Third World voices in four key UN debates on the status of individual petitions between 1947 and 1971. First, it examines the advocacy of the right to petition by figures like Charles Malik, Hansa Mehta, and Carlos Romulo in the late 1940s and early 1950s. Against daunting Western and Soviet opposition, these delegates campaigned doggedly for petitions to be heard by the Commission, and for their inclusion in the proposed covenant on human rights. Second, it evaluates the pivotal impact of African decolonization on UN willingness to accept a right to petition in the 1965 International Convention on the Elimination of All Forms of Racial Discrimination. It then analyses the subsequent debate on petition in the International Covenant on Civil and Political Rights, where profound divisions within the Afro-Asian bloc position emerged. Finally, the chapter demonstrates the indispensable role of Third World diplomats in the eventual success of reforms to the Commission on Human Rights in the late 1960s, when a universal right of petition was finally accepted, albeit with few immediate consequences.

Malik, Mehta, and Romulo: The Lonely Fight for Individual Petition in the 1940s and 1950s

During the late 1940s and early 1950s it was primarily a limited group of the Third World states then represented at the UN that sought the recognition of individual petitions. Delegations from the Philippines, Egypt, Syria, India, and Guatemala all sponsored various proposals on petition, both as part of the international covenant on human rights and as a basic prerogative of the Commission on Human Rights. [4] They were led by Charles Malik, the Lebanese philosopher so crucial to the successful completion of the 1948 Universal Declaration, and an icon of the early human rights program.

Malik was almost fanatical in his advocacy of a right to petition. At the very first session of the Commission in January and February 1947, he assailed skeptics of petition, which included chairperson Eleanor Roosevelt.

I can assure you, Madam Chairman, most of them [the petitions] will be nonsense, and they will be thrown into the wastebasket. That is perfectly all right, but then at least we assure the world that we are not going to disinterest ourselves in them; we are not going to disclaim our immediate interest in them as purporting to deal with human rights. Therefore, Madam Chairman, it seems to me it is of the utmost importance for us as a Commission to tell the world that we have a small body which will look at these documents as we receive them . . . I believe that as Commission of eighteen members whose only duty is to look after every aspect of human rights, we ought to receive, as a Commission, not as individuals, these communications, no matter how foolish and irrelevant and unfounded some of them may be.[5]

He was adamant that the Commission should be empowered to study petitions, no matter their provenance or credibility.

One of Malik's strongest arguments was directed at the symbolism of how the Commission treated petitions—failure to act would severely compromise the prestige and credibility of UN human rights activity. He expressed his shock and astonishment at the notion that no action would be taken beyond the cataloguing of petitions, which was the then accepted process.

I would be absolutely amazed if the one international body—namely, the Commission on Human Rights . . . if that one international body which is specifically set up for the purpose of looking after these . . . things, were to say, "All we do about these communications, regardless of whether one per cent of them or one millionth per cent of them is correct or not, is simply to list them and then leave them available to any person who wants to see them." I say I would be absolutely amazed if our conscience as a Commission, regarding our duty to everything which appertains to human rights, were to be aroused only to that extent.[6]

If the delegates adopted his plan for a special sub-committee to study petitions, Malik argued, then "at least the world will know that this Commission is not uninterested in problems of human rights." The pleas might go unanswered, but at least they would be read.

Although slightly more restrained in her rhetoric, Hansa Mehta (India) was almost as passionate as Malik on the subject of petitions. During the first two weeks of the 1947 session, she urged the Commission to focus on making rights a reality. Her concern was for the physical situation of persecuted individuals, and she made her distaste for extended philosophical digressions abundantly clear during the debate. On the afternoon of the first day of the inaugural session of the Commission, Mehta pressed Eleanor Roosevelt and Director of the Human Rights Division, John Humphrey, on the question of petitions, which were being threatened with excision from the agenda.

We have received a number of communications from individuals as well as organizations all over the world on matters pertaining to the work of this Commission. I believe very strongly that some of these communications from individuals and organizations which have been received by the Secretariat must be of profound interest to my colleagues on this Commission, and that they should be circulated.[7]

As the session continued with no progress on petition, Mehta intervened in the debate repeatedly. She argued that the actual realization of rights was "the most important thing."[8] Citing the precedent of the League of Nations minorities treaty, Mehta warned that without measures like a petition procedure, the Commission's work would "lack reality and content."[9] She had not come to the UN to quibble over empty abstractions.

The very next day, Carlos Romulo put forward a proposal to study how the Commission on Human Rights might investigate the petitions.[10] He was enthusiastic about setting up a pseudo-court for examining letters from the victims of human rights abuses, thereby giving some level of protection to all those who could appeal to the UN.[11] His suggestion for a sub-committee on petitions was adopted, with Malik, Roosevelt, and José Antonio Mora (Uruguay) appointed to examine a future procedure for dealing with the problem. On Romulo's part, there seemed a definite expectation that they would come up with a positive solution to the problem of the thousands of accumulated letters.

However, the pleas of Mehta, Malik, and Romulo were rebuffed by the Commission, which was then dominated by Western and Soviet members. Opponents of petition seized on an observation made in the report from Romulo's Sub-Committee, which recognized that there was currently no power to take action on any allegations of human rights abuse.[12] Instead of taking remedial steps, the Commission agreed on the notorious self-denying ordinance, which banned the investigation of any petitions received. It set up a mechanism virtually identical to that which Malik had mocked in his speech, but weaker and more secretive in its operation.[13] Led by Roosevelt, the Western bloc could call on a comfortable majority to pass the ordinance, which won additional support from the Soviet members, and was subsequently endorsed by the Economic and Social Council as Resolution 75(V).[14]

From the second meeting of the Commission on Human Rights, Roosevelt had rejected the suggestion of studying complaints.[15] The enthusiasm for petitions exemplified by Malik, Mehta, and Romulo was easily outvoted by an alliance that brought together both the Commission's persuasive chairperson and Valentin Tepliakov of the Soviet Union.[16]

Despite the sentiment represented by the self-denying ordinance, the struggle for petition soon resumed, with a number of Arab, Asian, and Latin American proposals for its inclusion as an article in the international covenant on human rights. When the Commission turned its attention to the covenant in 1949, following the successful passage of the Universal Declaration, India, the Philippines, Lebanon, and Guatemala all supported a right of individual petition, but their ideas won little favor among the Western states. In May and June 1949, Humphrey recorded his despair at the "sorry discussion" on petition, and complained that only a handful were interested, notably Mehta, with whom he had discussed individual petition privately.[17] If the situation did not improve, Humphrey complained that the UN "may as well give up the sponge" and abandon the idea of a serious covenant.[18]

At the 1949 session, Lebanese and Indian support for a right of petition again faltered when confronted with almost unanimous opposition from the Western and Soviet powers. At the session on 8 June, described by Humphrey as "one of the most significant" meetings in the history of the Commission, two tied votes again saw petition fail.[19] Eleanor Roosevelt was "the chief opponent" of petition for the duration of the debate, according to Humphrey. India, Lebanon, and the Philippines all voted in favour of individual petition, as did Guatemala, Denmark, Uruguay, and Australia.[20] Of the major powers, only France, represented by Cassin, voted in support. The UK and the U.S. voted with the Soviet Union, Ukraine, Egypt, Iran, Yugoslavia, and China against petition. At the conclusion of the vote, Malik again complained about the lack of "a bolder lead" from the West.

This basic pattern persisted during the drafting of the covenant in the early 1950s, with a range of diplomats from the Arab, Asian, and Latin American states advocating a right of petition in the face of implacable Western and Soviet opposition. Some of the Commission's most vocal representatives from the Philippines and India, later joined by Egypt, stressed the necessity of accepting individual complaints as a means of making the covenant effective. At the same time, Malik and Mehta persisted in trying to remove the constraints of the self-denying ordinance. Privately, Humphrey agreed with the emphasis on petitions. Following discussion with Mehta and other members from the Indian delegation in 1951, he reflected, "a good precedent here might, of course, be more useful for the international protection of human rights than any blue-print of implementation the Commission will ever prepare."[21]

Mehta and Malik promptly seized the initiative on petitions at the May 1951 session, with efforts to bypass the hollow mechanism set-up under 75(V). Mehta argued that a list of the petitions should be sent to the Economic and Social Council for their consideration, a measure that Humphrey praised as "a radically progressive decision," though it was not ultimately pursued.[22] Instead, the Commission adopted a compromise suggested by Malik, which raised the matter of petitions for the council's consideration, admittedly to little effect.[23] Further attempts to reverse the Commission's approach to petition failed comprehensively. Compared to 1949, observed Humphrey, "it was clear . . . that opposition to an effective right of petition was hardening."[24]

Yet a number of Third World voices persisted in their calls for a right of petition well into the 1950s. In a sharp departure from Egypt's 1949 vote, Mahmud Azmi (Egypt) made a number of attempts to overturn the embargo on studying petitions while serving as chairperson of the 1953 Human Rights Commission.[25] In May 1953, he introduced a resolution to empower the Commission to forward allegations of human rights abuse to the Economic and Social Council. The Commission voted to do nothing.[26] Undeterred, Azmi took his draft text to the Third Committee that November—where it was comprehensively defeated, much to the delight of the U.S. delegation, which reported Azmi's failure as the highlight of the session.[27] Azmi did not get another chance to present his petitions resolution, and he died in a Security Council debate the following year.[28]

With Azmi's death, and Malik's absence from the Commission, Philippine jurist José Ingles emerged as the leading advocate for the right of petition in 1954. Ingles was one of the more capable members of the Commission and widely respected by Western diplomatic personnel.[29] His skillful advocacy and cosponsorship of a draft petition article represented the most promising attempt to resurrect the issue since the splitting of the covenant into separate political and economic drafts in 1951.[30] At the Commission's morning meeting on 16 March 1954, Ingles urged the delegates to accept the basic principle of the individual being protected by international law.[31] If the political covenant was to guarantee individual freedom, a right of petition was required:

The real question was whether States would undertake to respect the right recognized in the [political] covenant. In the very terms of the covenant, the individual was plainly a subject of international law and its exact purpose was to protect him against abuse of power by the State . . . The Philippines delegation was in favour of any proposal for the inclusion of the right of petition in the covenant . . . and for that reason had sponsored the joint draft article [on petition].

To illustrate the necessity of petition, Ingles referred to the defunct League of Nations Upper Silesia Convention, once used by Franz Bernheim to challenge Nazi discrimination.[32]

Support for the political covenant's petition article came from another outspoken younger member of the Commission, Egyptian Ashraf Ghorbal. He protested "it was inconceivable now to retreat from the point reached by the United Nations, and to claim that the right of petition would constitute an encroachment of the national sovereignty of States."[33] Ghorbal denounced the double standard that permitted petitions from a limited number of trust colonies to be heard by the Trusteeship Council, while the Commission ignored those from everywhere else in the world.

Yet the most forceful champion of the proposal was Rajeshwar Dayal, the Indian Permanent Representative to the UN and its delegate to the Security Council.[34] He was a veteran of the British Civil Service in India, with extensive experience in the pre-independence government.[35] Dayal argued that a human rights program without a petitions procedure was a pointless farce.

If . . . individuals, groups of individuals and non-governmental organizations could not complain against violations of human rights, no effective implementation machinery would be available to prevent such violations, and the covenants would be no more than a series of platitudinous statements which would in no way serve the cause of human rights.[36]

Dayal's colleague, Rajan, cited the precedent of colonial petitions to the Trusteeship Council as evidence of the utility and feasibility of such a system for human rights communications.[37]

Leading the Western opposition to individual petition was the U.S. representative, Mary Pillsbury Lord, the flourmill heiress, by her own acknowledgment a novice on human rights matters. Shortly after her nomination, Lord claimed that the U.S. had not supported the Universal Declaration because it was excessively focused on economic and social rights "at variance with U.S. ideals."[38] She had been appointed after her support for Eisenhower's election campaign, and her first performance in Geneva in 1953 had been weak.[39]

During the afternoon meeting that followed the speeches from Ingles, Ghorbal, and Dayal, Lord argued that individual petitions were not only premature, but potentially harmful to the cause of human rights. Petitions would "inevitably" lead the proposed human rights committee to "examine the operation of the judicial systems" of those who were party to the covenant. This risked, she said, "a disruptive influence on the administration of justice."[40] Yet a "disruptive influence" on the sort of "justice" that was being delivered to many petitioners was precisely the point. Her response to the advocates of petition was replete with the sorts of platitudes Dayal had feared. She declared "that the debate had shown that all the members of the Commission were working towards the same goals," and that "the only disagreement was about the ways of attaining them."

More skeptical still was her British ally, Sir Samuel Hoare (UK), who warned on 17 March that individual petition could "bring about a highly dangerous situation."[41] Hoare was among the more experienced and capable Western representatives on the Commission. Yet he adopted consistently negative views on most major human rights proposals, and appeared to hold a deeply pessimistic view of the UN program. John Humphrey privately lauded him as one of "the two best brains" in the Third Committee, but also complained of Hoare's "inherent conservatism," and his "almost completely negative" attitude.[42] Humphrey later identified Hoare as "the most conservative (read reactionary) influence in the Commission."[43] He also described Hoare's arguments as "less than honest, particularly to the informed ear."[44]

Unsurprisingly, Hoare rejected the idea of petitions as unworkable for the age of Cold War. The public, he claimed, must not be trusted with a right of complaint when "lies and half-truths had become a means of influencing public opinion."[45] Modern democracies had yet to find a solution to errors induced by propaganda. He dismissed the relevance of the Upper Silesia petitions procedure under the League of Nations, because it was from a period when the world was more advanced on human rights matters, and the situation had subsequently degenerated. Not without reason did Humphrey lament that Hoare's mind was "Byzantine" and "more negative each year."[46]

Arab and Asian supporters of individual petition also faced opposition from the Soviet bloc, which shared much of the West's hostility toward the draft covenant article and petitions in general. V. I. Sapozhnikov (Ukrainian SSR) was adamant that petition in any form exceeded the bounds of the Charter. "The examination of complaints," he argued in his address of 16 March "was a matter within the domestic jurisdiction of States."[47] Henryk Birecki (Poland) attacked the proposed right of petition as "fraught with dangers."[48] He exhorted the Commission to "admit the principle that every State was itself responsible for the observance of its international obligations." Both Polish and Ukrainian delegates strenuously defended the hearing of colonial complaints to the Trusteeship Council and argued there was no inconsistency because the petitioners involved came from colonies, not fully sovereign states.

Nor was the Arab-Asian group united on the value of petitions. Close Western allies Pakistan and Turkey were highly critical of the draft article. Akbar Tyabji (Pakistan) denounced the proposal as "a regrettable attempt . . . to bring undeniable moral pressure to bear on the Commission," and contrary to the basis of international law, which "was concerned only with States, and not with individuals."[49] Turkish diplomat Vahap Asiroglu warned of abuse from "agitators and demagogues."[50]

Another prominent critic was Lebanon, which had previously led the petition campaign.[51] The new Lebanese representative, Edward Rizk, was especially concerned with the potential abuse of petition. He had replaced Charles Malik, who was increasingly occupied serving in the political and security committees. Rizk seemed much less confident about the good intentions of human rights advocates, and he challenged the presumption of the "State as being essentially and inevitably tyrant."[52] An individual armed with the right of petition was more dangerous than state oppression. Rizk made the deeply implausible assertion that there was probably "much more reason to fear abuse of the right of petition by individuals than failure by States to comply with obligations they had freely assumed under the covenants." Governments were, apparently, more worthy of trust than their citizens, and were at the very least entitled to the trust of the Human Rights Commission.

By the conclusion of the session, the proposed right of petition had stalled, without any major action, primarily due to the obstructive role played by the Western states that held the majority, backed by a Soviet bloc that had vastly more to hide. Since the first debates on petition in 1947, the Western group had consistently voted against its introduction. Given the institutionalized racism of the southern United States, a right to individual petition was liable to cause considerable embarrassment.[53] Equally, members of the British Foreign and Colonial Offices feared petitions from British colonies.[54] Both of these fears were compounded by the expectation that the open political systems of the West would be placed at a disadvantage when compared to the Soviet Union, which, it was assumed, would block any petitions coming from its territory.[55] For the U.S. in particular, defeating any petition article was among the highest priorities in the Commission; it was an explicit feature of State Department instructions.[56] Given the determination of the U.S. and the UK to stop the study of petitions, it was hardly surprising that Mehta, Malik, and the small band of Third World supporters found so little success.

Despite the obvious self-interest in the arguments of the Western group, their objections reflected the problems of a human rights program where liberal democracies faced unrelenting pressure from totalitarian dictatorships and increasingly militant and numerous anticolonialists. Hoare's arguments about the Cold War corrupting the process were not without merit. In the negotiations for the 1950 European Convention on Human Rights, the democracies of Western Europe, led by Great Britain and France, had, albeit with great difficulty, indicated their willingness to open themselves to a stunning level of scrutiny. When the European Convention came into force in 1953, it created a stronger petition system than anything being proposed in the UN.[57] To a lesser extent, the U.S. had demonstrated its readiness to surrender sovereignty to the Inter-American Commission on Human Rights. The sacrifices in sovereignty that these states were prepared to make when they had confidence in the process were unparalleled. Their determination to block petitions to the Commission on Human Rights owed much to the nature of General Assembly politics.

The Third World and Petitions in the 1960s: No Standards to Double Standards, the ICERD and the ICCPR

Between 1954 and 1960, little progress was made in advancing the cause of individual petition. Consideration of petitions was again officially rejected in ECOSOC Resolution 728F, which was passed by a comfortable majority of the Economic and Social Council in July 1959.[58] The Council's vote was indicative of the impasse over communications that had become an established feature of the program by the late 1950s, despite the continued efforts of a small group of Third World delegations. The 728F procedure was nothing more than a streamlined version of that provided by the Council under Resolution 75(V), a system Humphrey aptly described as "the most elaborate wastepaper basket ever designed."[59] As with 75(V), Resolution 728F outlined a formal process for politely ignoring communications.

Yet only one year after 728F was promulgated, the influx of African states began a radical transformation of the UN approach to petitions. With the decisive voting strength of the new African states, the right of the UN to study human rights communications was dramatically extended by the creation of two new committees in the early 1960s. Their respective mandates reflected the two main preoccupations of the new African group, *apartheid* and colonialism. The first, the Special Committee on Decolonization, or Special Committee of 24, was created to monitor compliance with the landmark 1960 Declaration on the Granting of Independence to Colonial Countries and Peoples.[60] The second, the Special Committee on *Apartheid*, was focused on the plight of those suffering discrimination and abuse in Southern Africa.[61] Unlike the Commission on Human Rights, both of these bodies were permitted to hear petitioners and launch investigations.[62] The *Apartheid*

Committee, for example, began hearing petitioners from its second meeting.[63]

These two committees were among the most vocal in the UN, and almost certainly the most militant. Topics in the Special Committee of 24 included meetings devoted to the Centenary of Lenin's Birth, lengthy eulogies to guerrilla leaders in Portuguese African colonies, like Agostinho Neto and Amilcar Cabral, and praise for the Palestinian Liberation Organization.[64] Representatives from national liberation movements, including Cabral himself, often addressed the Special Committee. By the 1970s, members of the Committee would even visit liberated zones under insurgent control and report on the situation on the ground. Such powers were an astonishing contrast to the Commission on Human Rights, which was not allowed to study the tens of thousands of communications sent to it, let alone fly investigators into sovereign states. Members of the Commission were not even able to see the stamps on the letters—which were, at least for a period, excised and sold to amateur philatelists as part of the Secretariat's annual Christmas fundraising efforts.[65]

The two new committees were treated with considerable hostility by the Western states, which were rapidly alienated by the radical rhetoric that inflamed debate in both bodies. U.S. Ambassador Seymour Maxwell Finger was the last U.S. ambassador to the Special Committee of 24. In his explanation of the U.S. withdrawal from the Committee, Finger argued that it had been captured by an "extremist coalition" which dictated the agenda with "uncompromising domination."[66]

Resolutions have normally been worked out by a group of communist members and anti-Western African and Arab states. The latter, being militant and persistent, dominate the twelve member Afro-Asian caucus of the Committee. With the twelve Afro-Asian and four communist members there is little disposition to compromise or negotiate within the committee. "Decisions" are presented on a take-it-or-leave-it basis to the three Latin American members and the "other" (Western) members. . . . If such resolutions are changed from one year to the next, the change has usually been in the form of adding or inflating objectives or inserting still more unattainable provisions.[67]

For the Western states, the conduct of the two committees was not the most encouraging example for a right to individual petition in the Commission.

Nor could they find much more comfort in the next major Afro-Asian human rights initiative, the International Convention on the Elimination of All Forms of Racial Discrimination (ICERD), which was further evidence of the new majority's narrow human rights agenda. Although the draft convention extended an optional right of petition universally, its primary focus remained the particular abuses of *apartheid* and co-lonialism. It singled out colonial territories for special protection; and referred to the abuses of *apartheid* and segregation by name.[68] The draft-ing process had served as a forum for Soviet abuse directed against the Western states.[69]

Yet the ICERD also represented significant progress when compared to the resolutions that set up the earlier two Special Committees. Unlike those committees, the draft convention set standards that applied uni-versally and were not expressly limited to Southern Africa and colonial-ism. The draft text generally avoided emphasis on particular forms of racism, elaborating instead the general principle of non-discrimination as it applied to both political and economic rights.[70] In its enforcement article, the convention raised the question of the limits of state sover-eignty, albeit only in the specific case of racial discrimination. Yet even this restrictive infringement on domestic jurisdiction was enough to fracture Afro-Asian solidarity.

Throughout November and December 1965, when the Third Com-mittee debated the convention's enforcement, there was again a deter-mined group of Third World delegations that demanded an individual petitions mechanism. Representatives from Ghana, the Philippines, and Nigeria all championed the creation of a committee to receive com-plaints from the victims of racial discrimination through the inclusion of an optional article in the draft convention. They argued for the need for a proper implementation plan, frequently over objections from other Afro-Asian states which had so often been reliable partners in more lim-ited rhetorical forays against *apartheid* and colonialism.

For the first time, there was also serious Western support for indi-vidual petition, driven by the opportunity to gain a tactical advantage over hostile Afro-Asian states and the Soviet bloc. The West's reactive stance on petitions was highlighted in an Australian diplomatic cable. By exploiting the petition issue, Western diplomats sought to regain the initiative they had lost to the Third World group.[71]

Western countries are almost unanimously in favour of supporting strong im-plementation measures for the Racial Discrimination Convention in the hope of putting both the communist countries and the Afro-Asians on the defensive. Afro-Asian countries have in recent weeks shown increasing concern at the pos-sibility that their own domestic record on human rights questions will be ven-tilated in United Nations bodies; and strong implementation measures might prevent some of these countries from ratifying the Convention.[72]

There was "a general desire to put Afro-Asians on the spot by press-ing for strong implementation clauses," such as those allowing for petition.[73]

Western interest in a petition article for the race convention was further motivated by an awareness of the pivotal role that African votes would have in the impending debate on the International Covenant on Civil and Political Rights (ICCPR). The New Zealand delegation relayed the importance of the race issue for the broader program.

Consensus in the Western Group is that a firm stand should be taken in favour of strong implementation in the context of racial discrimination item. It is argued that if proposals of this kind do not repeat not commend themselves to the Africans in this convention then the battle will have been lost on the Covenants.[74]

A victory on the ICERD might improve the chances of a similar procedure being adopted for the ICCPR, the main object of Western concern.

Yet the most effective champion for the convention's right to petition was not from the West, but from Nkrumah's Ghana.[75] George Lamptey (Ghana), a leading moderate in the Afro-Asian bloc, was central to the success of the convention, and the eventual adoption of its optional petition system. When discussion of petitions was raised, Lamptey "outbid [the] West by [a] strong and competent statement" that "suddenly increased momentum" in the entire debate on implementation, as later reported by the Australian delegation.[76] Lamptey tried to harmonize competing draft texts, and arrange compromises to ensure the passage of a strong but widely acceptable Convention. He was clumsily assisted by Western diplomats who realigned themselves in support.[77]

Unlike more cynical Afro-Asian representatives, Lamptey approached the drafting process with the hope of achieving an outcome acceptable to the West, not a "dead letter" condemnation for Afro-Asian edification and Soviet propaganda.[78] He castigated those, from the United Arab Republic, Tanzania, and the Soviet bloc in particular, who sought to limit the right to petition to colonial territories, to allow it nowhere else.[79] Such a blatantly one-sided gesture, Lamptey warned, merely guaranteed that Western states "would have an excuse for not signing it."[80] Lamptey mocked the hollowness of the Arab, Soviet, and Tanzanian position, and the basic absurdity that these states which "abstained even on an optional petition clause should now sponsor a mandatory clause."[81] Equally, he was not willing to weaken the text so excessively that it became meaningless, and was especially critical of the suggestion that the enforcement article should be transposed to an optional protocol separate from the convention.[82]

By contrast, Waldo Waldron-Ramsey (Tanzania) used the issue of petition to embarrass the West, with a series of anticolonial speeches and amendments. Waldron-Ramsey was a capable Barbados lawyer in the service of Tanzania, reported to have a personal dislike of Lamptey.[83] According to the Australian delegation, he had a "well deserved reputation . . . even among his African colleagues—for recklessness and irresponsibility."[84] He was also one of the most vocal opponents of *apartheid*, though it was claimed that he did not always end up actually attending all of the special *apartheid* seminars the UN flew him to first class.[85]

Unlike Lamptey, Waldron-Ramsey seized the convention's implementation debate as an opportunity to denounce the West's human rights record, which was exquisitely vulnerable when it came to race.

The record of the Western countries in the matter of human rights gave those countries absolutely no right to take a patronizing attitude toward others . . . the Western world clearly had nothing to teach the developing countries in the matter of human rights; indeed, it was the Western world that had given birth to colonialism and slavery, while the developing countries had suffered as a result. The most flagrant violations of human rights still occurred in the so-called open and free societies, and they were often allowed by the authorities on the very pretext that the societies were "free" and "open."[86]

Dismissive of the universalist language of the draft text, he regarded any discrimination in African countries as outside the ambit of the convention.[87]

According to Waldron-Ramsey, the right to petition, which would be invoked primarily against colonial powers, was an essential part of any system of enforcement. Removal of the draft petition article, he argued, ran contrary to the whole purpose of the convention:

the fundamental aim of the Convention was, after all, to protect individuals against discrimination in their own country, and not to confer new rights of States. It was therefore indispensable to guarantee the right of petition, without which the scope of the Convention would be greatly reduced.[88]

The violation of state sovereignty entailed by petitions was less important than upholding this human right. Waldron-Ramsey conceded that such measures were probably contrary to domestic jurisdiction, but claimed that the exceptional gravity of racism warranted outside interference: "In cases of racial discrimination, such infringement was justified."

Not all Waldron-Ramsey's colleagues in the Afro-Asian bloc agreed with his support for an individual petitions article. Despite the relatively restricted terms of the ICERD, which dealt with abuses typically associated with European colonialism, and the optional nature of the petitions clause, a number of members of the Afro-Asian group baulked at any curbs on sovereignty.[89] Particularly concerned were diplomats from countries with large ethnic and linguistic minorities, which could theo-retically face embarrassment from the complaints procedure.

Foremost among the skeptics were the Indian and Iraqi delegations. Krishna Chandra Pant (India) argued in the Third Committee that compliance with the ICERD was "essentially voluntary."[90] He asserted that it "was very difficult to go further" because "sovereign States were hesitant to accept the scrutiny and judgment of an international body over their actions."[91] Pant reminded his audience that "great care" was required, because allowing individual petition for the ICERD "would create precedents" with serious implications for the future.[92] Ironically, it was India that had first raised the question of *apartheid* in South Africa in 1946—over similar objections from the South African government.[93]

Far more vehemently opposed to the ideas of the draft enforcement article was Iraqi delegate Hasan Al-Rawi. He denounced the text as "a very dangerous adventure."[94]

Their adoption might disturb international peace and impair friendly rela-tions between States. It might serve to extend the cold war by permitting any State, person or non-governmental organization to submit a petition against a State and to interfere in its domestic affairs. The articles were contrary to the principles of the Charter of the United Nations, particularly Article 2, paragraph 7.[95]

Al-Rawi's dismay was predictable. Earlier in 1965, the Iraqi army, di-rected by the Baath Party, had launched a full-scale military offensive against Kurdish separatists.[96] The 1965 onslaught provoked scandal in January 1966 when an official UN Secretariat document was issued in-cluding allegations of the Iraqi atrocities—yet it was the fact that the document existed, rather than its content, which caused the contro-versy.[97] Claims regarding the massacre were reproduced and distributed by the UN "as an example of an allegation of genocide," provoking a storm of abuse from Iraq, and subsequently a series of concessions from the secretariat that absolved the Iraqi government without any debate or investigation. Under the regulations the UN staff had no other option. "We didn't have a leg to stand on," according to John Humphrey.

Despite these objections, the ICERD was adopted by the General As-sembly on 21 December 1965. It was celebrated as a promising sign for the future by Humphrey, who expressed his hope that the petition ar-ticle would provide a useful model for the ICCPR.

It is fortunate that the General Assembly should have adopted this convention before dealing with the implementation of the two covenants, because the new countries whose voting strength is now so important in the United Nations are obviously much more interested (and with cause) in the eradication of racial discrimination than in most of the individual rights defined by the covenants, and they were therefore much more likely to agree to implementation procedures for that convention than for the covenants. However, these measures having been adopted for the convention on racial discrimination, they create a precedent for the future; and it will be difficult for the majority not to follow a similar pattern in the covenants and in other human rights conventions.[98]

Yet the precedent of the ICERD did not necessarily ensure that such a system would be adopted for the ICCPR. There was no guarantee that Afro-Asian majority would accept the logic that had proven decisive in the case of the racial discrimination for rights in the general case.[99] Even Third World ratification of the ICERD was, in many cases, much more halting than the grand rhetoric that issued forth so freely in the debate.

Fractured Solidarity: The Afro-Asian Bloc's Divided Opinion on Petition in the ICCPR

After the conclusion of the ICERD in 1965, the Third Committee turned its attention to the completion of the long-deferred human rights covenants and the intensely controversial matter of implementation. For the ICCPR, there were hopes among many in the Western group of delegations that the ICERD mechanisms would be adopted; though there was no prospect of this for the International Covenant on Economic, Social and Cultural Rights (ICESCR). When the covenants came up for their final debate in October 1966, U.S. representative Patricia Roberts Harris cited the ICERD as a precedent for introducing individual petition to the ICCPR. Harris, the Johnson administration's new appointee to the UN General Assembly, had served as co-chair of the National Women's Committee for Civil Rights. She was the first African American woman to achieve the title of Ambassador.[100] Her forthright advocacy of individual petition and human rights marked a discernible break from the lassitude and obstructionism of the Eisenhower and Dulles era. Harris's proposal for enforcement procedures was closely derived from the article in the ICERD.[101] When challenged, she defended it by shrewdly reminding her colleagues of its provenance. "If that wording caused concern," she argued, "it was the fault of other drafters and of a Convention which the Committee had already adopted."[102]

Although Harris's strategy for extending the Convention's precedent to the ICCPR was skillful, it was hardly sufficient to persuade the majority of Afro-Asian states. A chorus of Third World delegations, many of whom had supported the article when it had been in the race convention, now objected to its inclusion in the ICCPR. They sought either deletion or removal to a separate, optional protocol. Their arguments were a testament to the limits of the new powers supposedly won in the battle against *apartheid* and colonialism.[103] Tanzania, having been among the leaders of the fight for individual petition in the ICERD, essentially as an anticolonial weapon, was now among the leading voices of opposition for its incorporation in the ICCPR, where its political value was less obvious.

Tanzanian representative Malecela did not repudiate the advances made against *apartheid*, and conceded that "the principle of petitions was a noble one, especially when applied to the disenfranchised people in colonial countries, including South Africa."[104] However, when explaining her vote, Malecela asserted that it was not appropriate to apply these measures to independent Asian and African governments.

With regard to the implementation of the Covenants, she said that the problems faced by the newly independent States were not only different from those of other countries, but were sometimes the heritage of the colonial past. . . . Furthermore, while the newly independent countries had to ensure respect for the rights of the individual, what they to ensure above all was the security of the State, for Africans had learned from bitter experience that human rights could not be guaranteed unless the security of the State was guaranteed. That was why the African countries were primarily concerned with the security of the State, in other words, the security of the greatest number, sometimes at the expense of the individual.[105]

She also took the opportunity to question the content of the ICCPR, which she claimed "had been drafted by bodies which would no longer be regarded as representative of the United Nations."[106]

Her statement was endorsed by a number of other African delegations, many of which represented states with far from exemplary human rights records. Abdoulaye Diallo, who served Guinean dictator Sekou Touré, warned that the enforcement committee would serve as a pretext for neocolonial interventions. It would be "a sword of Damocles hanging over the heads of the young nations, which would fear that that committee might at any moment intervene in their domestic affairs."[107] There was certainly scope for such a committee to report on Touré, who had recently executed the nucleus of a Guinean political opposition that sought to contest presidential elections.[108]

Rwandan representative Simeon Sibomana asserted that "national structures were still too different for States to be able to judge one another" in the human rights area.[109] He refused to countenance the suggestion that human rights should be monitored in decolonized countries, and declared "the newer nations in particular should not permit any intervention by countries which did not understand them." In an implicit attack on the West, Sibomana lambasted states that "could not conceive of anyone wishing to live differently from themselves." Since

Rwandan independence in 1962, President Grégoire Kayibanda had engaged in a systematic campaign of persecution against the Tutsi population of his new country.[110]

A collection of delegations from still more repressive African regimes insistently asserted the primacy of the state above individual rights. Many of the dictatorships they represented were only months old. One of the more vocal supporters of the need for "strong" government ahead of rights was Nygesse, who represented the regime of African military dictator, General Mobutu Sese Seko, who had murdered his way into power in the Congo in 1965.[111] Mobutu's emissary paid lip-service to the idea of petition, but explained that "many new States were not yet able to defend themselves," and therefore "needed strong governments."[112] Nygesse objected that any "system which might weaken the authority of national governments should be avoided."

Togolese representative Akpo defended his country's negative vote in similar terms. Akpo declared that "to allow the right of individual petition was to impart the authority of Governments" to individuals.[113] This was perilous, he argued, because "States which had recently become independent needed strong Governments, in order to consolidate their new structures and combat under-development." The new leader of Togo's one-party state, Nicolas Grunitzky, was himself consolidating power after the 1963 assassination of President Sylvanus Olympio.[114] Akpo acknowledged that the concept was "excellent," but solemnly warned that, for Togo, "the national interest must take precedence over individuals' interests."[115] To allow otherwise "might lead to a kind of blackmail" and could "undermine the authority of Governments."

Colonel Sangoulé Lamizana's Upper Volta also joined the growing gallery of opposition. In January 1966, Lamizana had deposed the elected President Maurice Yaméogo and installed a military dictatorship.[116] Upper Volta's UN representative, Sanon, argued that it was not yet possible for his government to respect the human rights the petition article would protect. "At the current state of its existence," he advised, Togo's "primary emphasis should be placed on the State," and "at a later stage due attention should be paid to the needs of the individual."[117] African conditions demanded a period of unchallenged state power for securing human rights in the future, and hence, no system of petition was yet possible.

Nevertheless, there were some strong expressions of support for the petition article from major African and Asian countries. Perhaps the most powerful endorsement was that by Nigerian representative Adam Mohammed, a zealous critic of *apartheid*. Mohammed had been appointed by the democratic Nigerian government, but continued to serve at the UN after the 1966 military coup by General Ironsi.[118] On 29 November 1966, as the debate approached a vote, Mohammed implored his Afro-Asian colleagues to lend their support to the right of petition. In one of the longest and most impassioned addresses of the session, punctuated by an interjection from the Indian representative, he declared that it was unthinkable to vote otherwise.

In view of the nature of the Covenant under consideration it seemed incomprehensible that there could be any refusal to grant individuals the right of petition in cases of violation of the rights which were specifically guaranteed to them by that instrument . . . unless the individual was permitted to exercise his rights fully, the Committee would be wasting its time.[119]

He rebuked those who had made pronouncements on the absolute authority of the state, and argued instead that in some instances "the individual must come before the State."[120]

Mohammed asserted that his concern was not with the reputations of governments but with the rights of people. "Every individual," he urged, "must be given the possibility of defending himself if the need should arise, even against his own Government." Mohammed, who served as an independent expert on the Sub-Commission on Discrimination, also expressed his distaste for the previous proceedings, which saw "everyone endeavouring to safeguard the rights of his own Government while being at the same time hesitant about protecting the rights of the individual."[121]

When the proposal to excise the petition article from the ICCPR was put to a vote, Mohammed voted against it. Nigeria was joined by several other Third World states, which voted with the Western countries and much of Latin America for the article's retention in the political covenant. Among them were the Philippines, Ivory Coast, Ceylon, and Ghana. However, Afro-Asian opponents of the article were far more numerous, and the implacable opposition of the Soviet bloc bolstered their ranks.[122] The article was removed to an optional protocol, which allowed countries to ratify the covenant, with the attendant prestige it brought, while at the same time evading any risk of embarrassment from petitions.

"A Precedent of Some Importance": Petition and the 1967 Reform of the Commission

While the petition article failed to win inclusion in the ICCPR, its defeat revealed the significant shift in Western attitudes toward individual petition that had taken place since the initial phase of the debate in the early 1950s. Driven by constant Third World pressure on *apartheid*, and the loss of most colonial territories, European powers opposed to the idea in the 1950s were now cautiously transforming their position on the relationship between human rights and sovereignty. Most of the Western states were now willing to support the examination of petitions, as illustrated by their arguments and voting in the 1966 debate on the ICCPR and, to a lesser extent, the ICERD. Although not as bold as the sacrifices a decade earlier in the ECHR process, it was a major step forward, given the much less friendly audience that prevailed in the UN.

A prominent example of the shift in attitude was that of the UK. Opposed to petition in the 1954 session, it reversed that position in 1966, and supported the draft petition article in the ICCPR. This change was presaged by earlier reversals on the matter of *apartheid*. In an April 1961 address to the Special Political Committee, Peter Smithers (UK) had announced his government's recognition of a special exception to Article 2(7) on domestic jurisdiction. Smithers asserted that although the UK "had always attached the greatest importance to the observance of Article 2, paragraph 7 . . . the question of *apartheid* was unique."[123] *Apartheid* marked the first breach in the UK policy on domestic jurisdiction and human rights, as Smithers' explained, "it regarded apartheid as being now so exceptional as to be *sui generis*."

By 1966, that single tactical concession to Third World activism had broadened to a total revision of UK policy on human rights and sovereignty at the UN. This radical change was never officially outlined in a speech to the UN Human Rights Commission, but applied to human rights questions from May 1966 onward.[124] The director of the Human Rights Division, Marc Schreiber, was privately informed of the UK stance in late May, and related the details in a confidential memorandum to the Secretary-General.

Mr. Taylor of the United Kingdom mission came to see me to announce informally that the present British Government has decided to change the position of the United Kingdom in relation to the consideration of human rights questions by the United Nations. The British Government had considered until now that Article 2, paragraph 7 . . . prevented the United Nations from dealing with specific complaints of violations of human rights in individual countries. An exception was made in regard to the *apartheid* problem in South Africa for political reasons, and under pressure. As from now . . . they would consider that the United Nations is competent to intervene when there is a specific pattern of violations of human rights.[125]

For the next four years, in a series of complex debates across a variety of human rights bodies, this became a majority-endorsed doctrine of the United Nations.

The new phase of the petition campaign was much more significant than the ICERD or ICCPR debates because it represented a potential challenge to the sovereignty of every member state, not just those which ratified the treaties and their optional petition mechanism. Between 1967 and 1970, advocates of an improved system sought to reverse a firmly established rule of the Commission on Human Rights, which had denied itself the power to study individual complaints in 1947. While states could choose whether they adopted the ICERD and the ICCPR, or could choose to sign but reject the petitions component, there was no equivalent mechanism for rejecting the competence of the Commission on Human Rights. Although initially driven by a variety of ad hoc procedures on *apartheid*, victory here held the possibility of exposing every government across the world to charges made by their citizens.

When the debate began in the newly expanded Commission in March 1967, the Western democracies generally supported the Afro-Asian group's initiative for expanded powers, albeit with little hope and less enthusiasm.[126] Within the Western Group there was the expectation that any new procedures, such as the investigation of petitions, would simply end up being devoted to further attacks on *apartheid*.[127] The examples of the *Apartheid* and Special Colonial Committees stood out not as precedents to expand upon, but rather as cautionary demonstrations of the danger of reform.[128] Given the climate of the Commission on Human Rights, now dominated by Third World and Soviet blocs, there was a logical presumption from Western diplomats that any change would probably be for the worse.

However, changes were now inevitable given the increased African representation on the Human Rights Commission. Robert Quentin-Baxter, the experienced New Zealand representative, approached the reform process with resignation. Even if there were simultaneous improvements to the Commission's general powers, and those of the Sub-Commission, they would only occur in the context of bolstering the anti-*apartheid* effort.[129] Opposition to new prerogatives like petition on the grounds of state sovereignty, he advised, was pointless; the time for "dragging that anchor" had passed.[130]

Cooperation with moderate Afro-Asian delegations was the best chance for the West to salvage something from the reform process, according to Quentin-Baxter. He proposed that the West should concede the competence of the Commission on Human Rights to study individual petitions, and then attempt to work with the majority as much as possible "to obtain a balanced treatment of all human rights issues."[131] There was overwhelming sentiment among the African and Asian members for major reform to "the annual farce" of reading about "individual complaints on which the Commission may not comment."[132] He identified many delegations that, for various reasons, wanted at least gestures toward impartiality in the new investigative powers.

There is a notably wide sympathy for this position [of going beyond *apartheid* abuses] among other groups—partly because many realize that the United Nations authority must be damaged by a situation which provokes perpetual Western dissent. It would be fair to say that more than 20 of the 32 Commission members are actively interested in trying to promote 'across the board' solutions. Among the leaders are Dahomey, Senegal, Nigeria, Jamaica and the Philippines. The question is how this potential majority can be harnessed.[133]

Although the West could no longer dominate human rights votes, it still held meaningful power when it chose to exercise it. For the moderates of the Afro-Asian alliance, Western endorsement had unique value that could not be reproduced by even the most overwhelming bloc majorities.

Yet there remained a collection of powerful enemies to reforms granting a universal right to petition. Almost as soon the battle began in the Economic and Social Council in May 1967, the arguments of Indian, Soviet, and Tanzanian representatives vindicated more pessimistic Western commentators. Ambassador N. N. Jha (India) swiftly introduced an amendment that limited the proposed reform to communications dealing with *apartheid* and colonialism:[134]

the Commission would do better than to concern itself solely with *apartheid*, colonialism and other similar manifestations and accomplish something really positive in that direction than to transform itself into an unwelcome busy-body. . . . For those reasons, he proposed that the words "in areas where apartheid is practiced" should be inserted after the words "violations of human rights" . . . and that the words "in any country" . . . should be deleted as redundant.[135]

Jha's proposal won support from the Soviet bloc and also from Waldron-Ramsey, who "presumed" that the original text was actually referring solely to *apartheid* anyway, even if it was not specified as such, and moved amendments to limit the powers to Southern Africa and colonial territories.[136] Evgeny Nasinovsky (USSR) objected that the original agenda item, which had been added by the Soviet Union, was "concerned with such gross violations of human rights . . . as racial discrimination."[137] The reference to "all countries" was only made to cover "that particular evil" all over the world, and not human rights generally. Seemingly alarmed at the direction of the debate, he protested that "those words [in all countries] were now being used for the attainment of different and tangential objectives." Those "tangential" objectives were, self-evidently, the construction of a useful system for the global protection of human rights.

Not all Afro-Asian members of the Council were inclined to the narrow view of Jha, Waldron-Ramsey, and Nasinovsky. One of the most effective proponents for broad reform was Salvador López (Philippines), an influential diplomat who had been at the UN working on human rights since 1946. In March 1965, Humphrey had privately described López the best ever Chairman of the Commission on Human Rights, ahead of such eminent figures as Charles Malik and Eleanor Roosevelt.[138] By 1967, López had taken the lead role in pushing the Council resolution that would overturn the ban on studying individual human rights complaints. Responding to Jha's restrictive amendment, López strongly defended the original text, which his delegation had co-sponsored. Studying communications for a consistent pattern of violations was, he asserted, part of a shift "beyond the academic study of human rights" and into the realm of reality.[139]

On 25 May 1967, after several days of intense debate, the first tentative victory for the new communications procedure was won. A clear majority adopted the text López had championed.[140] Yet with the opponents of a general communications procedure unwilling to concede, it was apparent that the question was far from resolved. Despite the unequivocal nature of his defeat, Jha immediately demanded that another vote be taken on his submission for a committee to study the issue before any action was taken. His motion failed. Nasinovsky, who had supported Jha's call for another vote, warned that the change "had not been considered with sufficient care," and indicated that the Soviet Union would challenge the decision in other UN bodies.[141] Waldron-Ramsey had succeeded in his demand for the text to emphasize communications relating to *apartheid* and Southern Africa, though his other amendments failed in a tied vote.

When the issue of the Commission's new powers reached the plenary session of the Economic and Social Council two weeks later, Jha and Nasinovsky again tried to block action on communications. Having failed to restrict the application of the new communications procedure to *apartheid* and racial discrimination, Jha now proposed that reference to communications be deleted from the resolution altogether.[142] His Soviet ally Nasinovsky endorsed the amendment, and threatened to vote against the entire resolution if the communications text remained.[143] There would be a double standard, or there would be none at all.

Once more López successfully defended the proposed extension of the Commission's power to investigate complaints. Deletion of the reference to communications, he argued, "would deprive the paragraph of all meaning."[144] For López, access to the letters from the victims of human rights abuse was critical to any improved system. If the Commission were to play a useful role in defending human rights, "it must be allowed to see the information contained in the communications." Maxime Zollner (Dahomey) highlighted the basic absurdity of the Indian amendment, remarking that the Human Rights Commission "could already use all sources of information, except the communications."[145] As the body supposedly charged with defending rights, the Commission "should have access to the information [the petitions] contained." Former skeptic Samuel Hoare (UK) also urged the retention of the reference to communications. His views had evolved considerably since the previous debates in the 1950s.[146]

Through the struggle of these representatives, the first universal procedure for examining complaints was approved on 6 June 1967. Under the terms of Economic and Social Council Resolution 1235, the Commission on Human Rights and the Sub-Commission were permitted to study communications when examining situations "which reveal a consistent pattern of violations of human rights."[147] Individual petitions were specifically identified as a legitimate source of information in paragraph 2 of the final text. There were no formal obstacles to studying allegations of violations from anywhere in the world: a complaint could notionally be from the Soviet bloc, South Vietnam, Senegal, or Denmark.

Yet the rhetorical and political framework that surrounded the procedure remained closely tied to the question of Southern Africa, and directed those conducting investigations to limit their attention to *apartheid* and similar racist abuses. In a concession to the unrelenting demands of Waldron-Ramsey, both major paragraphs added a clause that specified that the gross human rights violations under discussion were "exemplified by the policy of apartheid as practised in the Republic of South Africa" and "racial discrimination as practised notably in Southern Rhodesia."[148] Racial discrimination remained the centrepiece of the resolution, and a potential source of conflict when the procedure began its operation in the sessions of the Commission and the Sub-Commission.

During the September–October 1967 meeting of the Sub-Commission on the Prevention of Discrimination, the first skirmishes over the meaning of the Resolution 1235 resulted in partial victory for the proponents of universality.[149] A wide range of petitions were circulated, including allegations of human rights violations in Southern Sudan, Egypt, Israel, Zaire, Indonesia, Greece, and Haiti.[150] Debate over human rights violations in Greece and Haiti was consistent with an expansive reading of the new standard.[151] John Humphrey, now serving as the Canadian expert on the Sub-Commission, acclaimed these otherwise fruitless discussions as "a precedent of some importance."[152] The polemical exchanges regarding the two countries were actually of considerable significance, because according to Humphrey, they "broadened the current debate in the United Nations on violations of human rights to include situations unconnected with *apartheid* or racial discrimination in South Africa and colonial territories." Intervention on the substance of the charges from those who had opposed the passage of 1235, notably the Soviet Union "sanctioned a broad interpretation of the Council's 1967 resolution as applying to parts of the world other than southern Africa and thus implicitly rejected the double standard."

Winning the Battle for a Global Right to Petition

Those first battles in the usually temperate chamber of the Sub-Commission on the Prevention of Discrimination and the Protection of Minorities were the prelude to a vastly more rancorous 1968 session of the Commission on Human Rights, where the fate of the petition mechanism was again placed in the balance. Many of the same figures from the ECO-SOC debate were present, including Nasinovsksy and Waldron-Ramsey, who had yet to give up the fight to restrict the procedure to *apartheid* and racism. López and Hoare resumed their familiar roles in defense of a universal communications procedure, as they had in the meetings the previous year. Morris Abram, who was President Johnson's appointee to the Commission, and his alternate, John Carey, augmented the defense of Resolution 1235 considerably. Endorsement for the universal interpretation of the new mandate was also given by major Third World figures in the Commission, including Nigerian Adam Mohammed and Iranian human rights expert Manouchehr Ganji.[153]

Tension between the political origins of the 1235 procedure in anti-*apartheid* activism and its expanded terms of reference were evident from the opening of the Commission's deliberations on 20 February 1968. The strange evolution by which the system was arrived at was encapsulated in the title of the relevant agenda item, which was a mélange of anti-*apartheid* and universalist language.

Question of the Violation of Human Rights and Fundamental Freedoms Including Policies of Racial Discrimination and Segregation and of Apartheid, in all countries, with Particular Reference to Colonial and other Dependent Countries and Territories.[154]

Human rights in Greece, Haiti, South Vietnam, and the Soviet Union were all debated under this item. Ironically, for the first time in almost a decade, Southern Africa was overshadowed, its prominence in the agenda description notwithstanding. The beginning of the meeting was consumed instead by mutual antagonism from the U.S. and Soviet representatives. Abram condemned the injustice of the recent show trial of Soviet dissidents Yuli Daniel and Andrei Sinayvsky.[155] For his part, Soviet delegate Morozov attacked U.S. imperialism and the dictatorship of the Greek colonels.[156]

Far more important for the future of the UN human rights project was the speech from Adam Mohammed (Nigeria), who made a compelling case for a universal approach to the study of individual petitions. Although he was highly critical of the comparison between Greece and Haiti and Southern Africa—the exemplar of human rights violations referred to in Resolution 1235, Mohammed extolled the virtues of consistency and the need for an even-handed attitude to communications. Given that complaints from individuals were central to ascertaining which situations warranted attention, the Commission had to study them all.

If the communications received were felt to be an adequate basis for discussing the situation in Greece, the two or three hundred communications relating to eastern European countries should in all fairness be treated in the same way. . . . If the situations in Greece and Haiti were considered without any prior definition of "gross violations" or "consistent patterns of violation," logic would require that the Commission investigate all the charges [for all countries, including U.S. and USSR] . . . although such action would clearly be intervention in domestic affairs.[157]

It was a striking intervention from a figure who had spent much of his career focused on the plight of those suffering under *apartheid* and European racism.

Mohammed's comment provoked outrage on the part of Waldron-Ramsey, who rejected the discussion outright as illegitimate, and demanded that the Commission restrict its focus to *apartheid* and racism. Waldron-Ramsey chastised the Sub-Commission's 1967 forays on Greece and Haiti, which "clearly exceeded its terms of reference" under Resolution 1235 and the related Commission resolution.[158] Those terms of reference "related essentially to southern Africa" alone. Resolution 1235 had not, he argued, permitted such activity, rather it had directed both the Commission and Sub-Commission to "consider those situations in southern Africa which revealed a consistent pattern of violations of human rights." With respect to violations outside the orbit of the racist southern African regimes, the Commission was allowed to keep doing what it had been doing before, which was virtually nothing of note.

Such was Waldron-Ramsey's outrage that he introduced a resolution that formally condemned the Sub-Commission for enlarging its area of interest beyond southern Africa.

[The Commission . . .]

1. *Regrets* that the Sub-Commission failed to prepare a report on information relevant to gross violations of human rights and fundamental freedoms,

as exemplified by the policy of *apartheid* as practised in the Republic of South Africa . . .

4. *Rejects* the findings of the Sub-Commission that the situations in Greece and Haiti, *of all possible States*, represent glaring examples of situations which reveal consistent patterns of violations of human rights and fundamental freedoms as exemplified by the policy of *apartheid* . . . on the basis of the evidence provided by the Sub-Commission.[159]

His text was a transparent attempt to reimpose the restrictions of previous UN practice.

Waldron-Ramsey's attitude to the 1235 procedure was subject to fierce criticism from other diplomats, spearheaded by a representative from within the Afro-Asian bloc. The first to respond was Moroccan delegate Ahmed Kettani, who rejected an exclusive focus on southern Africa because "the references made to those countries and Territories in the various resolutions were illustrative and not restrictive."[160] Kettani's primary concern, Palestine, was well outside Africa. To support his position that all complaints were admissible, he invoked the arguments of Cassin, who had claimed that "studies, investigations, and reports" were permitted under the Commission's mandate and allowed by the UN Charter. Kettani was contemptuous of the invocation of state sovereignty; those who consistently violated human rights could not "take refuge in what was referred to as the domestic jurisdiction of States."

Hoare followed Kettani with a blunt dismissal of Waldron-Ramsey's speech and its reliance on "legal quibbles." The Tanzanian speech was "an effort to evade the fact that the relevant resolutions covered any situation involving a violation of human rights." The violations referred to, Hoare said, "were not confined to those occurring in southern Africa," which were provided to "only as an example."[161] The next to speak, Felix Ermacora, an Austrian academic expert on human rights, was harsher yet in his scornful assessment of Waldron-Ramsey's proposal, which gave "preference" to "politically useful" human rights violations.[162] Although Waldron-Ramsey "might prefer to have the Commission deal solely with violations occurring in southern Africa," such a view was not faithful to the instructions that had been given by the General Assembly.

In response, the opponents of universal petition intensified their assault on the text, and began to direct threats of investigation against the proponents of a broad interpretation of Resolution 1235. Stung by criticism of his arguments, Waldron-Ramsey reacted in the afternoon session of 23 February 1968 with a more provocative suggestion. Tanzania, he said, "would be quite prepared to make an amendment to its draft resolution," directing the Sub-Commission "to determine whether a consistent pattern of gross violations of human rights existed in the United States and Vietnam."[163] Nasinovsky backed Waldron-Ramsey, and complained that the Commission "had never asked and could not be asked" to study human rights abuses "'in all countries.'"[164] Predictably appalled was the delegate from the Ukrainian Soviet Socialist Republic, Petr Nedbailo, who cautioned that the universal approach would "alter the whole direction of the Commission's debate, which was essentially concerned with *apartheid* and racial discrimination."[165]

As the first to be embarrassed by the new procedures, delegations from Greece and Haiti embraced Waldron-Ramsey's attempt to outlaw investigations outside southern Africa. Zotiades (Greece) warned on 26 February that "certain representatives seemed to have been endeavouring to create a new precedent" by moving beyond southern Africa and racism.[166] In a comment clearly aimed at Mohammed's earlier address in support of universality, he cited the human rights situation in Nigeria, presumably in reference to the continued mass starvation in the secessionist state of Biafra. To illustrate the potential difficulties he might cause Mohammed, Zotiades cited a communication received by the Commission "that very day" containing allegations of "gross violations of human rights in Nigeria." Less outspoken were Haiti's delegates, Duplessy and Antoine, who relied more on extreme and circular legalism as compared to Zotiades' preferred strategy of menace. Particularly absurd was Duplessy, who claimed that the phrase "exemplified" restricted the powers essentially to those states that practiced racial discrimination and *apartheid* in precisely the same form as the regimes in southern Africa. Only Southern Rhodesia and South Africa were sufficiently close examples to fit the criteria they exemplified.[167]

However, Waldron-Ramsey's coalition did not prevail, and the general consensus was that communications from all countries could be studied. His resolution was amended into oblivion, and finally collapsed. Third World proponents of universal petition had been decisive. Along with López and Mohammed, Manouchehr Ganji, the Iranian expert, endorsed studying petitions from areas other than southern Africa. Recognizing that *apartheid* had been the Commission's previous focal point, he asserted that "there was no reason why similar procedures should not be employed elsewhere."[168] As the session edged towards its close, it was Ciss, the Senegalese representative, who advised Waldron-Ramsey to compromise and abandon his hard-line on southern Africa; adoption of the Tanzanian resolution would produce unnecessary "confusion."[169]

When the right to study petitions was again challenged at the October 1968 meeting of the Sub-Commission, it was Mohammed Abu Rannat, the Chief Justice of Sudan's Supreme Court, who made one of the most compelling pleas for the development of the new power. Abu Rannat, who had been part of a three person working group on petitions with Humphrey and Polish delegate Slawomir Debrowa, argued for a committee to study the communications and then pass them to the Sub-Commission where there was a case to be answered. He unequivocally rejected the old system.

The argument that the Sub-Commission had no jurisdiction in the matter . . . would make it powerless to safeguard the interests of millions of people who looked to the United Nations for protection, and would leave the international community without any machinery for the consideration of genuine complaints. If the confidence of people throughout the world in the United Nations and its subsidiary bodies was to be restored, the Sub-Commission's duty was clear.[170]

His speech was consistent with his independent character, and the generally high regard in which members of the Sub-Commission held him.

By the end of 1968, the right to petition had made the precarious transition from the armamentarium of political measures against *apartheid* to the human rights program more generally.[171] Working in a UN revolutionized by African decolonization, figures like Abu Rannat, López, and Mohammed had succeeded where Mehta and Malik had not. In the following decade, their advances were slowly and tentatively consolidated and institutionalized into a comprehensive system well beyond that envisaged by most members of the Commission on Human Rights in the 1940s.

"Frantic politicking": Securing the Right to Petition in the 1970s

Between 1969 and 1971, uncertainty persisted about the study of petitions, primarily due to relentless opposition from the Soviet states and some members of the Arab group. The March 1969 meeting of the Commission on Human Rights saw a resumption of the 1968 battles over petition. Rita Hauser, the new U.S. appointee to the Commission, reported back on the "frantic politicking" required to save the report on petitions issued by the Sub-Commission, and growing Soviet anger at the continued existence of the fledgling system.[172]

However, the Soviet-Arab diplomatic campaign was now primarily concentrated on the purportedly "independent" Sub-Commission, which had been expanded in 1969 with a view to improving the voting strength of the non-aligned.[173] With the assistance of Waldron-Ramsey, the Soviet-Arab opposition tried to obstruct all action related to individual communications, two years after the apparent triumph of the universal petition system implicit in Resolution 1235. They were aided by an escalation of tension between Arab and Israeli diplomats, which proved a formidable distraction from the complaints item.

Opponents of a universal right to petition almost certainly hoped to exploit the altered balance of the Sub-Commission, and in particular the two African members who were serving for the first time in September 1969. Waldron-Ramsey suggested as much when he reminded the experts that they "in reality represented Governments," a remark that was received with scorn from the other members.[174] The behavior of the two new African experts, Paul Nikiema (Upper Volta) and Nicodème Ruhashyankiko (Rwanda) was likely a disappointment to Waldron-Ramsey, who presumably expected to gain a pair of quiescent allies. Nikiema swiftly delivered a humorous rebuke to Waldron-Ramsey's insult on his independence. He explained that on his departure from Upper Volta, "he had forgot to ask for instructions because he did not realize that he would be representing a state, [and] so would have to vote according to his own ideas," which he undoubtedly did over the course of the debate.[175]

With the gradual erosion of significant Afro-Asian opposition to petitions, the Soviet bloc resorted to increasingly desperate obstructionist measures. After June 1970, and the adoption of ECOSOC Resolution 1503, which further sanctioned the use of petitions, Soviet diplomacy shifted to procedural delaying tactics. At the Sub-Commission meeting for 1970, communist efforts to stop an institutionalized right to petition reached their apotheosis in the figure of U.M. Rybakov, the newly appointed Soviet "expert."[176] Evidently a loyal Soviet diplomat, as opposed to an independent expert, Rybakov attacked the right to petition relentlessly, using personal insult, filibuster, and banal legalism. Such was the disgust of UK Sub-Commission representative Peter Calvocoressi that he decided to wait out most of the session in the UN lounge.[177] Humphrey, who chaired the 1970 Sub-Commission, privately described Rybakov as "much worse than Vishinsky," the notorious prosecutor in Stalinist show trials who had led the Soviet campaign against the Universal Declaration.[178] Little significant work occurred on complaints, but neither was there any sentiment for rescinding the powers granted in 1967.

Growing Third World diplomatic support for a universal petition procedure swept away Rybakov's obstructions. By August 1971, the Sub-Commission was approaching unanimity in its support for the study of petitions. U.S. Sub-Commission expert Carey later reflected on the triumph of individual petition at the 1971 meeting, and the decisive position of the Third World, which determined its success or failure.

The Egyptian member, formerly a staunch ally of the Soviet opponent of human rights investigation, took the floor early and pleaded for action on the admissibility rules and screening group. For support, he quoted the poet Yevtushenko, and all present knew that times had changed. Egyptian leadership was instrumental in securing Third World sponsorship of the form of draft rules [on petition] which were ultimately adopted with no dissent.[179]

The creation of a universal petition system had been contingent on the consent and support of the Afro-Asian states.

By the early 1970s, a majority of Third World states had decided that upholding a universal right to petition was the most advantageous policy to pursue. They had voluntarily surrendered the *apartheid* specific mechanisms that had guaranteed immunity for their own regimes. The political value of a more general approach had been judged by most to exceed the modest risk that their own human rights abuses might become the focus of UN attention. New Zealand delegate to the Commission, Robert Quentin-Baxter argued that the success of petitions was a testament to the residual power of reason and justice, even in a UN dominated by bloc politics.

The need to declare a general position, instead of voting inscrutably on a particular issue, might pose a problem of consistency for a delegation which was vulnerable to reason . . . That is why some delegations find it worthwhile to uphold a single standard—knowing that a vote won under these conditions has an enhanced value. For similar reasons, and believing in their cause, delegations may welcome the institution of a complaints procedure. A verdict against *apartheid* in a semi-judicial proceedings is worth more than the registration of an automatic majority vote.[180]

There were victories that could not be won by numerical superiority alone.

Conclusions: A Strange Success

The unpredictable political dynamics of decolonization allowed the creation of a human rights system that few governments had originally wanted. Western states, always fearful of the potential disadvantage they faced with their open societies, much less their colonies, were hardly enthused by the prospect of individual petitions when they held control of the General Assembly in the 1950s. They remained cautious once they had lost control of the agenda in the 1960s, and had witnessed the operation of the *Apartheid* Committee and Special Committee of 24. However, once the prospect of such powers being extended to the Human Rights Commission emerged in the late 1960s, Western delegations had little option but to support the investigation of individual communications and campaign for universal application. Continued passivity carried the vastly greater threat of such powers being introduced anyway by the Afro-Asian majority, but being explicitly limited to human rights violations in European colonies and those of the *apartheid* regime. Like their Western counterparts, the Afro-Asian states were compelled to accept sweeping new human rights procedures that were, for many of them, far from ideal. Their quest for more effective weapons against *apartheid* and colonialism necessitated the acceptance of the 1235 and 1503 measures, which held out the possibility of investigating complaints about their own regimes. Excessive politicization was also, counterintuitively, a threat to Afro-Asian human rights priorities. Without some minimum degree of Western support, or at least acquiescence, the credibility of their campaigns was tarnished.

The most stunning paradox in the history of the human rights program was that a UN dominated by dictatorships should prove more successful in expanding human rights monitoring than one occupied by a majority of democracies. Only in an environment of Afro-Asian solidarity, where repressive states could be confident of the immunity granted by bloc voting, was such an impressive reform of the Commission's powers possible. Perversely, the most impressive achievements of the Afro-Asian bloc in the international sphere occurred when human rights were approaching their nadir in many of the countries across Asia and Africa. The diplomats of the undemocratic Third World had inadvertently succeeded in accomplishing what their democratic predecessors had begun. Hence the extraordinary irony of the 1960s, where an alliance of African and Asian dictatorships facilitated the construction of a human rights system that contained unprecedented potential for the future investigation of their own regimes.

Chapter 4
"It Is Very Fitting": Celebrating Freedom in the Shah's Iran, the First World Conference on Human Rights, Tehran 1968

> While we still revere the principles laid down in the Universal Declaration, it is nevertheless necessary to adjust them to the requirements of our time.
> —*Shah Reza Pahlavi, Opening Address to the Human Rights Conference, 22 April 1968*

> The [Universal] Declaration, although universal in scope, had come into being at a specific date in the development of the United Nations; indeed, only much later had most of the then colonial countries achieved independence. It also corresponded to a certain moment in the evolution of ideas about human rights.
> —*Princess Ashraf Pahlavi, President of the Human Rights Conference, 22 April 1968*

In April 1968, exactly thirteen years after the Bandung Conference, the first UN International Conference on Human Rights opened in Tehran. Even by the standards of the chaotic UN program, it was an extraordinary event. Connections between Nazism and Zionism, *apartheid* and slavery, were frequently made, and often met with a mixture of bored acquiescence and raucous enthusiasm. In the Algerian delegate's speech, Che Guevara joined Martin Luther King, Jr., and Mohandas Gandhi in the pantheon of human rights martyrs. Haitian dictator François "Papa Doc" Duvalier became a human rights activist in another, and not a word of protest was issued. Radical delegates extolled violence as the path to true freedom, with the Vatican observer serving as a lonely voice of dissent.[1] Only rarely did the Western states contest such claims.

Convened to commemorate the twentieth anniversary of the Universal Declaration, the conference would symbolize instead the diminished status of that document and the declining respect for traditional human rights across the developing world. Tehran opened not with praise for the rights it was meant to celebrate, but with skepticism and even hostility. Several Third World delegations sharply questioned the Universal Declaration's validity. They were led by no less a dignitary than the President of the Conference, Princess Ashraf Pahlavi. Others called for the Declaration to be rewritten, including the host, Shah of Iran, Reza Pahlavi. UN Secretary-General U Thant, who attended the conference for barely a day, offered no defense of the rights supposedly central to the aims of his organization. According to Thant, the fate of the Universal Declaration "depended on the human rights conference," and he was unable to "anticipate what the conference might decide in this regard."[2] Little better were the timorous and virtually mute Western delegates, though at least they attended. A number of Latin American states ignored Tehran entirely. So too did Carlos Romulo of the Philippines, the grand defender of Universal Declaration at Bandung. 1968 saw him appointed foreign minister for the Marcos regime, whose "New Society" was then emerging as a blueprint for precisely the kind of developmental dictatorship Romulo had so eloquently denounced in 1955 (see Chapter 1).[3]

Among academics and human rights advocates, the conference is now an obscure event, which many neglect to even mention.[4] A recent compilation of human rights documents from the UN has excised the conference Proclamation from an otherwise voluminous collection of resolutions and conventions. Much of the reason for this neglect can be found in the nature of Tehran's outcomes. To many human rights advocates, the conference was a failure. An International Commission of Jurists report on Tehran was scathing in its assessment. It was approved by ICJ chief Sean McBride, who attended the conference. Describing the Proclamation of Tehran as "a document which hardly merits a full-scale three-week international conference," the report was unsparing in its criticism of the final outcome.[5] For human rights NGOs like the ICJ, Tehran was worse than useless. The ICJ report wrote in its despairing summation that the Tehran Proclamation addressed "less than half the rights enumerated in the Universal Declaration" and went "no further in defining and enlarging these rights." Worse still, the Proclamation "in some cases may even be said to limit the pronouncements of the Universal Declaration."[6] As disappointing as the Proclamation was for human rights advocates, however, agreement on anything at all was, according to U.S. delegate Bruno Bitker, "a minor miracle."[7]

This absence of positive results from Tehran does not diminish its significance.[8] Its failure reveals much about the state of the human rights program in the late 1960s. New Zealand representative Robert Q. Quentin-Baxter, one of the staunchest defenders of human rights in the

Third Committee, opined that, as was so often the case in the UN, "once again, the great political preoccupations got in the way of progress."[9] *Apartheid* and Arab-Israeli conflict consumed most of the meetings, foreclosing the possibility of any progress on the rest of the human rights agenda: "There was not much time for other things . . . people left this Conference with a feeling of genuine disappointment . . . each initiative falters at the barriers of national sovereignty and of the issues which divide mankind on racial and regional lines."[10]

Veteran Jamaican UN Ambassador Egerton Richardson, a driving force behind the organization of the conference, described Tehran as "our moment of truth, when we came face to face with the nature of the beast—when we saw what it means to be promoting the cause of human rights by working mainly through governments."[11] A majority of those governments were now outright dictatorships, especially across Asia and Africa. The conference derived its significance not from its achievements, but from the magnitude and nature of its failures.

This chapter argues that Tehran crystallized the new human rights priorities of these Third World states and exemplified the transformation of their role in the human rights program in the years since Bandung. The optimistic postcolonial democrats of 1955 were, with a few exceptions, now confirmed adherents to various authoritarian systems. A Third World whose delegates had once embraced the Universal Declaration now questioned its legitimacy. Concern for individual rights was virtually obliterated by a preoccupation with collective goals like development and national liberation. Consensus about the balance of political and social rights was increasingly replaced by formulations that asserted the primacy of economic development. Bitter anti-imperialist rhetoric dominated a majority of the sessions. Double standards and selectivity, which had been cautioned against at Bandung, began to threaten the credibility of the UN program.

This decline was shaped by the ideological and compositional shifts that occurred between the early 1950s and the late 1960s in Asian, African, and Arab states. Many of the countries that had formed the original nucleus of the Afro-Asian coalition had undergone dramatic political change since 1955. To this original group of 29, more than 40 other states had been joined. As a consequence, Tehran's Afro-Asian group was radically different from its counterpart in the Bandung era. The Third World of Bandung was not the Third World of Tehran, even if the latter proclaimed its fidelity to the Bandung legacy.

The group's capacity to impose its will on the UN agenda had also been magnified by the progress of decolonization. Although Afro-Asian diplomats already wielded considerable power in 1955, by 1968 they essentially controlled the human rights agenda. In the intervening period, the UN had been revolutionized by the influx of new member states from Africa. The Commission on Human Rights had been expanded to increase the role of African and Asian voices in 1967.[12] Since 1964, the Afro-Asian bloc had been the dominant force in the General Assembly, and commanded a more reliable majority than the West had done in the early years of the organization.[13] States that were yet to gain independence at the time of Bandung now constituted the bulk of a coalition that dictated the direction of the human rights program.

From across Asia and Africa, these triumphant representatives reflected on the dramatic impact they had made in the dozen years since decolonization begun to reshape the UN. Several invoked the legacy of the 1955 Bandung Conference.[14] Shoja Eddine Shafa, an Iranian academic and advisor to the shah, paid tribute to the revolutionary impact of decolonization. He recalled that "only twenty-four countries, six of which were African, had participated as independent nations in the Bandung Conference. Today more than sixty Afro-Asian states were members of the United Nations."[15] This transformed United Nations "had adopted a clear-cut attitude of opposition to colonialism and racial discrimination."

Yet those in Tehran who championed the spirit of Bandung had not even been at that first conference, and they exalted a highly selective version of the Bandung heritage. Adib Daoudy (Syria), who praised the Bandung group's recognition of the Universal Declaration, complained, quite reasonably, that the "hopes raised at the Bandung Conference had not been fulfilled."[16] But Daoudy was also a ferocious critic of Israel and a major proponent of the supposed parallels between Nazism and Zionism.[17] The vehemence of his criticism here was glaringly inconsistent with the reality of Bandung, where even moderate expressions of concern for the Palestinian cause struggled for adoption.[18] Israel itself had almost been included as the thirtieth member of the Bandung conference, and had voted with the Afro-Asian bloc on human rights issues in the early 1950s, a laughable proposition by 1968, when Israel was locked in the crosshairs of the anticolonial majority.

White Revolutionaries: The Absolutist King of Human Rights and Princess of the Third World

The very location of the two conferences was symbolic of the contrast between the two eras of Third World diplomacy. At Bandung, the delegates arrived in a country that was in the midst of a transition to pluralistic multiparty democracy, with all its attendant difficulties. A vibrant free press reported their debates.[19] Conventional army and police forces protected the delegations; there was no formal secret police apparatus.[20]

There was, however, a parliamentary opposition, which complained about the cost of financing the conference and demanded answers from the government.[21] There was no lavish accommodation. Indian Prime Minister Nehru worried about the provision of enough toilets.[22]

In Tehran, delegations assembled in the New Majlis building, which normally housed the two authorized parliamentary parties created by Shah Reza Pahlavi in the late 1950s.[23] Officially titled the New Iran and Merdom parties, they were widely rechristened among the population as the "Yes" and "Of course" parties. Accommodation was luxurious, at least for the delegations that could afford it. Cables were sent to investigate the best hotels.[24] Such arrangements were of themselves an ironic endorsement of the shah's contention that economic development was more important than political freedom. Western representatives notionally meant to defend the values of constitutional government ensured they were at least comfortable while attending a human rights conference in an autocratic state.

Delegates to the Tehran conference held their meetings in a city with considerably more toilets than Bandung, but fewer basic civil liberties.[25] Their security was ensured by the SAVAK secret police, which had a reputation for torture.[26] Press freedoms too, were severely limited. When newspapers published editorials on "Constitution Day" calling for the slow transition to liberal democracy, they were sharply rebuked by the regime. New editorials were promptly written, claiming that Iran had "no desire to pursue western-style democracy so long as in practice it merely encourages treachery and leads to tyranny by a minority."[27]

The conference opened on 22 April 1968 with the spectacle of the UN secretary-general fawning over the dictator who was to give the opening address. In his introductory speech, U Thant expressed his "warmest appreciation" to the shah for his hospitality, and remarked on the symbolic significance of holding a celebration of the Universal Declaration in Iran. Thant, who would soon instruct UN posts worldwide not to accept human rights petitions from Soviet citizens, remarked that it was "very fitting that we should commemorate such an anniversary in a land whose culture and civilization are among the oldest in the world."[28] The secretary-general's official script then mandated that he thank the shah for his "most inspiring and moving address," and express gratitude for the "honour" of the royal "presence."[29]

In an ironic sense, Thant's praise for the "fitting" location was indeed appropriate. Bandung had been the capital for the revolutionary democratic nationalists who won Indonesian independence. It had profound historical resonance for the generation of nationalist leaders who assembled there. Equally, Tehran was an emblem for the prevailing mentality among authoritarian Third World elites, exemplified by the policies of the Pahlavi regime.

There was the shah himself, who probably used his oil wealth to attract the UN conference away from other candidate cities, notably Nice and Vienna.[30] He was, by the late 1960s, increasingly hostile toward democracy and political rights. Soon after the conference closed, he eliminated even the cosmetic multiparty democracy that had once existed and instituted a formal one-party state. According to Economic Minister Alinaghi Alikhani, as Pahlavi's reign continued, "the mere word 'democracy' came to produce and allergic response in him."[31] Memoirs were re-ghostwritten to amend earlier statements in support of pluralism.[32] Liberal democratic government became the focus of the shah's vicious and sarcastic attacks: "Freedom of thought, freedom of thought! Democracy, democracy! With five-year-olds going on strike, parading in streets. Is that what you call democracy? Freedom? . . . It's all yours, you can keep it, don't you see? Your wonderful democracy."[33] Human rights fared no better; according to the shah they were little more than a plot by Western states "to establish their hegemony throughout the world."[34]

As the shah took the rostrum in his own sham-parliament to open the conference, he addressed an audience all too comfortable with autocratic government. More than two-thirds of the eighty three countries that attended Tehran were undemocratic. It was a lecture from a dictator to an audience with considerable expertise in the language of dictatorship. In this setting, far from praising the Universal Declaration, the shah attacked its relevance to the postcolonial era.

In a world of explosive transition, where everything is changing at an ever-faster pace, a twenty-year interval is a considerable period and gives occasion for reflexion. While we still revere the principles laid down in the Universal Declaration, it is nevertheless necessary to adjust them to the requirements of our time.[35]

Central to the shah's proposed "adjustment" was a greater emphasis on economic development, and a consequent diminution in civil and political rights. This was consistent with his authoritarian modernization program, or "White Revolution." The shah challenged the primacy of political liberty, transforming human rights into social and economic entitlements, rather than individual freedoms to be wielded against the power of the state:

The conditions of man's political and material life have been changing throughout these two decades, and the very notion of human rights should consequently be regarded in a new light. In our day . . . political rights without social rights . . . and political democracy without economic democracy no longer have any true meaning. Viewed in this light, the real progress of our time consists in breaking daily some more of the chains which privileged minorities have for centuries imposed on the less fortunate masses.[36]

Despite being wrapped in the evasive language of interdependence, his address clearly identified some rights as more dependent than others. One of the wealthiest hereditary absolutists in history found the Soviet philosophy of rights much less threatening than the Western variant.

Yet it was not the shah but his twin sister Princess Ashraf who proved the most potent critic of the Declaration. Already an experienced and prominent member of the UN human rights program by the time of the conference, she was confident, tough, and aggressive. When the monarchy negotiated with Stalin in 1946, Ashraf was sent instead of Reza. She was widely regarded by palace observers to be tougher than her brother, dominating him to some extent.[37] In 1965, the princess was chair of the Commission on Human Rights, and by the time of the conference she was probably lobbying for the proposed position of High Commissioner for Human Rights, U.S. diplomats later reported.[38]

In her inaugural address as conference president, Ashraf included the obligatory passages of self-congratulation, but approached the Universal Declaration with significant reservations.[39] She amplified the themes introduced in her brother's preceding speech, and highlighted the anticolonial revolution that separated the conference from the era of the Declaration.

The Conference must also be one of questioning. Twenty years was the time for coming of age, the time at which to question the road one was following. The Declaration, although universal in scope, had come into being at a specific date in the development of the United Nations; indeed, only much later had most of the then colonial countries achieved independence. It also corresponded to a certain moment in the evolution of ideas about human rights.[40]

Ashraf's speech portrayed the Universal Declaration as an irrelevant artifact from a past age, and strongly suggested that a new document was needed to meet the demands of a mature, postcolonial order.

The princess's address highlighted her self-proclaimed role as the champion of a distinctive Third World human rights ideology. Despite her luxurious lifestyle, Ashraf's solidarity purportedly remained with the people of the impoverished global south. Coming from a state that "has experienced the problems of a have-not status," she felt "affinity with others who are struggling through similar problems."[41]

Like the shah, the princess was no enthusiast of liberal democracy. Westerners who agitated for its implementation in Iran, she claimed, "failed to comprehend the enormous differences between our cultures, particularly the historic roots of the monarchy in a society where children for centuries have learned the words for 'God-Country-Shah' as indivisible."[42] Basic human needs, as opposed to political liberties, were the object of her "Third World" human rights vision:

When I came to the UN it was with this issue of human rights foremost on my mind. . . . While my primary concerns were hunger, illiteracy, and women's rights, I saw myself in a broader sense as a spokesperson for the Third World point of view. . . . Now, in the UN, I felt I had found the natural forum for discussing and solving the problems that concerned me most. . . . In my own country I had developed my own ideas about what the most fundamental human rights were: the rights to food, shelter, clothing, work, medical care, and a basic education. In my own country these areas had been my principal concern.[43]

Over the next decade, Ashraf would become one of the most prolific and articulate exponents of "Third World" rights, most famously as chair of the Consultative Assembly at the 1975 International Conference on Women in Mexico City.[44] The 1968 conference would close with an appropriate image of the Iranian princess being congratulated by a fellow servant of the authoritarian cause. Alexandre Demetropoulos, who represented Greece's colonels, praised the royal conference president. Ashraf, he declared, "took a rightful and honoured place" alongside such figures as René Cassin.[45]

All the Shah's Men: Third World Diplomacy at Teheran

Although the shah and his sister had spearheaded the onslaught against the Universal Declaration, a number of other delegations also made powerful assertions of Third World skepticism. Mauritanian diplomat Abdallahi Ould Erebih paid lip service to the older generation of human rights activism, but asserted the need for significant change. He complained that "most of those instruments had been drawn up without the new independent countries and before their accession to international life."[46] Documents like the Universal Declaration "did not always take account of the special circumstances of the developing countries and their well known problems."[47] Erebih's claims reflected the new priorities of President Moktar Ould Daddah's Mauritania, which had degenerated from a multiparty democracy to a one-party state under the Parti du Peuple Mauritanien.

The conference, ostensibly called to commemorate the anniversary of the Universal Declaration, instead became a forum for celebrating the virtues of the shah's White Revolution.[48] Their praise seemed to indicate shared political philosophy at least as much as diplomatic protocol. Rafael Salas, from Marcos's Philippines, "considered it a good augury for the success of the Conference that it was being held in a progressive

country like Iran."⁴⁹ The Philippines "New Society" program of land reform and modernization, at the expense of political rights, was directly
comparable to the style and aims of the White Revolution.⁵⁰ Similarly,
Ahmed, representing General Ayub Khan's Pakistan, "was glad that the
Conference was being held in a country whose sovereign and Government had given repeated proof of their devotion to the cause of human
rights" through "measures which an admiring world had described as
the 'white revolution.' "⁵¹ The representative from Argentina, which was
two years into military dictatorship, voiced his support for the shah's
view "that political democracy without economic democracy no longer
had any true meaning."⁵²

Iran's own conference delegation insisted on the centrality of economic rights, echoing the arguments of the king who presided over
them. At the forefront of the offensive was Nasrollah Entezam, a member of the Iranian delegation originally involved in the drafting of the
Universal Declaration. Once a reformist, his human rights activities had
attracted unwelcome attention from the shah.⁵³ By the time of the conference, Entezam had reconsidered his position, and now extolled the
primary importance of economic development in the pursuit of human
rights. He invoked the *White Revolution* published volume as a guide to
his country's human rights policy.⁵⁴

As the shah's example demonstrated, a framework that equated
human rights with development could be embraced by even the most
traditionalist regimes. Absolute monarchs had nothing to fear from
"White Revolutionaries." Ethiopian Emperor Haile Selassie's emissary, Ato Solomon Tekle, advocated a view of human rights that was
once the exclusive preserve of the Soviet bloc. Economic and social
rights, Tekle argued, "formed the basis for all other human rights."⁵⁵ A
highly conservative monarchy was now presenting the arguments that
only Soviet diplomats like Vyshinsky and Pavlov would have offered
in 1948.

Such ideas on economic and social rights went well beyond the
speeches of a handful of apologists for authoritarian regimes, and were
formally codified as the official position of the conference. The Proclamation of Tehran proposed an unmistakable hierarchy of rights. While
Article 13 asserted the "indivisible" quality of human rights, the phrasing suggested strong priority for economic development, masquerading
as deference to the Universal Declaration's vision of equal and interdependent rights. Under the terms of the Proclamation, "the full realization of civil and political rights without the enjoyment of economic,
social and cultural rights is impossible."⁵⁶ Yet there was no equivalent
statement regarding the enjoyment of economic, social, and cultural
rights. Respect for human rights, the article stated, was "dependent

upon sound and effective . . . economic and social development." Development, not rights, was the most fundamental goal.

The second defining element of the new Afro-Asian human rights agenda at Tehran was the cause of national liberation. This versatile category managed to encompass the trinity of Asian, Arab, and African human rights preoccupations: *apartheid*, Zionism, and imperialism. It had no general case application beyond the specific political situations agreed upon by the Afro-Asian bloc. Instead of a universal rights claim, it often served as little more than a political weapon for lambasting unpopular enemies. National liberation was not a right that could be invoked by the Czechs, and it certainly had no application in Biafra, Baluchistan, or Kashmir.[57]

National liberation also provided ideological coherence to the disparate Afro-Asian bloc by linking the issues of Southern Africa and Palestine. Through the terminology of national liberation, the immediate concerns of Asian, African, and Arab members became manifestations of a common cause—and provided a rationale for reciprocal support. Arab solidarity with Africa against *apartheid* and imperialism ensured African solidarity with the Arabs on Israel. This was especially important for the numerically weak Arab group, which despite Soviet backing, still required African support for its initiatives. U.S. Ambassador to Tehran Armin Meyer, although impressed by the "Arab-East bloc steamroller," was equally well aware of its heavy dependence on African votes for success.[58] Meyer reported from Tehran that the "Arab-Soviet entente dominates Human Rights Conference" but only "as long as it marches in step with Africans."[59] Arab delegations had to be careful not to overemphasize the Occupied Territories alone, and thereby distract from African priorities, *apartheid* and imperialism. On at least one occasion, Arab insistence on a specific Occupied Territories draft resolution caused some African delegations to complain that it was taking up too much time reserved for *apartheid*, racial discrimination, and colonialism.[60]

By grouping these two distinct regional issues under the rubric "national liberation," such internal bloc tensions were reduced. Transforming the respective violations practiced by South Africa, Israel, and Portugal into a shared conspiracy to suppress national liberation movements served a useful purpose for coalition unity. As Daoudy (Syria) explained in his speech of 5 May, there existed a "conspiracy of Zionism, British colonialism, and American imperialism" practicing an agreed policy of aggression and domination:

It was high time that Africans and the Third World became aware of the existence of an unholy alliance between world imperialism, European colonialism and the racist Western entities established in the Asian African countries. Members of this alliance had common interests, followed the same strategy and pursued a common purpose: to dominate the peoples of the Third World and thwart their aspirations to political and economic independence and the restoration of their dignity.[61]

Alfozan (Saudi Arabia) "denounced the collusion between Zionism and *apartheid*" and highlighted the similarities between Southern and Portuguese Africa and the occupied territories.[62] Al-Sani (Kuwait) was unequivocal about the parallels between the Middle East and Southern Africa, claiming that the situation in the occupied territories was "in no way different from that of South Africa and Rhodesia."[63] A number of others spoke on the interrelated plight of those living under *apartheid*, colonialism, and Israeli occupation, sometimes in terms of a quasi-conspiratorial relationship or "axis."[64]

National liberation also had considerable appeal for more radical delegations, which could then promote violent insurgents as heroic freedom fighters. Mohamed Yazid (Algeria) invoked Che Guevara and Patrice Lumumba in his catalogue of human rights heroes.[65] Foremost in his speech was the value of the armed struggle. Although "the Declaration of Human Rights had been a help and an inspiration to those [who] were coming of age at the time of its adoption," Yazid argued that "events since 1948 had shown that man had progressed only through struggle."[66] It was freedom fighters, not human rights visionaries, that ultimately granted rights:

Men of goodwill had drafted the principles of the Declaration, but others had striven for the triumph of those principles sometimes by shedding their blood. . . . The proclamation of human rights could not be separated from men's struggle to win respect for principles. In actual fact, rights were not granted; they had to be won.

Ould Erebih (Mauritania) urged the donation of "arms and concrete help to freedom fighters."[67] Kanyeihamba (Uganda) endorsed that view, suggesting all money collected for UN work on *apartheid* be donated to the warriors of the liberation movements.[68]

Cuban delegate Alfaras argued support for the national liberation struggle was the most fundamental human rights issue. Abstract discussions were far less important than enabling violence in the cause of national freedom:

The greatest contribution which could be made by States sincerely desiring to enforce respect for human rights was to give the maximum moral and physical support to peoples which, with weapons in their hands, were fighting for the conquest of those rights.[69]

Alfaras's logic was shared by Nefissa Laliam (Algeria), president of the Algerian Women's Association, who rejected the discussion on women's equality, a major item on the agenda, as irrelevant and trivial.[70] In Vietnam, Southern Africa, and Palestine, she protested, "there could be no question of promoting women's rights."[71] As a result, Laliam argued, the "the order of priorities must begin with independence, self-determination and racial equality."

Few Western states were willing to challenge the assault on traditional human rights from the confident, and numerically superior, Afro-Asian bloc. This was especially true for the U.S. delegation, who did little to defend the legacy of Eleanor Roosevelt and the Universal Declaration.[72] They chose instead to flatter the prejudices of their audience with prophylactic doses of self-criticism.

In the wake of the assassination of Martin Luther King, Jr., less than three weeks earlier, the delegation seemed hypersensitive to the possibility of a major attack on U.S. race relations. Two days after King's murder, Meyer privately cabled Secretary of State Dean Rusk in the hope of getting a civil rights march on Washington delayed. Fear of criticism from a gallery of what were, by this time, mostly authoritarian regimes had the ambassador defensive about protests in his own country.[73]

The Washington demonstration undoubtedly will help give ammunition to those at Human Rights Conference whose chief purpose will be to pillory U.S. Presumably there [was] no way we could prevail on Washington marchers to defer their affair?[74]

An unimpressed Rusk replied that the protest "should be viewed as pertinent to the attainment of progress toward full justice for all Americans, through democratic means."[75] In a sharp rhetorical conclusion, he asked whether "states which deny democratic freedoms [can] claim as much for their own people?"

For all Rusk's encouragement, nothing so bold was heard from the U.S. representatives in Tehran.[76] Civil and political rights were hardly referred to in the major address to the conference by Roy Wilkins, chief of the U.S. delegation. Wilkins himself was a tireless champion of civil rights, and one of the most senior figures in the National Association for the Advancement of Colored People. But in a well-received speech he made few references to civil and political rights.[77] Instead, he emphasized the great progress made in racial equality, and the steps being taken to grant economic and social rights in the United States. Given his own experience of the civil rights struggle, this was hardly surprising.[78]

State Department officers in Tehran, fearful of international criticism, acclaimed the success of Wilkins's defensive posture to their superiors in Washington. In what Secretary of State Rusk described as a "glowing report," Meyer issued a detailed cable on the apparent triumph and its consequences:

Delegation believes Wilkins visit a major success from US standpoint. It undercut any tendency here to use King assassination and aftermath as springboard for criticism of US. Highlighted broad American unity in facing up to admitted US race problems: and projected calm conviction that US would work through its problems by democratic means, to successful solutions. We have been immensely helped by his presence.[79]

Joseph Sisco, head of the International Organization Branch of the State Department, sent an understandably jubilant memorandum. He was delighted with Wilkins's performance, and relayed the delegation's news of "extraordinary success" to the White House.[80] Sisco went so far as to suggest an official reception with President Johnson. Wilkins had decisively forestalled any serious attack on the problem of U.S. race relations.[81]

Yet in the process he and the rest of the U.S. diplomatic team had done little to challenge the radical Third World campaign, and had instead willingly abrogated the role as chief defender of civil and political rights barely three days into the conference. Daniel Patrick Moynihan would later single the conference out as a key moment in the collapse of U.S. human rights diplomacy. Events like Tehran convinced Moynihan of the need for a much more assertive policy in the General Assembly, which he successfully implemented when serving as U.S. ambassador in the mid-1970s. His view of the entire episode was much less flattering than that of the career State Department officers.

For whatever reason, apart from this new word [racism], the delegation brought little along with it, conceding almost the whole initiative on human rights to dictatorships, avowing American failings at every opportunity. Language depreciated rapidly. "All recognized," the Afghan *rapporteur* of the conference noted, "that the tragic situation in southern Africa constitutes the vilest and most flagrant violation of human rights ever recorded in history." Worse than the age of Hitler, presumably, or of Stalin, or of Idi Amin. No American asked for precision. No American took exception as Israeli occupation of Arab territories, now a huge fact of Middle East life, was continuously associated with the situation in southern Africa.[82]

According to Moynihan, Tehran was a principal exhibit in the long list of failures of a State Department that lacked the courage to seriously contest Afro-Asian and Soviet supremacy in the human rights bodies of the UN.[83]

Only two delegates made serious, explicit statements challenging the general Afro-Asian assault on human rights. The first defense of the "old" approach to human rights came from French delegate René Cassin. Cassin, who won a Nobel Prize later that year for his work on the Universal Declaration, warned of the perils of the emerging Third World rights framework. Although he had for a brief period advocated differentiating between the rights enjoyed in the "developed" metropole and those in colonial territories, Cassin now argued for universality:

Human rights could not be different for Europeans, Africans, Americans and Asians. . . . It was necessary to avoid the existence of two categories of human rights applicable to developed and to developing countries.[84]

Cassin attacked the triumvirate of sovereignty, development, and violence that seemed to constitute so much of the new human rights vision:

As a senior participant, not only in age but also in experience in the struggle for human rights, he wished to make a personal appeal to States not to confuse independence from the economic or political domination of other States with absolute sovereignty over the rights of their subjects. . . . He was convinced it was possible to defend human rights without having recourse to violence.[85]

No other Western ambassador was prepared to go this far. They defended their human rights achievements in comparatively timid and bland language, with little by way of direct response to the vicious invective of Afro-Asian and Soviet diplomats.[86]

The passivity of the other Western delegations was highlighted by the fact that the most poignant plea for the value of civil and political rights was issued by one of the reformers of communist Czechoslovakia, where the Prague Spring was in full bloom. Professor Rudolph Bystricky was the head of the delegation from Dubček's Czechoslovakia, and rector of Charles University in Prague.[87] Bystricky addressed the full plenary session late in the afternoon on Monday 29 April, the final session in the first week of meetings. With Cassin temporarily taking the role of chair from Ashraf, Bystricky embarked on a remarkably frank analysis of the state of human rights and democracy in his home country. Socialism had resulted in "contradictory developments," and "political liberties that had been limited or suspended" were not always "re-introduced when they should have been."[88]

Bystricky proceeded to emphasize the primacy of political rights, "the rights of the individual," and the efforts being made to restore them to the Czech people through the Action Program adopted only weeks earlier by Dubček:

The program of the new Czechoslovak Government . . . aimed to develop the rights and freedoms of its citizens, especially their political rights and freedoms . . . A wide range of legislative and institutional changes were being prepared and significant changes were being made. . . . Fundamental civic and political rights, in particular the freedoms of assembly and association and the freedom of opinion and expression were already being exercised more than ever before.[89]

At the conclusion of his speech, the main hall of the conference erupted in what the U.S. delegation reported as "heavy applause, in which the Russians barely participated."[90] Few paid attention to the speech from South Vietnam that followed.[91]

"Outgunned": The Dynamics of Third World Dominance at Tehran

The Tehran conference was a symptom of the Third World dominance already apparent in the regular sessions of the UN, and the equally obvious tendency toward Western passivity.[92] The Afro-Asian bloc had its already decisive power enhanced by the absence of the Latin American states, and exaggerated by special rules of procedure, which demanded only a simple majority for the adoption of all resolutions.[93] The West was, in the phrase of the U.S. delegation, "outgunned."[94]

As a direct consequence, misrepresentations that were impossible in the regular human rights program became acceptable in Tehran, most grotesquely in the speech of the Haitian delegation. Much of one afternoon meeting was consumed by a lengthy address from René Chalmers (Haiti) on the landmark human rights implications of dictator François "Papa Doc" Duvalier's legislative efforts, which were nominated as the zenith of over 150 years of human rights achievement. Only weeks earlier, Haiti was one of a handful of states to be indicted for gross human rights violations during the new individual complaints procedure in the Commission on Human Rights, but in Tehran its delegation could make such claims without reproach.[95]

Chalmers boasted about the human rights record of the Duvalier regime. He "described the gradual evolution of the essential human rights throughout that period [from 1804], a process which had culminated in the François Duvalier Labour Code, [and] the François Duvalier Land Code."[96] These two landmark acts, he claimed, "represented, according to the experts, a veritable monument of labour legislation." Haiti stood firmly in the "vanguard of progress" on labor. What Chalmers failed to mention was that the same labor policy saw President-for-Life Duvalier export Haitian laborers to American sugar plantations as virtual slaves, pocketing a large portion of their wages for himself.[97] Civil servants had their pay docked to pay for a special second edition of Duvalier's collected works, which was kindly distributed to all of them. Those who resisted were tortured to death by Papa Doc's Tonton Macoutes. School-children learned a strange version of the Lord's Prayer, with Duvalier standing in as God, and notions of forgiveness redacted out.[98]

Diplomats from the radical Arab wing, which drove so much of the Afro-Asian bloc's diplomacy, also exploited the uniquely advantageous situation at the conference. Ambassador Meyer reported that "the Arabs evidently recognize they have better forum here than in UN General Assembly or UN Security Council in sense that all their best friends are present while many other UN General Assembly members are not."[99] Emboldened by the favorable composition of the Tehran audience, and encouraged by Western weakness, the radical faction of Arab delegates lobbied with considerable aggression. In his assessment of the Arab group's tactics of 1 May 1968, Meyer detailed how these delegations "used covert blackmailing techniques and threats to convince weak delegations to vote their way or absent themselves."[100] He complained that although the "Westerns, Latin Americans, and some Africans reacted with distaste to these tactics, most remained silent."

The numerically stronger African group, while seemingly less insistent in their diplomatic technique, were similarly uncompromising in their determination to attack *apartheid*. Given the arrangements, coupled with Western acquiescence, there were few incentives to encourage moderation. As a consequence, the African section of the Afro-Asian bloc pursued a maximalist approach on *apartheid*. Reporting on the drafting of the Final Proclamation, Meyer described the hard-line of the African delegations, and their willingness to forgo moderation.

Informal meeting to review draft final statement . . . opened with small bomb-shell this morning as Africans announced they insisted on inclusion of verbatim quote of three critical paragraphs. . . . These paragraphs declare *apartheid* a crime against humanity punishable in accordance with provisions of relevant instruments dealing with such crimes; declare *apartheid* a threat to international peace and security; and declare vigorous support for "patriotic liberation movements in Southern Africa" . . . we asked Africans whether they realized that inclusion in final statement of provisions we had opposed would make it impossible for us to accept statement—in other words, that they were jeopardizing possibility of unanimous approval of [the] statement. They replied very firmly that they had decided that appropriate strong language on *apartheid* was their overriding objective.[101]

Given the simple majority required for adoption, winning Western support was unnecessary. With the bloc politics so heavily weighted toward the Afro-Asians, the language of compromise was becoming more expendable. Consensus and Western support remained desirable, but it ceased to be mandatory.[102]

The sheer preponderance of Asian, Arab, and African states also made still further collapse in the Western position more likely. Comfortable majorities could now be assembled on questions of *apartheid* and colonialism without consulting the so-called West and Others Group, let alone gaining assent. Negative votes or abstentions became increasingly embarrassing in such a context, even if the language proposed bordered on that deemed unacceptable. As Ambassador Meyer noted on the Tehran conference's *apartheid* text, the U.S. was willing to capitulate on "extreme African demands" simply to avoid the humiliation of joining a friendless set of states abstaining.[103] The ambassador advised the secretary of state that he had "in mind the unfortunate impression which would be created if we were one of very few absentees."

An astonishing testament to the isolation of the Western states at Tehran was the secret makeshift entente concluded between Soviet and U.S. diplomats. Frustrated by the tight control exercised by the Afro-Asians, the head of the Soviet delegation, Tchikvadze, and his American counterparts arrived at a *modus vivendi* proposal for both superpowers to "take it easy" on each other and "collaborate to subdue small nation prima donnas" that had seized control of the conference.[104] As part of the agreement, the Soviets promised not to attack the U.S. specifically in return for equivalent restraint.[105] Meyer reported to the Department of State that "the Soviets have made it clear to US privately they will damp down their criticism of US on Vietnam and other issues if we on our side maintain low-key approach."[106] This agreement seems to have been honored, with Ambassador Popper noting that Soviet rhetoric on Vietnam had been "extraordinarily low key." Relative moderation from the Soviet delegation reportedly provoked angry missives from Moscow demanding its conference staff launch more denunciations of imperialism.[107]

Both delegations were apparently irritated by the aggressive style of the Third World representatives, and their firm command of the proceedings. In response to this strange inversion of the world order, Tchikvadze made repeated overtures for cooperation with the U.S. Powerful states like the U.S. and the USSR had a mutual interest in regaining control, argued Tchikvadze, and he tried to persuade the U.S. diplomats "that if we two great powers would collaborate [the] small powers would be put in their place." He also warned that "when we are at odds both of us get exploited."[108] His entreaties found a sympathetic ear in Meyer, who reported back to Secretary of State Rusk that it was "comforting to know that even [the] Soviets have their troubles and annoyance with small-time prima donnas who gang up to throw their weight around at conferences such as current human rights conclave."

Despite Soviet conduct in the open sessions, where they almost invariably backed the most extreme Afro-Asian position possible, the desperate U.S. delegation was nonetheless receptive to the offer of a joint effort to rein in the Third World.[109] Meyer cautiously indicated his approval for U.S.-Soviet collaboration, and reported back to the secretary of his belief in "an underlying, if unreliable, desire [on the part of the Soviets] to meet us part way (not half) in [the] interests of subduing rambunctious reps from small nations who get quite intoxicated at these conferences."[110]

By the last week of the conference, the two delegations were enjoying lunch together in the U.S. Embassy, and drafting their own Proclamation of Tehran. The hosts were willing to consider many of the Soviet ideas, which were in turn, "drawn up with view to gaining assent of Asians and Africans," according to Soviet delegate Ostrovsky.[111] The Americans approached it as a meaningless document, "patched together," in the words of Ambassador Meyer, "for optical purposes" only.[112]

The Spirit of Tehran: Human Rights in the 1970s

The events of Tehran were emblematic of fundamental changes that had emerged in political systems that characterized much of the Third World, with a tendency toward the diminution of democracy and individual rights. Sandwiched between the oppression of the colonial era and the oppression of postcolonial dictatorships, the early and mid-1950s were unique for their relatively widespread support for human rights. As the decade wore on, many of Bandung's democracies had collapsed into authoritarianism. Indonesia, Egypt, Burma, Iraq, Pakistan, the Philippines, Sudan, and Ghana were all more authoritarian in 1968 than they had been in 1955. The spirit of Tehran was radically different from the legendary "spirit of Bandung."

As the International Year for Human Rights drew to its close, even the chair of the Commission on Human Rights, Senegal's Ibrahima Boye, was urging renewed emphasis on development ahead of political rights. On the twentieth anniversary of the Universal Declaration, when the realm of democracy in Africa had withered to little more than his own country and Botswana, Boye expressed little interest anything other than economic modernization: "How can a poor people, physically, morally and intellectually unhealthy, enjoy civil and political rights?"[113] According to Boye, the Third World needed different human rights.

Just as important as this preoccupation with these supposedly "Third World" rights were the telling silences of the conference. Although humanitarianism had been a key agenda item, no one had mentioned the Biafran conflict, the crucible of the modern humanitarian movement.

As the diplomats declared their respect for self-determination, Federal Nigerian forces continued a ruthless aerial bombing campaign on Biafran civilians, with a mixture of British and Soviet arms.[114] No longer under French domination, Benin's aborted transition to democracy had also been politely overlooked.[115] Nor did anyone investigate Egypt's recent referendum, in which President Nasser had won a remarkable 99.989 percent of the vote.[116] Certainly there was no reference to the imprisonment and abuse of students and professors from Tehran University, despite letters of protest from NGOs, including one from Roger Baldwin, head of the International League for the Rights of Man.[117] Such complaints, explained Human Rights Director Humphrey, were "of course," dealt with "in the usual way."[118] The "usual way," of course, involved no meaningful action whatsoever.

Silence on the part of the Western delegations at Tehran was indicative of the growing imbalance between assertive Third World diplomacy and its quiescent Western counterpart. Afro-Asian supremacy accelerated the disengagement of the Western states, which had essentially abandoned the promotion of their ideas, and facilitated still further tightening of Afro-Asian control. Marc Schreiber, director of the UN human rights division, remarked on the damaging effects of this tendency in an April 1969 memorandum to the secretary-general on the state of the Human Rights Commission.

I also believe that active confrontation of views and national attitudes on human rights problems is important for debates . . . and by far preferable to a system that seemed to develop, of draft resolutions being agreed upon, sometimes with some difficulty, by those belonging to the Afro-Asian group, with little possibility of change left to the others. This resulted, and still results in certain cases, in somewhat fatalistic attitudes of helplessness by representatives not belonging to the Afro-Asian group, many abstentions in voting and lack of interest in compliance with decisions reached in this manner.[119]

Such a dynamic produced a spiral of Third World power and Western apathy. The less the West tried, the more the Afro-Asian bloc could dictate, and the less appealing and effective future Western efforts became.

Tehran's extraordinary failure was a harbinger of the fate of the human rights program in the 1970s. It provided a glimpse of a UN where democracies were a dwindling and perpetually embattled minority. The issues that defined the conference consumed General Assembly debate for much of the following decade. Rarely did consideration stray from the relationship between rights and development, abuses in the Occupied Territories, Southern Africa, and racial discrimination.[120] Initiatives that promised to enhance the status of all individual rights, such as the proposed office of high commissioner for human rights, would languish for session after session. This was the political geometry of the "beast" Jamaican Representative Richardson had discussed; the reality of an unchecked authoritarian majority running an international human rights program.

Chapter 5
"According to Their Own Norms of Civilization": The Rise of Cultural Relativism and the Decline of Human Rights

Human Rights: A Western Construct with Limited Applicability.
                                        —*Adamantia Pollis and Peter Schwab, 1979*

Differences of culture and tradition were no obstacle whatever to the universal application of the provisions of the covenant . . . nowadays it could no longer be claimed that some civilizations were essentially different from others.
—*Bedia Afnan, Iraqi delegate, UN Third Committee, 27 October 1950*

There is no debate more persistent or more fundamental to the study of human rights in the Third World than that between cultural relativism and universality. Nothing less than the legitimacy of human rights for African and Asian peoples rests on its outcome. For more than five decades, universality has been the site of bitter academic and political controversy. Since the very beginning of the UN human rights program, the application of rights to those outside the West has been under assault. Even before the Universal Declaration was completed, the American Anthropological Association (AAA) had launched a scathing 1947 denunciation of such a document's relevance for "the Indonesian, the African, the Indian, [or] the Chinese."[1] Earlier that same year, in the Commission on Human Rights itself, Carlos Romulo (Philippines) was forced to defend the universality of rights against charges that they were "quite useless" to "the primitive inhabitants" of Asia and Africa.[2] It was a claim that persisted throughout the early 1950s.

Beginning in the late 1960s, a more radical attack on human rights began to emerge. The rise of identity politics and the related "cultural turn" contested claims to universals in any human experience. An academic climate that emphasized the primacy of identity and culture, and the plurality of values, was naturally skeptical of any claims to universality. By the close of the 1970s, this more extreme cultural relativist case would be epitomized in the famous assertion from Adamantia Pollis and Peter Schwab that human rights were "a Western construct of limited applicability."[3]

Proponents of radical cultural relativism contest the very idea that human rights have a role to play in Third World countries. They have charged that human rights constitute a form of imperialism, a neocolonial method of control. Since the foundation of the UN, cultural relativism and these accusations of human rights imperialism have been nearly inseparable. It was a link first made in the AAA statement of 1947, and reiterated more explicitly by anthropologist Julian Steward in a 1948 open letter. According to Steward, the Universal Declaration was tantamount to "advocacy of American ideological imperialism."[4]

Within the growing discipline of human rights scholarship, the association between human rights and imperialism has become an academic commonplace. Issa Shivji, author of a leading study of rights in Africa, has lambasted human rights as "an ideology of domination and part of the imperialist world outlook."[5] Human rights, claims Shivji, represent "a very important component in the armoury of imperialist ideology." No less hostile is Makau Mutua, former chair of the Kenyan human rights commission, who has located human rights "within the historical continuum of the European colonial project."[6] For Mutua, the link between colonialism and human rights is indisputable: "the white human rights zealot" is connected through an "unbroken chain . . . to the colonial administrator." Sonia Harris Short, an academic specialist on indigenous rights, has echoed Mutua's refrain. She has lamented that human rights "remain deeply entrenched in the imperialist mindset," with attempts to impose universal standards "distinctly reminiscent of the ethos of colonialism."[7]

This chapter analyzes the historical development of cultural relativism in UN forums and its relationship to the Third World. Although an immense body of scholarship exists on cultural relativism and human rights, it is predominantly theoretical in nature, with little reference to actual use of cultural relativist arguments outside the academic context.[8] No scholars to date have documented the evolution of cultural relativist discourse as it was practiced by government delegations to UN human rights bodies. Such a study is an essential corrective to the current body of literature, which is dominated by competing theses on the philosophical aspects of the cultural relativist question. By emphasizing this philosophical dimension, both advocates and critics alike have neglected an important dimension of cultural relativism: its use by political leaders and its close association with authoritarian practices.

The First Battle over Universality: European Imperialist Against Anticolonial Nationalist

The compatibility of human rights with non-Western cultures has always been a central issue in human rights debates. From the very beginning of the human rights program in 1946, when the UN was dominated by Western states, the problem of cultural difference was the subject of heated argument. Cultural relativism did not appear with the influx of African, and to a lesser extent, Asian states into the UN in the late 1950s and early 1960s. On the contrary, in the early 1950s, it was driven by the imperial powers and strongly opposed by the few Third World delegates then present in the UN. The first struggle for universality was the exact opposite of what academic proponents of cultural relativism hold as orthodoxy.

In the opening years of the 1950s, cultural relativism was the language of the Western colonial powers, which resisted any attempt to extend human rights to their colonies.[9] Diplomats from Great Britain, France, Belgium, and the Netherlands explained to the UN Third Committee why particular human rights treaties could not be applied to the colonies under their control. René Cassin, a Nobel laureate and arguably the single most influential figure in the drafting of the Universal Declaration, exemplified this tendency when he complained during a 1950 debate on the human rights covenants that it would be improper to subject "countries inhabited by different peoples to uniform obligations" especially those "at the lowest stage of development."[10] As the Belgian representative protested in October 1950, human rights were for advanced "civilized" countries, not for Africans.[11] For the colonial powers, which included some of the most established liberal democracies in Europe, rights were an anticolonial threat, not a neocolonial weapon.

Western colonial delegations attempted to evade their human rights obligations through a feigned reverence for the traditional culture of indigenous inhabitants. Their arguments to this end constituted a distinct subspecies of cultural relativism. Unlike the pioneering anthropological relativism of Franz Boas or the radical relativism that emerged in the 1970s, colonial cultural relativism was essentially conservative. It did not explicitly challenge the philosophical basis of human rights, only the feasibility and speed with which they could and should be realized. Older notions of cultural evolutionism, the theory Boasian relativism had attacked, were still a major part of colonial rhetoric, as were ideas of Western paternalism and outright racism. Such features were antithetical to classic relativist theory. Yet colonial cultural relativism shared one fundamental similarity with the other, more typical forms of cultural relativism. Both were constructed around an unshakeable belief in the essential differences between cultures.

Opposition to colonial cultural relativism came from a broad co-alition of non-Western delegations, many of whom were outspoken in their support for universal human rights and anti-colonialism. Some of these figures were genuine champions of human rights. Peng-Chun Chang (Republic of China: Taiwan), the expert on Confucianism who had exerted such influence on the preparation of the Universal Declaration, was among the first to attack the abuse of cultural difference by the Western powers. He was also unquestionably one of the most impressive figures in the history of the early human rights program. Humphrey privately observed in December 1948 that in "intellectual stature [Chang] towers above any other member of the committee."[12] But Chang was not alone, with a number of less commonly recognized human rights advocates featuring heavily in the debates of the early 1950s. Although rarely mentioned in human rights scholarship, Bedia Afnan (Iraq), Lakshmi Menon (India), Begum Rana Liaquat Ali Khan (Pakistan), and Mahmud Azmi (Egypt) all played a major role in the first struggle for universality. They were consistent supporters of human rights, in some cases for many decades. Begum Rana would later risk her life to oppose the abuse of cultural relativism by Pakistani dictator General Zia Ul-Huq.

Fighting for universality alongside these human rights champions were other Third World delegations with more problematic human rights credentials. Symbolic of these was Minerva Bernardino (Dominican Republic), a vociferous proponent of women's rights, both domestically and internationally, and one of the most aggressive and effective participants in human rights debates. She was one of the few bold enough to confront the imposing Saudi delegate Jamil Baroody, whom she once reportedly denounced to the chairman of the Third Committee as "that son of a bitch."[13] A long-time advocate of women's equality, Bernardino had attempted to have the phrase "sisterhood" inserted into the Universal Declaration, but was apparently prevented from doing so by a quip from Stalinist show trial prosecutor Andrei Vyshinsky, who complained that he didn't want to treat all women as sisters.[14] She used her influence with the authoritarian regime of Raphael Trujillo to gain suffrage for Dominican women in 1942, and seemingly exploited the dictator's vanity and desire to appear "progressive" to further her agenda on nondiscrimination. But Bernardino, venerated as a hero in official UN history, holds a much more ambiguous status when her links with Trujillo are considered. Her activism in the Third Committee and the UN Commission on the Status of Women sits uneasily with the way she cooperated with caudillo-style governance at home.

The overwhelming majority, however, were just career diplomats, with varying levels of personal enthusiasm for human rights. It was the politics of anticolonialism, and to a lesser extent antiracism, that explained their support for universality. The appeal of anticolonialism meant that some of the loudest supporters of universality in the 1950s debate were not necessarily sympathetic to traditional notions of human rights. Both de facto leaders of the Arab-Asian bloc, Baroody (Saudi Arabia) and Abdul Rahman Pazhwak (Afghanistan), were not the most natural supporters of universality. Baroody had registered one of the eight abstentions on the vote to adopt the Universal Declaration. His objection to the freedom to change religion was at that time framed in relativist terms. In December 1954, Pazhwak tried to add a relativist amendment to Resolution 843, which was aimed at eliminating harmful traditional practices against women.[15] That same year, he also criticized the phrasing of Article 18 of the draft covenant, which provided for freedom of religion. Less than three decades later, Baroody criticized universal human rights as a Western construct.[16] Pazhwak was unable to lend him support; after the 1978 Saur Revolution he was preoccupied with a more immediate human rights issue: the new regime had ordered his arrest. Philosophically, both men were among the most committed critics of the classical liberal human rights project.

During the first major battle over universality, colonialism and cultural relativism were intimately connected. The source of the rift was a special colonial application clause in the 1950 draft covenant on human rights, the successor to the Universal Declaration. This colonial clause had the potential to exclude colonial territories from the ambit of the covenants, while at the same time allowing their ratification by the metropolitan power. Many viewed the clause as an attempt by the British, French, and Belgian governments to avoid the application of the human rights covenant to their colonies, but without the tremendous political difficulty of opposing the idea outright. Such a clause would also allow the Western colonial powers to use the covenant against the Soviets while retaining their colonial possessions, thus resolving a key tension in their foreign policies.[17] As was discussed in Chapter 2, the clause also precipitated the introduction of a right to self-determination into the covenants.

When the debate on the colonial clause began on 25 October 1950, claims of cultural difference were the centerpiece of Western European justifications for the clause's inclusion in the covenant. In a condescending speech, Soudan (Belgium) argued that the colonial clause "was especially justified" for the covenant, because its "purpose . . . was to prescribe . . . rules of conduct which, as they supposed a high degree of civilization, were often incompatible with the ideas of peoples who had not yet reached a high degree of development."[18] Far from helping those in the colonies, Soudan declared, the rights in the covenant "ran the risk of destroying the very basis of their society." The "civilized nations of today," not least Belgium, had attained the standards of the covenant "after a lengthy period of development" that could not be "abruptly" forced onto the indigenous inhabitants. Application of human rights to the colonies was, he claimed, contrary to the Charter. According to Soudan, colonial people "should only be led towards civilization in a progressive manner which was adapted to their varying degrees of development and to the special conditions of each country."

Next to speak on behalf of the clause was Cassin, who had hitherto been an ardent defender of universalism. He nevertheless adopted a similar approach to that of the Belgian delegate, albeit with much greater subtlety. Cassin conceded that most of the rights in the covenant were basic and should be applied universally. The first eighteen articles of the covenant, he said, were "essential human rights," and for these "there should be no question of France's requesting or availing itself of the territorial clause."[19] Yet according to Cassin, the clause should still be included in the covenant because it might be needed later. He urged the other delegations to think of future instruments and the problems that might emerge when transforming the Universal Declaration into binding law:

It should not be forgotten . . . that it was a first covenant which would be followed by others that would include all the rights set forth in the Universal Declaration of Human Rights. The Committee should anticipate the situation that would arise when, some years later, it came to study, for example, a convention to protect the rights of the family, in the case of France, for instance, would not be the same for a Christian family as for a Moslem family. . . . He warned the Committee against omitting any territorial clause, which would represent a double alternative disadvantage. It might subject countries inhabited by different peoples to uniform obligations, and the standards that they adopted for legislation would be those applicable to peoples still in the lowest stage of development.[20]

This was a remarkable contrast to the uncompromising universality he had proclaimed in his contributions to the Universal Declaration.

Colonialism had trapped Cassin on the losing side of the universality debate. One day prior to this speech, Humphrey had presciently observed the difficulties colonial policy posed for the eminent French delegate with respect to the covenant. Humphrey thought Cassin's situation "maddening because his instructions do not permit him to do the things which he believes should be done."[21] There was an obvious contradiction between his conscience and his status as a representative of the French government. Humphrey privately reflected that "a less loyal

Frenchman would take fewer pains to hide the fact that the position of France in this business of human rights is as reactionary as the worst of the other governments."[22] Difficult as it was for him, in the Third Committee Cassin was French representative first and human rights champion second. After demonstrating excessive enthusiasm for human rights initiatives inconvenient to the French government, he had been placed under instruction earlier in the year.[23] Just as the colonialism had made the likes of Pazhwak a temporary, and profoundly unlikely, enthusiast for universality, so too did it make Cassin a reluctant cultural relativist.

For the Third World supporters of human rights, there was no such tension between principle and politics. Peng-Chun Chang (China) opened the offensive against colonial cultural relativism on the afternoon of 27 October 1950. His performance warranted a special mention from Humphrey, who noted it as "perhaps the best" among an already good selection of speeches against the clause in the Committee.[24] Chang dismissed the Belgian and French rhetoric about the incapacity of colonies to accept human rights as "something that had been dignified by the name 'levels of civilization'," even though it represented little more than European prejudices.[25] He emphasized the fundamental nature of the rights involved, and their legitimacy across cultures: "The draft covenant did not deal with such matters as road traffic, customs duties or narcotic drugs: it dealt with human rights and no one could assert such rights should be qualified."[26] The most revealing presumption for Chang was the colonial presumption that indigenous peoples would have rights forced upon them unwillingly. This fear was totally unfounded, chiefly because "there would surely be no reason to suppose that the people of the territories involved did not desire human rights."[27]

In a less diplomatic response to Cassin and Soudan, Lakshmi Menon (India), a lifelong advocate of women's rights and member of the Indian parliament, offered a frank assessment of the colonial clause. Once described by Humphrey as highly capable but "mischievous and dangerous," Menon seemed to care little about causing offense to other delegates.[28] She bluntly asserted that the elaborate explanations presented for the colonial clause "attempted to justify what could not be justified," the selective denial of human rights to some groups of people.[29]

The most passionate denunciation of colonialist cultural relativism came from an Iraqi woman little recognized in human rights scholarship. Bedia Afnan, who represented Iraq in the Third Committee and the Commission on the Status of Women, was one of the delegates most directly responsible for the inclusion of Article 3 of the draft covenant, which guaranteed gender equality.[30] Press attaché to the Washington embassy in the 1950s, she was a vocal critic of U.S. foreign policy on

Palestine and notorious in the State Department for her anti-American views, but personally friendly with Eleanor Roosevelt.[31] Although the Iraqi government of Nuri Al-Said had only recently declared a one-party state under the so-called "National Pact," Afnan herself had been appointed during one of the most liberal periods in Iraqi history.[32] Her diplomatic career began in the second half of the 1940s, when Prime Minister Tawfiq al-Suwadidi had relaxed press censorship, freed many political prisoners, and permitted the development of a limited multiparty democracy.[33] Periodic experiments with political liberalization continued into the early 1950s, with the June 1954 elections perhaps the freest ever held.[34]

Afnan immediately launched into a stinging tirade at the afternoon session on 27 October 1950, which made the speeches from Chang and Menon seem tame by comparison. She dismissed the claim that cultural factors should provide an excuse for not extending the covenants to colonial territories, and took aim at the essentialist reasoning that underpinned Cassin's arguments. Afnan questioned "how the degree of evolution of a people could prevent it from enjoying the rights which that representative," namely Cassin, "had admitted to be inherent in human nature." Contrary to the objections of the French, Afnan declared that "differences of culture and tradition were no obstacle whatever to the universal application of the provisions of the covenant." She explicitly rejected claims of intractable cultural difference:

the Moslem world would certainly be able to respect human rights. The differences between Roman law and Islamic law, for example, were wholly foreign to the field of human rights; nowadays it could no longer be claimed that some civilizations were essentially different from others.[35]

Over the next few years, Afnan became one of the Third Committee's most consistent defenders of universality, especially when it came to the issue of women's rights.

Echoing Afnan's attack on colonial cultural relativism, delegations from across Asia, the Middle East, and Latin America denounced the colonial clause for the remainder of the afternoon. Representatives from Indonesia, Lebanon, Cuba, the Philippines, and Chile all expressed their opposition to setting up different categories of people. Human rights were universal, and the covenant should reflect that in its scope. Artati Sudirjo, the delegate from Indonesia, where the parliament was then debating the place of human rights in the new republic's constitution, was adamant that the clause be scrapped.[36] Acceptance of the colonial article, she argued, would be "betraying the ideal . . . unwearyingly pursued" in the Indonesian struggle for freedom.[37]

A similar assessment of the clause was given by Carlos Valenzuela

(Chile), though the parliament of his country was then debating not human rights, but measures against suspected communists by President Gabriel González Videla.[38] A colonial clause, argued Valenzuela, would formalize discrimination and give official sanction to the idea that "a second category of people in the world . . . called natives . . . were regarded as unfit to enjoy the minimum rights which the covenant was to guarantee."[39] The imperial powers would perpetuate the subjugation of colonial peoples under "the pretext of respect for their customs."[40] It meant nothing less than abandoning the concept of universality for decades to come.

One of the last to speak against the colonial clause was Mahmud Azmi (Egypt), an Egyptian lawyer and former journalist for *Al-Misri.*[41] Azmi played a significant role in the human rights program of the 1950s, exemplified by his tireless work on the right to petition. He acted as the leader of the moderate wing of the Arab-Asian bloc, privately attempting to find compromise on such fraught issues as the right to self-determination.[42] Azmi's friend John Humphrey described his work in the Commission on Human Rights as both "useful and important."[43] The U.S. State Department, which worked closely with Azmi, described him as "keen, shrewd, and good humoured" and as "one of the outstanding personalities in the Committee."[44] According to the delegation's 1952 report, Azmi was "a champion of the underdeveloped countries . . . and again one of the most influential members of the Committee."[45] They also noted his moderation on self-determination. Yet he was certainly no ally of the West. The U.S. diplomats singled out Azmi as "one of our most vocal and skilful opponents," and he had certainly proven so when it came to the fate of petitions.

Azmi invoked the specter of the Holocaust and Nazi racism as a warning against the consequences of cultural relativism. He argued that the sort of differential application of human rights standards proposed by the imperialist powers was "only too reminiscent of the Hitlerian concept which divided mankind into groups of varying worth."[46] A colonial clause would not mean the freedom of colonial people to choose human rights, but the freedom of the administering power to deny them. Its inclusion threatened the whole enterprise of human rights protection.

A mixture of anticolonial hostility and, at least from a small selection of delegates, genuine concern for human rights ensured the triumph of universality in the first battle over cultural relativism. When the colonial clause was put to the vote several days later, on 2 November 1950, it was easily defeated. Basic human rights, as laid out by the covenant, were now automatically extended to colonies upon the metropolitan power's ratification. This was, as Humphrey observed, more than just the deletion of the colonial clause but "the inclusion of such a clause pointed in the other direction."[47] Colonial powers had to apply human rights law to all their citizens if they acceded to the covenant. This development had repercussions that extended beyond the covenant itself, because the article adopted would become the model formula for future human rights instruments. That article mandated equal treatment of peoples, irrespective of claims of cultural difference. The struggle against colonialism had set the legal contours for a much more universalist program than might otherwise have emerged.

Women's Rights and Colonial Cultural Relativism: The 1952 Convention on the Political Rights of Women

Despite the resounding triumph for universality in 1950, the bitter debate over culture resumed scarcely two years later. Once again, it was provoked by the attempted inclusion of a colonial clause, resurrected from the covenant and proposed by the United Kingdom in the draft text of the Convention on the Political Rights of Women, the first major UN initiative on women's rights. Much less comprehensive than the later Convention on the Elimination of All Forms of Discrimination against Women (1979), this convention was solely directed at securing political equality for women, and consisted of only three substantive articles.[48] It was one of the shortest and simplest human rights instruments ever proposed, and acted as little more than an explicit reiteration of two principles already elaborated in the Universal Declaration.[49] Nevertheless, over the course of eight meetings of the Committee between 12 and 17 December 1952, the convention precipitated debate over the role of cultural difference in human rights law that paralleled the furor over the human rights covenant two years earlier.

Representatives from Britain and France rehearsed the same arguments about the durability of deeply rooted customs and the catastrophic effects of inflicting human rights to their colonies. Stéphane Hessel (France), who had worked alongside Cassin in the drafting of the Universal Declaration, asserted that there was strong opposition to the convention among the colonial inhabitants, and argued that it would be wrong to override their wishes.[50] France, he boasted, "prided itself precisely on not resorting to violence for the purpose of changing deeply rooted customs. Education was better than force."[51] Hessel neglected to mention that force was the solution of first resort when withholding political rights.[52] Equally vulnerable to claims of hypocrisy was C. A. Meade (UK), who warned other members of the Third Committee that "customs could not be radically changed overnight without damaging the body politic."[53] The Kenyan "body politic" was at the time wracked by the beginning of harsh colonial counter-insurgency operations against those suspected of taking the Mau Mau oath.[54] Customs were hardly the sole obstacle to women's political rights in colonial territories, which often failed to extend even the most basic civil rights to any of their population, male or female. This was especially true of the African examples that the British and French delegates tended to focus on.

H. L. T Taswell, representative of the South African *apartheid* regime, went farther still than the British and French delegations, claiming that women's rights were a unique and distinctive feature of "advanced civilizations" such as those in Europe. In sharp contrast to the platitudes about education mouthed by Hessel and Meade, Taswell openly dismissed the applicability of the convention to non-Europeans. Implementing women's rights, he argued, "would be harmful" to indigenous societies. Although the "rights might seem to be fundamental," no action should be taken.[55]

Taswell's hostility toward the convention exemplified the affinity between the essentialist logic of colonial cultural relativism and that of *apartheid*. By December 1952, most of the key legislative pillars that would come to define the *apartheid* system were already in place. At the core of the new system was the 1950 Population Registration Act, which attempted to impose fixed raciocultural categories on the South African population.[56] The act's tests are a study in the inability of essentialist discourse to describe the dynamism and complexity of real multicultural, multiracial communities. Justifications for the 1953 Bantu Education Act, which consigned tens of millions of Africans to a life of poverty and manual labour, relied heavily on the rhetoric of essential cultural difference. In the 1951 Eiselen Commission Report, which formed much of the basis for Bantu Education, the emphasis was placed on cultural as opposed to racial difference:

Education practice must recognize that it has to deal with a Bantu child . . . trained and conditioned in Bantu culture . . . imbued with values, interests and behaviour patterns learned at the knee of a Bantu mother. These facts must dictate to a very large extent the content and methods of his early education.[57]

National Party ideologues designated culture as the determinant of an individual's future, and asserted that education "must be based on the culture and background and the whole life of the native himself in his tribe."[58] As the Grand *Apartheid* vision of the 1960s took shape, sham deference to African tribal cultures and the rhetoric of "multiculturalism" became the new weapons in a more sophisticated attempt to make white minority rule acceptable to the international community.[59]

In addition to South Africa, the British and French delegations were assisted by the more cautious approach to the convention adopted by many of the Arab states. Staunch proponents of universality two years earlier, most were much more circumspect when it came to women's rights, though none challenged the philosophical importance of gender equality. Egypt, Iran, Afghanistan, and Syria were skeptical of introducing reform too rapidly, with the place of local customs and traditions a central theme in their speeches.

Despite Syria having already granted women's suffrage in 1949, Toufic Huneidi (Syria) was concerned about the ramifications of the convention for his society and its traditions. On 16 December 1952, Huneidi warned that women's rights reforms could not be enacted immediately.

Due account should be taken of the special circumstances of each country and the degree of advancement of its people. Traditions, customs, attitudes and ways of life differed from country to country. A measure that was excellent for one might have deplorable effects in another. That had to be borne in mind if the work of the United Nations was to have practical and lasting effects. Social reforms, above all, had to be applied wisely, cautiously and gradually.[60]

Huneidi's criticisms of the draft text were amplified by the Iranian delegate, who emphasized that women's rights were contingent on "the cultural level of development and the customs of that country."[61] Conservative religious resistance to the rights provided in the convention had caused the government of Mohammed Mossadegh considerable embarrassment earlier that year. A bill granting equal political rights for women had been introduced to the Iranian *majlis* in 1952, to celebrate the 45th anniversary of the 1907 Constitutional Revolution. Over 100,000 signatures in support of the reform had been presented to the government, collected by the Society for Democratic Women, Iran's largest women's rights organization. But intense pressure from influential clerics forced the Tudeh party and Mossadegh to withdraw the proposal.[62] Struggling with domestic unrest and foreign policy problems, the Iranian government, then ruling by decree, had little interest in raising the issue again.

As had been in the case in 1950, a multitude of human rights advocates from the Third World denounced the cultural relativism of the colonial powers, South Africa, and the cautious Arab and Iranian delegations. This time, women delegates were the most outspoken, with Afnan (Iraq), Begum Rana Liaquat Ali Khan (Pakistan), and Minerva Bernardino (Dominican Republic) all defending the convention and its importance for those outside the West.

For Afnan, women's rights were not an unwelcome form of European cultural imperialism but an integral part of the postcolonial project of cultural reformation. Countries across Asia and the Middle East, she argued, were trying to "give new life to their cultural traditions . . . to borrow from the West elements which would raise the standard of living . . . woman's right to vote was one such element."[63] Women's oppression, claimed Afnan, was "not based on tradition or the laws of Islam," but instead an abuse of culture by Muslims.[64] Given that it was this misapplication of Islam that led to violations of women's rights, Afnan accordingly "did not believe the provisions of the convention contrary to Moslem law." The cause of women's rights was associated not with the imperial power, but with the nationalist movement, modernization, and a properly interpreted Islam. One of the few successes of the troubled Qasim nationalist government was the passage of the 1958 Personal Status Code, which dramatically enhanced the civil rights of Iraqi women.[65]

Afnan's argument was lent support from Pakistani delegate Begum Rana Liaquat Ali Khan, the founder of the All Pakistan Women's Association (AWPA), the leading women's rights organization in that country. Begum Rana, praised in the U.S. delegation's report for her "extraordinary intelligence, charm, and prestige," was highly critical of the claim the Convention was not suitable for Muslims.[66] Inequality of rights under Islamic law was a "widespread misconception," one being remedied in Pakistan by schools of jurisprudence that afforded women the rights they deserved.[67] She invoked the pro-equality writings of Mohammed Ali Jinnah, father of Pakistani independence, to demonstrate the impeccably nationalist character of women's rights.[68]

This speech on the Convention was one of the first in Begum Rana's lifelong struggle against the abuse of culture and religion. As early as 1956, during the hearings of the Pakistan Commission of on Marriage and Family Laws, religious conservatives were already proclaiming rights a Western invention. Conservative cleric Moulana Ihtasham-ul-haq Thanvi, clearly unaware of the Western states' attitude toward the Convention on Women's Political Rights, denounced the Marriage Commission's work against practices like polygamy, and protested that the "main cause of raising this question is inferiority of complex [sic] against the West and the desire to copy it blindly."[69] Intimidated by a vocal group of hardliners, the government was slow to implement the Commission's recommendations.[70] In 1972, the AWPA was still fighting for full protection of women's rights in the new constitution, though they met with much more success this time, at least until the constitution was suspended.[71] Even during the late 1970s and early 1980s, Begum Rana, well into her eighth decade of life, led the campaign against the emerging phenomenon of Islamic fundamentalism and the use of culture for repressive ends.

Among the last to speak against the cultural relativist case was Minerva Bernardino, who had been the driving force behind the convention in the first place.[72] Despite her problematic status as a human rights campaigner, Bernardino was a committed foe of cultural relativist arguments and a highly confident and experienced delegate with significant influence.[73] In the session on 15 December 1952, as one of the final speakers on the draft convention, she attacked the double standard inherent in the colonialist argument, which endorsed differential application of human rights according to tradition and nationality.

It was surprising that representatives who extolled the advantages which the women of their countries enjoyed should accept and support the proposals which were incompatible with the current movement to emancipate women and with the progress already achieved in their own countries. Other delegations quoted age-long traditions and claimed that adoption of the draft convention would compromise the normal development of the female population.[74]

Claims of cultural obstacles were "specious arguments invented for the purpose" of blocking the convention, Bernardino asserted, in her scathing assessment of the course of the debate.

Despite the breakdown of the anti-colonial, pro-universality alliance of 1950, the convention was nevertheless adopted without a dissenting vote. No state was prepared to explicitly challenge the idea of universal rights for women, even though many expressed reservations about implementation. Pakistan, Syria, Turkey, and Indonesia all voted in favour of the text.[75] So too did Afghanistan, then in the twilight of Shah Mahmud's modernizing quasi-democratic phase.[76] Egypt, Iran, and Saudia Arabia abstained, as did Iraq, a result that was surely disappointing to Afnan. Yemen also abstained, a wise decision given that its head of delegation Alkadi Mohammed Azzohieri was unable to speak any of the five languages used in the debate and, according to the U.S. State Department, "sat through the entire session without understanding a word that was said."[77] All the Western states voted for the final text, even though many had expressed severe concerns about its desirability for colonial territories. When the convention was opened for ratification in 1956, Bernardino's Dominican Republic was the first to accede to it.[78]

Militant Third World Universalism: Building Nations, Eradicating Harmful Customs

Support for universality grew throughout the 1950s and early 1960s as the domestic politics of many non-Western countries were transformed by revolution. New postcolonial elites of all persuasions tended to be much more sympathetic to the promotion of women's rights, even if their motives for doing so often stemmed more from the ideology of modernization and development than respect for the individual.[79] Nationalist movements focused on development were often hostile to customs and traditions perceived as outmoded or feudal, as exemplified by the introduction of the new Personal Status Code in Tunisia soon after independence in 1956. Within the Arab group in particular, willingness to modify or transform traditional culture increased considerably in the mid-1950s with the rise of Pan-Arab nationalist governments.

By the mid-1950s, non-Western states were at the forefront of UN activity to eradicate customs and cultural practices harmful to women. These efforts were exemplified by Resolution 843, adopted in December 1954. Resolution 843, titled "The Status of Women in Private Law: Customs, Ancient Laws, and Practices Affecting the Human Dignity of Women," established the supremacy of the Universal Declaration over traditional practices that violated the human rights of women. It was sponsored not by the Western states, but by an impressive coalition of Latin American and Arab countries, including Egypt and Iraq.[80] The colonial powers, and the United States, were highly critical of the proposed text, again engaging the category of culture to frame their opposition.

Introduced to the Third Committee by Minerva Bernardino on 14 December 1954, Resolution 843 was a clear expression of the modernizing spirit that animated many postcolonial elites during the period. It proclaimed the Universal Declaration as the guiding document for the treatment of women. From this premise, it noted the persistence "in certain areas of the world" of "customs, ancient laws, and practices" that were "inconsistent with these principles."[81] It urged the "elimination of such customs, ancient laws and practices," and then proceeded to list examples that failed to conform, and the required reforms. Practices such as bride price, child marriage, and arranged marriage were specified in the text as human rights violations.

Among its most enthusiastic supporters was Aziza Hussein (Egypt), who had recently been appointed to the UN delegation by new president Gamal Abdel Nasser.[82] Hussein played a major role in women's rights and welfare activities in Egypt, and later served on the Commission on the Status of Women.[83] Nasser himself nominated her as a model for his own daughters to emulate, though Hussein would later criticize the "top-down" approach to women's rights that characterized his regime.[84] First to speak on the proposed resolution, Hussein exalted the draft text as consistent with the grand project of national regeneration and reform, both of the social system and its Islamic foundations. While she conceded there had existed "dogmatic interpretations of some religious injunctions concerning women," Egyptian society was being remade and the "errors of the past were being rectified."[85] Reformed interpretations of Islam "provided no pretext for maintaining laws, customs or practices" that discriminated against women.[86] Education and development would ensure the human rights of all Egyptian women were respected.

Hussein's speech came at the close of an important year for Egyptian women, with the struggle for political rights almost won by independent action only months earlier. When confronted with a hunger strike from eminent Egyptian feminist Dora Shafik Regai, the then leader of the revolutionary Free Officers government, General Neguib, had held out the promise of full political rights for women. His successor Nasser ensured their inclusion in the 1956 constitution.[87] Under the new government, women gained the right to vote for the first time, but in a move typical of many authoritarian systems, they lost the right to independent political organization in the very same document.

Western colonial powers were much less enthusiastic about changing customs and traditions to meet human rights obligations. Belgium, the Netherlands, Great Britain, and Australia expressed support for the fundamental principles but objected to any immediate shifts in their colonies. They argued that the package of reforms suggested was potentially disastrous. According to the Netherlands delegate, these "practices were deeply rooted in the life of the people" and legislative reform would cause "serious social upheaval."[88] Gradual educational change, he conceded, might be possible "insofar as that was compatible with their way of life and standards of living." Ever anxious about stability and the limits on their policing power, postwar colonial administrations were hardly enthusiastic about imposing destabilizing or unwelcome rights on their subjects, or any measure that might cause dissent among the more powerful elements of indigenous societies. They had enough problems without radically empowering women and needlessly alienating traditional elites.

No less hostile was the U.S. representative, who questioned the right of the UN to make any judgment on specific cultural practices. Unlike the colonial powers, which framed their objections in terms of the speed of the proposed reforms, U.S. delegate James F. Green expressed his "fundamental disagreement with the very approach of the draft resolution."[89] He protested that Resolution 843 exceeded what the UN "could properly recommend," and argued that, "in such matters, recommendations of principle alone should be made." Green's defense of domestic jurisdiction came just nine months after the failure of the Bricker amendment in the U.S. Senate, which would have radically curtailed the executive's treaty making power, chiefly in response to the threat of "alien" human rights treaties. Only one unwell senator had prevented its adoption by the requisite two-thirds majority in February 1954, and the Eisenhower administration, led by Secretary of State Dulles, had retreated from much of the human rights program.[90] Even in the supposed heartland of the rights idea, powerful interests perceived human rights as a dangerous foreign imposition.

Despite these objections, an impressive majority adopted the resolution, including almost all of the African, Asian, and Middle Eastern states. The passage of Resolution 843 illustrated the aggressively reformist mentality that was typical of many nationalist governments in the Bandung era. Human rights, especially those that involved the elimination of outmoded and harmful customs, were generally embraced in the rhetoric of postcolonial emancipation. Indian academic and activist Devaki Jain, a veteran of several UN World Conferences on women, has argued that "political freedom, democratic rights for the people, and women's emancipation were often interlinked themes for struggle in these countries."[91] Jain cites the period beginning in the early 1950s as a landmark for women's rights, with a wave of enthusiasm from early nationalist leaders propelling a series of reform initiatives.[92] This surge in activity extended to specialized UN agencies, notably the WHO, which began to investigate female genital mutilation around this time.[93]

The support of Third World elites for the elimination of harmful customs persisted into the 1960s, when the influx of African states added a new set of voices to the human rights program, many of them optimistic supporters of universality. African delegations were the driving force behind the preparation of a draft Convention on Consent and Minimum Age for Marriage in 1961.[94] Numerous other states feared that drafting such an instrument would be too difficult owing to the vast range of "cultural and ethnological patterns in various countries."[95]

Some of the most hopeful proponents of the Marriage Convention were African women. Marie Sivomey (Togo) contended that the convention was a means of liberating African women "from the yoke imposed upon them by custom" and ensuring the realization of the rights granted to all under Article 16 of the Universal Declaration.[96] Martin (Guinea) expressed great faith in the Marriage Convention's power, and "hoped that African girls, knowing that they were protected by an international instrument, would not hesitate to refuse their consent to anyone who attempted to exert pressure on them."[97] Not all the African delegations embraced the move to set standards on marriage. Nigerian representative Jaja Wachuku was among the few in the Committee who raised serious objections to the text. He sought an adjournment of the debate, on the grounds that the draft "failed to take into account the physical, economic, cultural and traditional factors in each country . . . [being] based solely on the Western conception of marriage."[98] Sivomey and Martin opposed the adjournment, and seemed irritated by Wachuku's attack on the Marriage Convention.[99] Sivomey delegated her defense of the draft to another speaker on account "of the emotion the Nigerian proposal caused her."[100] The adjournment motion failed and Wachuku ended up in less than distinguished company. Only South Africa and Pakistan would repudiate the text, the former purportedly out of respect for "Bantu custom" and the latter nominally out of concern for its minorities.[101]

Yet another example of the Third World campaign against harmful traditions emerged in 1967, with the preparation of the Declaration on the Elimination of Discrimination against Women.[102] In response to the demands of the Guinean delegate, Articles 2 and 3 of the text were focused on the abolition of customs and traditions, rather than just legislative barriers to equality.[103] The first of these articles specified that "all appropriate measures shall be taken to abolish existing laws, customs, regulations and practices which are discriminatory against women."[104] Traditional practices were the sole object of the succeeding article, which mandated "all appropriate measures shall be taken . . . to direct national aspirations towards the eradication of prejudice and the abolition of customary and all other practices which are based on the idea of the inferiority of women."[105]

Jamil Baroody (Saudi Arabia) registered the only significant objection to the declaration. Although the anticolonial purpose of the campaign against the colonial clause had made him a temporary ally of universality in 1950, Baroody remained unconvinced of the practicality of universal human rights.[106] He objected that the draft text "had been drawn up from an exclusively Western point of view, partly because of the prejudices against certain traditional African and Asian institutions, which had long proved their worth."[107] Any implementation of its provisions would result in the dissolution of the family. As influential as Baroody's dissents often were, he failed to prevent the passage of the declaration by a large majority on 7 November 1967.[108] But his arguments would gain much more support in the coming decade, when the UN began to address a very different proposal.

A High Commissioner for "Western" Human Rights: The Rising Challenge of Radical Cultural Relativism

In the late 1960s and early 1970s, the complexion of the UN changed significantly. Unlike the shift of the early 1960s, which had been brought about by the influx of new states, this transformation was in the nature of the regimes that were represented. During this period there was a pronounced transition toward authoritarian or even totalitarian government across Asia and Africa. There were no fewer than twenty-six coups in Africa between 1960 and 1969, most after 1966.[109] In 1971, Idi

Amin seized power in Uganda and began eight years of unprecedented violence.[110] Similarly depressing trends were apparent in Asia and the Middle East. Ferdinand Marcos imposed martial law in the Philippines in September 1972, and would not lift it for nine years.[111] After a brief liberalization experiment with highly limited forms of multi-party democracy, the Shah of Iran incorporated all political organization into his Rastakhiz party in March 1975.[112] His collected works were then edited to remove disparaging statements made previously about one-party states.[113]

Across the border in Iraq, the personal rule of Saddam Hussein was established by the middle of the decade, following the Baath coup of July 1968.[114] After nine years of fledgling democratic rule, Afghanistan's second liberal experiment ended with Daoud's coup of 17 July 1973. With it went a genuine attempt at representative democracy, as well as the 1964 Constitution, which contained extensive human rights provisions.[115] Saudi Arabia still had no constitution, no parliament, and no trade unions, following the rejection of the Free Princes reform program in the early 1960s.[116] It had, however, abolished slavery in 1962, a little over two hundred years after the birth of Thomas Clarkson.

The UN halls were an increasingly controversial and violent place. Mobutu Sese Seko, the brutal leader of Zaire, addressed the General Assembly in October 1973 and was greeted with a standing ovation.[117] Less than a month earlier there had almost been a shootout in the Third Committee between the Cuban and Chilean delegations, after the bodyguards of Cuban Foreign Minister Raúl Roa drew their pistols during a particularly bitter exchange.[118] Most famously of all, PLO leader Yasser Arafat would address the General Assembly for the first time on 13 November 1974. With his own sidearm holster visible, he praised the new order in the UN as one "more nearly capable of implementing the principles embodied . . . in the Universal Declaration."[119] This was the context in which radical cultural relativism began to gain support among the Third World representatives at the UN.

The catalyst for the emergence of this new relativism was the proposed creation of the post of High Commissioner for Human Rights, which precipitated the most prolonged and controversial debate in the history of the human rights program. The meetings that addressed the High Commissioner proposal were characterized by an almost unprecedented level of animosity between the proponents of the office and the clique of states determined to prevent its establishment. There was at least one instance of physical violence in the Third Committee, when a fistfight between the French and Saudi Arabian representatives broke out during the 1970 session.[120] Another fight was only prevented by intervention from the observer from the Holy See.[121] There would be no resolution to the question until 1993, when the Office of High Commissioner was finally created, almost half-a-century after it was first put forward.[122]

The High Commissioner was the first human rights monitoring body with the prospect of genuinely embarrassing the non-aligned states, the Soviet Union, and indeed most other states in the Assembly, including the Western democracies.[123] It was perhaps a testament to the power of the office that much of the support came from human rights NGOs, with many governments, including the United States, reluctant to support it initially.[124] Only Costa Rica, Latin America's most durable democracy, was truly enthusiastic about the idea when it was revived in the mid-1960s. Although its functions were altered quite substantially as the proposal evolved, the High Commissioner envisaged in the 1960s and early 1970s would have been empowered to receive and investigate individual petitions, with powers greater than those accorded to the Commission on Human Rights and the Sub-Commission under Resolution 1235 (1967) and 1503 (1970) procedures.[125] Because the high commissioner was to be appointed by the secretary-general, and not directed by General Assembly resolutions, there was nothing to prevent him or her from examining human rights abuses anywhere in the world. Scrutiny would not be limited to pariah countries like Israel, the Portuguese colonies, Southern Rhodesia, and South Africa. The High Commissioner was to protect all individuals from abuse by the state.

Radical cultural relativism was central in the rhetorical armamentarium of the Arab and Soviet opposition, which worked tirelessly to obstruct the creation of the High Commissioner's office. The Arab-Soviet campaign was primarily designed to manipulate concerns about state sovereignty, Western paternalism, and European imperialism among the more moderate African and Asian states, which were uncommitted but generally thought to be sympathetic to the idea when it was first introduced. Gradually, the determination and cynicism with which this strategy was pursued enabled a minority opposition to cast sufficient doubt over the proposal to ensure its continued delay and very nearly its obliteration. The nature of the arguments so poisoned the atmosphere of the Committee that it became extremely difficult for any of the African or Asian states, even those with reasonable human rights records, to support the proposal.[126] Racial and non-aligned solidarity was often the overriding concern in Third Committee votes.[127]

The High Commissioner debate combined fears of Western neocolonialism, in the guise of human rights monitoring, with the radical cultural relativism championed by Saudi delegate Jamil Baroody. The High Commissioner became a Western initiative, and in the process human rights became "Western." Over the course of the 1970s, human rights would become suspect, a manifestation of Western colonial power, rather than an effective response to it. As police states proliferated across Asia and Africa, the coupling of imperialism and rights would also become a useful way of marginalizing and denigrating human rights discourse.

Baroody developed his cultural relativist argument to superb effect in the decade-long High Commissioner debate. In 1969, he objected to the High Commissioner on the grounds that, among other things, it would be impossible for one figure to be "fully conversant with many legal systems, many political ideologies, and the unspoken ethos of peoples in different continents," missing the fundamental point that the office would be guided by a single set of international standards.[128] Throughout the 1970s his objections would become progressively more philosophical, culminating in his 1977 assertion that even slavery was a "relative concept."[129] With continued exposure, a growing segment of his Afro-Asian audience began to use these ideas as their own, having displayed little interest in them previously. Undoubtedly many might still have objected to the High Commissioner, but the language and conceptual framework they used to attack it owed much to the Saudi delegate, chief theologian of radical cultural relativism. Baroody's academic objections were borrowed by a host of regimes that found them politically expedient.

After thirty years in the corridors of power at the UN, Baroody was arguably the most influential and effective delegate in the UN human rights program. He reiterated his arguments with great frequency, and wore down opposition through the sheer volume, intensity, and persuasiveness of his speech. Edward J. Derwinksi, who represented the U.S. at the 1971 General Assembly, commented that Baroody's "oratorical skill" was "almost overpowering."[130] "I am convinced" said Derwinski, "that if Mr. Winston Churchill in his heyday had debated Mr. Baroody, he would have come across second best." U.S. representative William F. Buckley observed the Saudi delegate's powers first-hand at the 1973 session. Although Buckley took an immediate personal dislike to Baroody, he was astonished with his simple but effective argumentative skill, and sheer intellectual energy.

Baroody is the most conspicuous figure in the United Nations, and it pays to ask oneself why. . . . His polemical trenchancy, his delight in ad hominem arguments, his addiction to pop history, and the persuasive arrangement of his arguments. . . . I would estimate that between us, [Assistant] Dino Pionzio and I heard, in the hundred days of the General Assembly, one hundred speeches by Jamil Baroody. One day he spoke six times: at four different committees, and twice at the Plenary. . . . It is in part because he has served there forever (he was at San Francisco), and in part because he talks ten times more than the nearest competitor; in part because he never tires of repeating what he has said.[131]

Buckley would later take to insulting the Saudi delegate during a debate on freedom of information when he claimed that while it might be "true that there are limits to expression, it is not true that Mr. Baroody has discovered them."[132] When not permitted to speak, Baroody had occasionally become frustrated, and was involved in a minor altercation with the under-secretary-general in December 1971.[133]

Baroody's confidence, independence, and superior knowledge of procedure allowed him to influence the Third Committee to an extent unmatched by any other delegate. With a single address he convinced the Afro-Asian bloc not to expel South Africa through the Credentials Committee—an extraordinary achievement given the strength of hostility toward Pretoria.[134] Even an indication of how Baroody planned to vote could swing a significant number of delegations to his position.[135] Such was his influence that U.S. representatives tried to remain on reasonably good terms with him, even though he was not averse to criticizing the U.S. position on a great number of questions.[136] In November 1970, he castigated a member of the U.S. delegation, which provoked a formal protest from Washington. The telegram expressed exasperation with "such Baroody capers" and advised a communication to Foreign Minister Omar Saqqaf in Jeddah, with the hope of "toning Baroody down" and putting an end to his "eccentric conduct" in the Committee.[137] This seems to have had little effect, perhaps because he appears to have enjoyed the personal support of King Faisal in Riyadh.

Buckley was greatly impressed by the pivotal role played by the assertive Saudi delegate, and attempted to dissect the sources of his power:

It is not a widely observed phenomenon that nobody, but nobody, ever replies to Baroody. It is supposed, by him and a few sycophants, that this is because of his encyclopedic knowledge of the UN (there is no denying it), his facile use of historical analogy, his sarcasm, and his relentlessness. There is probably still another reason. Baroody is not afraid of anybody . . . neither is he under any restraint. It is simply not conceivable that King Faisal would reproach him on account of anything he said. . . . In the UN there is a total fatalism about Baroody . . . .The Americans know that in the past he has voted with us on important issues, and that his vote is influential within the Arab bloc. The Africans are generally subservient to the Arabs, from whom they accept leadership in the non-aligned bloc. The Soviet Union is afraid of him for the same reason the Americans are—his can be the swing influence. All the individual delegates are afraid of his sarcastic and relentless attacks.[138]

As had been the case in the self-determination debate, this kind of independence, influence, and flexibility gave him a tremendous advantage over many of the Western delegations.

"A figurehead in a world in which no absolute standard of human rights could be said to obtain": The High Commissioner in the Early 1970s

The battle over the High Commissioner erupted in the 1969 and 1970 sessions, which set the pattern of arguments that would continue for the next decade. While there had been discussion in the preceding sessions, it had been drastically cut short by time constraints manufactured by representatives opposed or indifferent to the item. There was scarcely one session devoted to it in 1965, and debate had been conducted only in a piecemeal fashion before 1969, although the Third Committee had nonetheless managed to find sufficient time for consideration of a Draft Resolution on the Lenin Centenary, and speeches equating Zionism not only with racism but with Nazism as well.

The Arab-Soviet opposition successfully exploited the preoccupation with sovereignty that was common among the political elite in many recently decolonized countries. Opponents of the High Commissioner carefully portrayed the initiative as an example of resurgent Western imperialism, playing on legitimate sensitivities the Afro-Asian states had about interference. Early in the 1969 debate, Tarasov (USSR) reminded the Committee that the High Commissioner was promoted by those "very powers which, in the not too distant past, had subjected African and Asian countries to colonialist oppression," and that the High Commissioner's monitoring function might jeopardize their independence once more.[139] It was a dubious argument, but one with very considerable appeal to many of the African states, most of which had been colonies less than a decade previously, and in many instances were now governed by regimes with much to hide from any High Commissioner. The continued influence of the neocolonial spectre was exemplified by Sudan, where Gafaar Numeiri had just seized power by a military coup. The Sudanese delegation, which was now responsible to Numeiri's Revolutionary Command Council, "flatly rejected any form of supervision."[140] It was "fully aware" of its human rights problems and "perfectly capable of solving them" alone. The very term "High Commissioner" was subject to attack for its supposed colonial overtones. The debate was deferred, again, until 1970.

Under the influence of vigorous Soviet and Arab lobbying, these sentiments intensified when the Committee resumed its consideration of the item. The first session was hardly auspicious, with Baroody filibustering for over two hours.[141] The opening speaker for the following session, Ratnakirti Gunewardene (Ceylon) repeatedly characterized the high commissioner's proposal as a Western attempt at reasserting control over their former colonial possessions. His outburst against the

commissioner was illustrative of the growing hostility of many Third
World states:

Those who belonged to smaller non-aligned developing countries were particularly concerned at overt or covert attempts to limit their sovereign rights . . . the
African countries, which had been under imperial bondage for hundreds of
years, would have no wish to see a reversion to what was in effect gunboat diplomacy. . . . The countries that had tardily granted freedom to their former
colonies were constantly seeking ways of limiting that freedom . . . The smaller
countries did not want the "protection" of the great Powers imposed upon
them. Each country had its own system and no one had the rights to interfere
with it.[142]

As the U.S. delegation would reflect in its analysis of the High Commissioner item at the 1970 session, "the opponents . . . skillfully placed the
proponents on the defensive" with the item successfully discredited as a
"U.S.-inspired" plot among a solid section of the Afro-Asians.[143]

The committed core of Arab-Soviet opposition pursued this strategy
relentlessly, with progressively more explicit and crude denunciations of
the High Commissioner as a neocolonial initiative. Dia Allah El-Fattal
(Syria) argued that "under the banner of human rights, imperialism
and colonialism were depriving the people of their fundamental rights,"
especially that of self-determination.[144] What was needed instead was "a
high commissioner for national liberation." Individual petitions were,
under "objective analysis," simply an attempt by professional agitators
to "slander Governments."[145] Adopting a similar approach was the delegate from the UAR-Egypt, who "suspected the post of High Commissioner would be exploited by the allies of *apartheid*, colonialism, Zionism
and racism," and demanded an explanation of "certain vague terms,
such as 'human rights.'"[146] Speeches from the USSR and Ukrainian
SSR were somewhat more sophisticated but repeated the essence of this
charge.[147]

Senegal, one of the few remaining democracies on the continent,
tried to convince the swinging Afro-Asian states that the High Commissioner proposal was a positive measure consistent with the concerns
of the decolonized world. Boye (Senegal) mocked the Arab-Soviet fear
campaign, noting that "he could not take seriously attempts to persuade
developing countries that a High Commissioner for Human Rights
would be dangerous to them."[148] Where the Western powers spoke in
abstract terms, Boye spoke of Sharpeville and South African "concentra-
tion camps."[149] While almost every other advocate of the High Commissioner cited anniversaries of the Universal Declaration and the Charter,
Boye invoked another exalted resolution. The office, he argued, should
be created on the tenth anniversary of the Declaration on the Grant-

ing of Independence to Colonial Countries and Peoples, a resolution of unprecedented importance and meaning to the Afro-Asian group that had shepherded it to adoption in 1960. For all his efforts, the resolution was, as before, delayed for consideration, this time until 1971.

The radical cultural relativist case gained greater momentum in the 1971 and 1973 sessions as Baroody developed ever more provocative articulations of the basic theory, which were in turn seized upon by more cynical opponents of human rights in general. First to speak on the item in 1971, he raised the likely proposition that individuals would petition the High Commissioner for democracy as emblematic of the "awkward" and "insoluble" problems attendant to the office.

What, for example, would he [the High Commissioner] do if a citizen of a State with a one-party political system claimed that his Government was undemocratic because it did not allow a multi-party system? . . . Could a High Commissioner intercede with the Governments concerned? Most certainly not; he would be a figurehead in a world in which no absolute standard of human rights could be said to obtain.[150]

This was the essence of Baroody's case: in a divided world, there were simply no universal rights to be monitored. It was a claim that augmented the complex of arguments being made by other opponents of the High Commissioner, who had portrayed the office as a neo-colonial means of control and a secret "Western plot." The proposal languished for yet another year. When debate reopened in 1973, little progress had been made, despite attempts at compromise. Once again Baroody was quick to denounce the proposal, and cautioned that the Arab states "could never allow themselves to be lectured to by anyone who was not familiar with Islamic law."[151] They possessed instead "their own traditions, customs and ideology," leaving little place for a High Commissioner.

For the first time, the myriad objections made in the campaign against the High Commissioner coalesced into a single charge. Humam (People's Democratic Republic of Yemen) combined the assertions of neocolonialism, Western plots, and radical cultural relativism. As he delivered his address, the revolutionary government of the People's Republic had embarked on a campaign against so-called "Western" elements, attacking those in Western dress and eliminating political opposition to the socialist project.[152] His speech encapsulated the interdependent constellation of arguments that had emerged in the previous years.

The unproclaimed intention behind the creation of the post . . . [is an] attempt of certain Western Powers to impose their conceptions of human rights on other States through the creation of the post of High Commissioner.[153]

When synthesized into a single phrase, the significance of the High Commissioner debate becomes apparent. Despite the politicization of the previous two decades, on the philosophical level at least, universality had remained more or less quarantined from attack. But by the early 1970s civil and political rights were being flat-out dismissed as Western, and associated with an imperialist pattern of conduct. Baroody's arguments had been pressed into service by an anti-human rights coalition. Universality was now imperialist.

Alternative Ways and Means for Ignoring Human Rights: The Fate of the High Commissioner in the late 1970s

Although the previous years had hardly been positive, 1977 probably marked the nadir of the human rights program. In March 1977, the Commission on Human Rights voted against a study of atrocities in Amin's Uganda. Uganda was sitting on the Commission during the session, frustrating these efforts. The notoriously anti-human rights resolution 32/130 was passed by the General Assembly that December.[154] It was sponsored by a rainbow coalition of dictatorships from across the political spectrum: the shah's Iran, Marcos's Philippines, Videla's Argentina, and Castro's Cuba. Among other things, it made observance of civil and political rights contingent on economic development. Repressive regimes from both left and right exalted development as the primary justification for their powers. The ideological differences that divided them were superficial when compared to their shared adherence to a dictatorial model for development, and their desire to avoid scrutiny.[155] This was hardly a promising environment for the consideration of a High Commissioner, which had now been subsumed into another agenda item, titled "Alternative Approaches and Way and Means Within the United Nations System for Improving the Effective Enjoyment of Human Rights and Fundamental Freedoms." Ominously, Resolution 32/130 would also find its origins in this item.

Authoritarianism had found a new dimension with the rise of development discourse and the circulation of ideas on modernization that could give a certain pseudoscientific justification to dictatorship. Marxist-Leninist thought had always furnished the basis for antidemocratic modernization from the left, but the 1960s had seen growth in scholarship on the problem of modernization strategy in the more generic sense, in seminal work from Walt Rostow, Edward Shils, and Lucian Pye.[156] American theories of modernization, actively implemented by the U.S. government, often lost their nominal prodemocratic cast when they were carried out on the ground. The modernizing dictatorship evolved as a distinctive type, with top-down modernizers of left and right acting on their "backward" people. The problems of providing political stability for pro-Western economic "take-off," or managing the transitional Marxist "state capitalism," were not vastly different. Neither was friendly to individual rights.

The authoritarian development agenda that would be crystallized in 32/130 also began to be reflected in attacks on the High Commissioner. It served as an effective complement to the radical relativist push. Civil and political rights were Western, appropriate for Western cultural norms, and, with the incorporation of the developmentalist argument, wholly dependent on developed Western economies. Third World countries, on the other hand, had neither the culture for civil and political rights, nor the economic base to make them possible. In November 1977, Baroody characterized the world as a place without universals, but rather "relativity in the cultural, social and economic spheres, just as in the political sphere."[157] All the elements that would come to constitute the relativist campaigns of the 1980s and 1990s were now in place.

Radical relativism reached its most extreme theoretical elaboration in the 1977 session. Baroody developed his earlier theses into a comprehensive philosophical critique of the human rights concept. The resulting speech was arguably the most pessimistic appraisal of the UN program ever delivered. He condemned the Universal Declaration as embodying "an exclusively Western approach to the human rights question," the danger of which he had perceived at the time of its adoption.[158] Culture and the daily praxis of life were the sole determinants of what were and were not human rights. No cross-cultural standards had been agreed upon, much less any that could be monitored by the High Commissioner.

Cultural values were largely responsible for a country's concept of human rights. The Western countries want to impose a concept of those rights shaped according to their own norms of civilization. Those norms had no place in many countries where the concept of human rights was based on age-old customs and traditions. . . . He cited the example of the democratic values of which the Western Powers were so proud. . . . In Saudi Arabia there were no elections. . . . Nor were there any trade unions and the country was none the worse for it. . . . Even slavery was a relative concept, if one pictured the crowds of people who stuffed themselves into the subway at certain hours. If life-styles were radically different among countries, why should the third world countries necessarily accept the interpretation given to human rights by the Western countries? Why should there be a United Nations High Commissioner in a sphere which was essentially spiritual and educational?[159]

Always latently skeptical of the human rights concept, Baroody now rejected it outright. The state of the UN seemed proof enough that he had been right all along. His final withering critique of universality was made only two years before the resurgence of cultural relativism in academic discourse, with Adamantia Pollis's landmark 1979 essay that dismissed human rights as "a Western construct of limited applicability."[160] Baroody died in March that year, after an incredible 31 years as prime custodian of the relativist cause in the UN.

The rise of radical cultural relativism was epitomized by the November 1977 speech from Princess Ashraf, twin sister to the shah. Ashraf, once an enthusiastic supporter of the High Commissioner, now recited relativist arguments against it, introducing a procedural resolution designed to shelve the proposal once more. She had secretly lobbied to be the first High Commissioner in 1970, presumably with the backing of her brother.[161] Her candidacy, which had alarmed the U.S. delegation, probably explained earlier Iranian endorsement for the High Commissioner proposal. Emblematic of the ambiguity surrounding major figures in the human rights program, Pahlavi's election as chair of the Commission on Human Rights in 1970 had served as a depressing symbol of the condition of the UN program.

Pahlavi contended that the proposed High Commissioner was excessively focused on the "narrow" political rights of the West, which were not applicable in a world of vastly different economic and social conditions. She delivered her address to the Committee on 9 November 1977, less than a week before the shah's visit to the Carter White House.

Certain countries which had a tendency to lecture on civil and political rights had apparently forgotten the realities of a universe which did not belong to them. . . . While the Western countries stressed the rights of the individual, the developing countries were thinking of the rights of entire peoples. The former spoke of the immediate implementation of civil and political rights, while the latter strove to establish economic ones. It was important, therefore . . . to avoid planning new machinery solely on the basis of a narrow interpretation of concepts that were understood differently in a world which was divided by such great differences.[162]

This kind of justification for relativism would become more prevalent in the 1980s and 1990s, with the assertion of "trade-off" theories by confident East Asian elites, principally the government in Singapore.[163]

Several other African and Arab states espoused Ashraf's new variant of relativism, which was quite distinct from the older Soviet tradition of emphasizing economic and social rights. Radical relativism merged with the developmentalist ideology that placed economic modernization ahead of individual rights. Aminata Marico (Mali) was among those who asserted that "a universally acceptable definition had not been found" for human rights.[164] Civil and political rights were suitable only for an "individualistic" society. Human rights "for some . . . meant individual rights such as freedom of expression, in line with the individualistic concept of society. Praiseworthy as it might be, it was restrictive and had no claim to universal truth."[165] Mali had then been subjected to almost a decade of Lieutenant Moussa Traoré's military government, which had imprisoned and killed numerous members of the opposition.[166] Traoré's rule was remembered primarily for its assault on pro-democracy protesters in 1991.

Patrice Houngavou (Benin) pursued the Malian critique of universality, and complained that "the notion of human rights currently being discussed by the Committee was not shared by all members," with the rights of the individual being suitable only for "adherents of imperialism."[167] Benin, under Marxist dictator Mathieu Kérékou, was a favorite ally of the Soviet Union, which often used it as an intermediary for introducing anti-human rights proposals into the UN.[168] Nigeria objected that the High Commissioner "would encourage certain countries to accentuate the propagation of their own ideologies at the expense of those of other States."[169] All these criticisms were modest when compared to those of Kuwait, which denounced the High Commissioner as "a trojan horse from which sallies would be made against developing countries."[170] The "elitist" High Commissioner was irrelevant to the "millions of people throughout the world who were concerned with the problem of their very existence rather than the enjoyment of particular rights."[171]

More countries began to advocate Ashraf's relativist position in the 1978 and 1979 sessions. The Madagascar delegation, representing a government then preoccupied with crushing dissent against the ruling socialist AREMA party, protested that "the forces of imperialism and reaction had used the pretext of defending human rights when they had really been attempting to impose their own concept of such rights."[172] The delegate from Singapore reminded the Western powers that the "task of third world governments had been to ensure that basic human needs were met," and observed that "in such situations" respect for "total civil and political liberties would lead to the destruction of the fragile state."[173] It was almost a dress rehearsal for the official People's Action Party government line of the 1990s.

Despite this chorus of relativism, some Afro-Asian states persisted in their support for the High Commissioner and for universality. Particularly prominent were more liberal regimes, foremost Senegal.[174] However, the one country that spoke out above all others in favor of the office was outside the Western orbit. It was a state with the most recent experience of gross violations of human rights, and the utter failure of the existing UN system even to condemn those violations, let alone prevent them.

Throughout the 1979 session, delegate Eldad Wapenyi from Uganda pleaded for the Third Committee to take action on the commissioner.[175] His first speech on 26 October was delivered almost immediately after the Singaporean representative had promulgated the foundations of its "trade-off" theory. Uganda had only recently been liberated from the bloody rule of Amin through military intervention from Tanzania. More than 250,000 had been killed in the eight years since Amin took power from the democratically elected Milton Obote.[176] As they advanced, Tanzanian troops and Ugandan resistance uncovered appalling violations conducted by the Bureau of State Research, Amin's private police force. Amin himself fled to a comfortable exile in Saudi Arabia.[177]

Opening his address with thanks to Amnesty International and the International Commission of Jurists, Wapenyi catalogued the deficiencies of the existing human rights machinery. He passionately denounced "the tendency of States charged with human rights violations to become members of the Commission [on Human Rights] for the purpose of obstructing its work," which had been the case with the Amin regime.[178] Wapenyi desperately urged the establishment of a powerful High Commissioner. For human rights to be protected there had to be much stronger means of enforcement, and some sacrifice of national sovereignty. Wapenyi reflected that "his delegation was increasingly skeptical about the phrase 'interference in the internal affairs of States' because it was the phrase used by Amin to cover up his atrocities."[179] Later in the session Uganda again endorsed the High Commissioner, and complained that the UN Division of Human Rights "was not sufficiently powerful."[180] Protesting against the Afro-Asian focus on *apartheid,* the Ugandan representative warned the Committee that "violations of human rights were not limited by frontiers, or restricted to particular ideologies."[181] He concluded that "even when the situation returned to normal, it had proved impossible to prevent their recurrence. Wapenyi's observation was tragically perceptive, given the gross human rights violations practiced by the Obote regime that was returned to government in the 1980 elections.[182]

Conclusions: Cultural relativism as a Political Phenomenon

During the 1980s and 1990s, cultural relativism was codified as the officially sanctioned ideology of many Asian and African diplomats and leaders. In the lead up to the 1993 World Conference on Human Rights in Vienna, regional communiqués from African and Asian governments endorsed cultural relativism as part of their shared policy platform.[183] The Bangkok Declaration, drafted by government delegations from across Asia, with especially strong influence from Iran, China, and Singapore, declared that although "human rights are universal in nature" they had to be considered with careful reference to "the significance of national and regional particularities and various historical, cultural and religious backgrounds."[184] At the Vienna negotiations, cultural relativism served as the central stumbling block to an agreed conference program of action.[185] The idea of human rights as Western achieved unparalleled currency and power, threatening the first World Conference on Human Rights in a quarter-century with failure. The tensions over universality so prominent at the 1968 Tehran conference had arguably intensified in the intervening years.

Cultural relativism became a mainstay in the vocabulary of Third World dictators and former tyrants. In 2002, from his exile in Zimbabwe, former Ethiopian president Mengistu Mariam used cultural relativism to excuse the appalling political violence that characterized his Marxist regime. Mengistu, who killed thousands in his 1976-77 Red Terror campaign, justified his reign by claiming that "the traditions in Africa are different," though he failed to explain the place of Lenin in African customary governance.[186] Said Raja'i Khorasani, UN representative of the Islamic Republic of Iran, announced in December 1984 that the Universal Declaration of Human Rights "did not accord with the system of values recognized by the Islamic Republic of Iran" and that "his country would therefore not hesitate to violate its prescriptions."[187] Testimonies from the inmates at Evin prison confirm that the Republic had no hesitation whatsoever in violating human rights with acts of the most extraordinary brutality during this period, including arbitrary arrest, summary execution by stoning, and torture.[188] Chief ideologue for the Sudanese National Islamic Front, Hasan Al-Turabi, denounced Western human rights imperialism in 1994. Educated at the Sorbonne in the 1960s, Turabi attacked the notion of universal human rights as part of "an imperial tradition in the West, a colonial experience, deriving from Rome, of trying to impose one's culture."[189]

Following the Tiananmen Square massacre, cultural relativism formed the centerpiece of the Chinese diplomatic counter-offensive. The Governmental White Paper on Human Rights, issued in November 1991, scarcely two years after Tiananmen, explained that it was "normal for countries to have a different understanding and practice of human rights owing to varied historical, social, economic and cultural conditions."[190] Given these differences, it attacked attempts to "impose pressure" and "sell ideas" on human rights, which were part of the "anti-China plots of the West" and a tool for foreign enemies "to reach their sinister political purposes." Six years later, while defending China's human rights record to the Washington press corps, Premier Jiang Zemin adopted the same strategy. Jiang bristled when Tiananmen was raised, and clinically recited the standard relativist view to the assembled journalists: "Concepts on democracy, on human rights and on freedoms are relative and specific ones. And they are to be determined by the specific national situation of different countries."[191]

Asian and African dictators seem at least as fond of the relativist doctrine as the scholars who promulgated it in academic journals. This poses a significant problem for the Western adherents of cultural relativism, who often marry relativism with the protection of non-Western communities. The concept that relativists champion in terms of respect for Third World cultures has ended up providing a powerful excuse for those who murder, torture, and abuse Third World people.[192] It has been an excuse used by both colonial administrator and postcolonial dictator, invoked as both imperialist and anti-imperialist at different times. Cultural relativism as a philosophical discourse has its origins in opposition to European imperialism, but historically it has served authoritarian masters of all stripes.

There are those in the Third World, such as Begum Rana, who have opposed it in both its guises. When General Zia Ul-Huq seized power in 1978, backed by Saudi Arabian funding, he immediately co-opted Islam to bolster the legitimacy of his rule.[193] Begum Rana, founder of the women's rights movement in Pakistan, denounced the program of Islamicization, which had become little more than an excuse for the extension of Zia's control over the Pakistani state.[194] Through the new Islamic Ideology Council, dissent was suppressed and opponents jailed and executed. In September 1983, the octogenarian Begum Rana spoke out publicly against the new measures, describing them as "repugnant to the Holy Qur'an and Islam, which gives women equal rights with men in all public matters."[195] Her stature among the Pakistani population enhanced the prestige of the opposition movement considerably.[196] Ali Jinnah's words were again cited to demonstrate the nationalist character of women's equality, just as they had been in the 1950s, when the Western colonial powers were the main critics of universality.[197]

The history of UN human rights debates reveals that the political phenomenon of cultural relativism has had little to with the protection of African and Asian cultures from colonialism.[198] Far from being the defense against imperialism it is often held up to be, cultural relativism was once a favorite argument of Western colonial powers, who feared universal human rights as a threat to their rule, not an opportunity to perpetuate it. By contrast, those Third World states with recent experience of imperialism were often the most vocal critics of cultural relativism, at least when it suited their political interests to do so. This situation only began to change with the emergence of highly authoritarian regimes across Africa and Asia in the late 1960s and 1970s, and the simultaneous development of potentially more intrusive human rights monitoring. The rise of cultural relativism in the Third World is clearly associated with the rise of dictatorships, and the growing possibility of a human rights system that might cause them embarrassment.

For half a century claims of cultural difference have served as a generic response to the threat posed by universal human rights, one utilized by the full spectrum of repressive regimes. The fundamental similarity between states that assert cultural objections to human rights is not the culture of the people they represent but the authoritarian character of their governments. Misuse of cultural difference unites European colonial dictatorships, like the British in Kenya, racial police states like *apartheid* South Africa, African Marxist autocracies like Ethiopia, Islamic theocracies like Iran, and medieval absolutisms like Saudi Arabia. These widely divergent systems all share a fear of investigation and loss of power. Through their actions, they reveal their lack of respect for traditional culture.

The rise of cultural relativism in the UN was not then the inevitable result of decolonization. Colonial regimes had their own specific variant of cultural relativism, and early anticolonial nationalists were typically ardent supporters of universality. It was instead the product of the undemocratic and human rights abusive regimes that proliferated across the Third World from the second half of the 1960s. Just as their colonial predecessors had, these dictators abused the term culture to evade human rights scrutiny. They claimed to speak for their people, as the paternalistic arbiters of what was and was not consistent with the national culture, but without ever testing their legitimacy at the ballot box. Through their use of a notionally anti-imperialist doctrine, these postcolonial dictatorships had begun to resemble the colonial administrators that they professed to hate.

Conclusion

What good is our independence if it is only to imitate European totalitarianism, to replace external colonialism by domestic colonialism?
—Leopold Senghor

The principal triumph of the African, Asian, and Arab diplomats who entered the UN in the 1950s and 1960s was their successful struggle to make human rights truly universal. Prior to the battles of the 1950s, the notion of different human rights for African and Asian peoples had widespread currency, among defenders of European colonialism, and anti-imperialist critics alike. Well-meaning anthropologists like Boas, Benedict, and Herskovits cited insuperable cultural differences—a position enshrined in the American Anthropological Association's 1947 rejection of universal human rights. Patronizing representatives from the European colonial powers argued the same, albeit with a different inflection. As the Danish delegate explained to the Commission on Human Rights in 1949, "the interests of the peoples and territories themselves would require exceptions to be made to the application of certain rights and freedoms."[1] Even René Cassin, the great architect of the Universal Declaration, placed at least temporary limits on universality where colonial peoples were concerned.

When the Universal Declaration was adopted in December 1948, its universality was necessarily precarious. Although there had been crucial contributions from figures like P. C. Chang, Charles Malik, Hansa Mehta, and Carlos Romulo, much of Asia and most of Africa had not been involved in the drafting process. As the debates on the colonial clause of the human rights covenant illustrated, there was a very real possibility that the inferior status of colonial territories would be formally accepted in the International Bill of Rights. Equally, there was no guarantee that the rights enumerated in the Universal Declaration would be recognized as legitimate by those who had not participated in its creation. The passage of the Universal Declaration by a UN with only fifty-eight member states did not conclude the battle for universality, it was instead the first victory in a process that continued for more than a decade.

Much of the struggle for universality took place through the 1950s and early 1960s, as decolonization transformed the UN. The campaign to repudiate the colonial clause of the covenant was an early indication of the Third World's enthusiasm for universality. Led by a small coalition of Asian and Arab states, including conspicuously pro-Western countries like the Philippines and Lebanon, the idea of a separate status for colonies was emphatically rejected. In its place, they insisted on the inclusion of an "anticolonial" clause that explicitly ensured equal treatment for all colonies. At the 1955 Asian-African Conference in Bandung, the idea of universal human rights received one of its most significant endorsements, when 29 Asian and African countries recognized the Universal Declaration as "a common standard of achievement for all peoples," despite opposition from communist China. In the rise of the Universal Declaration as the definitive human rights document of the twentieth century, the debates of Bandung were almost as important as those of Lake Success and Geneva. Bandung advanced the legitimacy of the Universal Declaration for the emerging Third World, and insulated it from charges of cultural imperialism for more than a decade.

Through a mixture of idealism and political advantage, Third World diplomats of all ideological persuasions were united in their advocacy of universal human rights between 1950 and 1960. For some, the value of rights was essentially instrumental; they were a useful and potent weapon for advancing anticolonialism, or, as John Humphrey complained in 1951, "a stick for beating the western democracies."[2] Yet for others, supporting universality was clearly a matter of principle. Figures like Malik and Romulo were closely aligned to the West on most issues, but they were outspoken proponents of universality, irrespective of whether it ran contrary to the Western line, as it all too frequently did. To defeat the colonial clause in the Commission on Human Rights, Malik, a committed anti-communist, supported a Soviet-sponsored resolution.[3]

Whatever the motivation, this support for universality was decisive in a period when racism continued to compromise the West's policy on rights. Apart from the European colonial powers, major figures in the U.S. foreign affairs establishment advocated policies based on racism. They rejected liberal democracy in Africa on the basis of racial and cultural pessimism. At a 1960 meeting of the National Security Council, Vice President Nixon advised that "some of the peoples of Africa have been out of the trees only for about fifty years."[4] Others counseled that

"Africans do not understand Western-style ballot box democracy" and would be incapable of democratic government. Given the poor prospects for democracy, it was, they argued, better to "develop military strong men" than to encourage democratic regimes.[5]

Alongside the obvious problem of Western racism, there was also Western apathy. In the foundational years of the human rights program, until at least the mid-1960s, the great Atlantic democracies were ambivalent about the place of human rights in the UN. The United States pursued a deliberate policy of neglect from the early 1950s, which reflected the low status accorded to human rights in its foreign policy making. The State Department declared in 1952 that the Third Committee was nothing more than "a safety valve" for the small states to "let off steam."[6] The Cold War issues of the Security Council and the political committees were important, but rights were marginal. For almost a decade, the delegation from the most powerful democracy in the world sat more or less idle while the human rights covenants were drafted around it.

Third World leadership animated the moribund human rights project in the years after 1948. Figures like Mahmud Azmi, Bedia Afnan, and Salvador López provided the enthusiasm, energy, and ideas that so much of the Western UN group refused to contribute. Throughout the 1950s, the most vocal advocates of the supposedly Western philosophy of rights came from Egypt, Pakistan, the Philippines, India, and Iraq. Third World leadership also ensured the rise of self-determination and racial discrimination as priorities, but this was the price of Western disengagement. Both of these items deserved to be on the human rights agenda, even if the emphasis became excessive. The Third World captured the human rights program, but in the process they saved it from Soviet hostility and Western lassitude. Two human rights covenants with articles on self-determination were surely better than no covenant. A Commission on Human Rights that devoted too much time to debating *apartheid* was better than one that debated nothing.

So it was with the issue of self-determination, which was pressed forward relentlessly until politically transformed into a human right. Although clearly open to grave abuse, the initial phases of the self-determination struggle were not obviously distinct from a long-standing European and American tradition of linking national and individual liberty. The impassioned pleas that independence was the sole avenue to personal freedom would surely have found a sympathetic hearing from Mazzini, Gladstone, and Wilson. With a few eloquent exceptions like Cassin and Humphrey, a convincing repudiation of the case for a right to self-determination was never articulated. It was a hard case to make in an era of widespread colonial repression, particularly when the repression of endogenous African and Asian governments had yet to be so tragically and insistently proven, often under the very banner of "self-determination."

Even as the politicization of the human rights program intensified in the 1960s, many of the new African members were determined to take a reasonably even-handed approach. Ghanaian diplomat George Lamptey led efforts to conclude the ICERD, which included a pioneering, if ultimately ineffectual, individual petition article. Nigerian Adam Mohammed and Sudanese justice Mohammed Abu Rannat were both at the forefront of the struggle for a universal petition procedure in the late 1960s. These figures were just as likely to clash with their militant Afro-Asian bloc colleague, Tanzanian Waldron-Ramsey, as they were with the Western delegates. New experts to the expanded Sub-Commission from Rwanda and Upper Volta were sufficiently impartial to elicit a diatribe of Soviet abuse. Although properly renowned for its solidarity, the Afro-Asian bloc was never monolithic.

Nor was the much-vaunted authoritarian alliance of Afro-Asian, Arab, and Soviet regimes as persistent or durable as the entity imagined by Daniel Patrick Moynihan in his critique of human rights in the General Assembly.[7] The Soviet states desperately courted the newly independent states, but their successes were episodic, symbolic, and ephemeral. Weight of numbers ensured that the decolonized states were always the senior partners in any coalition. The Afro-Asian bloc was not hijacked by the communist states; rather, the communist states exaggerated their affinities with the Third World, and exploited a small number of genuine client regimes. They were never in control, as demonstrated by the struggle for petition, which was eventually won with Afro-Asian support, against Soviet obstruction.

The consequences of decolonization were necessarily contradictory and complex, involving a huge number of politically diverse states. In the 1960s and 1970s, revolutionary progress coexisted with catastrophic setbacks. On the eve of the disastrous 1968 Tehran Conference, the Commission on Human Rights was at last beginning to make progress on petitions, with Third World figures leading the fight. The Haitian delegation that boasted of Duvalier's human rights record in Tehran had been on the defensive scarcely months earlier as a range of states sought to study petitions regarding the human rights situation in Haiti.

Decolonization was the most powerful shaping influence on the human rights program between 1950 and 1979. In virtually every significant debate, Arab, Asian, and African delegations played a leading role, with their contributions central to the creation of major pillars of the modern human rights system: the covenants, ICERD, and the right to individual petition. At the UN, the activism of the decolonized world, propelled by both political advantage and idealism, radically and permanently transformed the status of the individual in relation to the state. The great tragedy was that an equivalent transformation was absent or deferred in so many of the former colonies. By a combination of accident and design, decolonization at the international level had delivered what few postcolonial regimes had provided their citizens domestically. Third World diplomats had secured the status of universal rights and greater scrutiny of state power. By the close of the twentieth century, Third World governments had proven beyond all doubt how urgently those protections were needed, and how limited they remained

Notes

Introduction: The Politics of Decolonization and the Evolution of the International Human Rights Project

Epigraph: Humphrey, *On the Edge of Greatness*, vol. 2, 129, 135.

1. Humphrey, *On the Edge of Greatness*, vol. 2, 129.

2. Glendon, *A World Made New*; Cmiel, "Human Rights, Freedom of Information, and the Origins of Third World Solidarity"; Lauren, *Power and Prejudice*; Lauren, *The Evolution of International Human Rights*; Waltz, "Universalizing Human Rights"; Waltz, "Reclaiming and Rebuilding the History of the Universal Declaration"; Waltz, "Universal Human Rights."

3. Abdullah, "UN Charter Review"; "Mahathir Warns of Superpowers' Scare-Tactics on Human Rights Review."

4. Mutua, *Human Rights*, 19.

5. Simpson, *Human Rights and the End of Empire*, 300.

6. Afshari, "On Historiography of Human Rights." For comments on anti-colonialism and human rights, see especially 51–55.

7. Lauren, *The Evolution of International Human Rights*, 174.

8. Henkin, "The United Nations and Human Rights," 512.

9. Quentin-Baxter, "International Protection of Human Rights," 136.

10. Ibid., 137.

11. Humphrey, *On the Edge of Greatness*, vol. 3, 8.

12. Report on the Third Committee of the General Assembly: 14 October–22 December 1952, 7 April 1953, 20–21, 320.13/14-753, Decimal File 1950–1954; General Records of the Department of State, Record Group 59 (RG 59), NACP.

13. Ibid., 20.

14. Ibid., 21.

15. This was a theme Humphrey returned to a number of times. In his diary entry of 17 November 1950, he again expressed his frustration at the lack of Western leadership. "My diagnosis remains the same. The great powers by their failure to accept their responsibilities lost leadership in the committee to countries like Mexico (Noriega), Pakistan (Bokhari) and Saudi Arabia (Baroody)." Humphrey was also highly critical of the consequences that flowed from Western neglect, and the rise of the so-called "little politicians": "The Arab bloc together with India (Mrs. [Lakshmi] Menon) have provided the leadership which the U.S.A., the U.K. and France abdicated; and that leadership has been incompetent, mediocre and irresponsible. My language is strong but not too strong. Little politicians have played havoc with great humanitarian questions." Humphrey, *On the Edge of Greatness*, vol. 2, 129, 131, 133, 143, 167; vol. 4, 15.

16. Ibid., vol. 2, 288.

17. Teltsch, "Private Appeals to the UN Barred."

18. Radio Transcript, "Today with Mrs. Roosevelt," 14 May 1950, 11, Charles Malik Collection, Box 39, File 8, Correspondence, Roosevelt, Eleanor, 1947–1960.

19. Malik persistently argued for greater Western leadership. At a speech at the Carnegie Endowment Round Table of World Affairs in September 1951, he again exhorted a more proactive Western policy: "You simply cannot afford to stand aside and plunging into the midst of things," and "you cannot afford to trail behind either." Human Rights in the United Nations, Address to the Round Table on World Affairs in Extension Education of the Carnegie Endowment for International Peace, New York, 19 September 1951, 6, Charles Malik Collection, Box 79, File 3, Seventh Session, Commission, Human Rights, Speeches and Writings, 1951.

20. Office Memorandum, Committee Three Activities—Delegate and Staff Comments, 27 December 1957, 2, 320.13/12-2757, Decimal File 1955–1959; General Records of the Department of State, RG 59; NACP.

21. Ibid., 4.

22. Ibid.

23. Ibid.

24. Humphrey, *On the Edge of Greatness*, vol. 3, 103.

25. Anderson, *Eyes Off the Prize*, 237.

26. Ibid., 239. Reports from the Commission on Human Rights were scathing about the "action plan" Lord introduced so unsuccessfully. "Neither of the United Kingdom and Australian delegations has been prepared to promise support for any of these proposals. . . . General objections to the proposals are—(a) that they would tend to be a substitute for action to complete, adopt, and implement, the Covenant, and indeed they are intended to be so far as U.S.A. itself is concerned; (b) that they would be superfluous in the event of the completion, adoption and implementation of the Covenant; and (c) that they are, in reality, but a political device to placate public opinion that has been disturbed by the Presidential withdrawal of support of the Covenant. Particular objections to (1) are . . . the reports would be innocuous and useless." From Australian Mission to the United Nations, Regarding US Human Rights Action Plan, 25 July 1954, National Archives of Australia, File 856/13/10/9, Memorandum 444.

27. Reproduced in Buckley, *United Nations Journal*, 259. See also Moynihan, "The Politics of Human Rights," 22; Moynihan, "The United States in Opposition," passim.

28. Quentin-Baxter, "International Protection of Human Rights," 137.

29. Humphrey, *On the Edge of Greatness*, vol. 3, 103.

30. Ibid., vol. 3, 157.

31. Abdul Rahman Pazhwak (Afghanistan) also appears to have had great latitude, at least for a period. See ibid., vol. 3, 98.

32. Buckley, *United Nations Journal*, 69–70.

33. Seebohm, *No Regret*, 254–55.

34. Ibid., 253.

35. Tree did make a notable contribution to the campaign for the creation of a High Commissioner for Human Rights, along with Costa Rican Ambassadors Emilia Castro de Barish and Fernando Volio Jiménez. See ibid., 256.

36. This dynamism had disappeared by the mid-1970s, when pro forma

denunciations of *apartheid* and imperialism had become the mainstay of the agenda. So repetitive were the speeches that UK representative Lady Gaitskell observed that the committee's meetings had become practically incomprehensible. "Over the past several years, the Third Committee had become a closed society with a language of its own, a language little understood in the outside world. The constant repetition of the words 'colonialism,' 'imperialism,' 'neocolonialism' and 'racism' had become an incantation and seemed to have a narcotic effect on some delegations." Summary Records of the Third Committee, 2088th meeting, 12 November 1974, A/C.3/SR. 2088, para 30.

Chapter 1. Human Rights and the Birth of the Third World: The Bandung Conference

Epigraphs: Romulo, *The Meaning of Bandung*, 53; for a detailed assessment of his position at the conference, see also Espiritu, "'To Carry Water on Both Shoulders'." Tasunosuke Takosake's speech is reproduced in Hassan, *Collected Documents from the Asian-African Conference*, 67. All opening and closing addresses are verified by cross-reference to Asian-African Conference, *Speeches and Communiqués*.

1. Kahin, *The Asian-African Conference*, 1. See also Burton, Espiritu, and Wilkins, "Introduction: The Fate of Nationalisms"; Jansen, *Afro-Asia and Non-Alignment*; Kimche, *The Afro-Asian Movement*.

2. Glendon, *A World Made New*, 215–16, 223–24.

3. Ibid., 215–16.

4. Ibid., 223.

5. Ibid., 224.

6. Lauren, *Power and Prejudice*, 223–29.

7. Ibid., 226–27.

8. Lauren, *The Evolution of International Human Rights*, 241, 243, 286.

9. Ibid., 241.

10. Humphrey, *Human Rights & the United Nations*, 203.

11. Nasser, *Egypt's Liberation*.

12. W. P. J. Handmer, "Afro-Asian Conference: Zhou Enlai's Report Text of Zhou Enlai's Assessment of the Bandung Conference Given at the Standing Committee of the National People's Congress, 13 May 1955," Department of External Affairs, Australia, Hong Kong, 18 May, 1955, 2, National Archives of Australia, A1838/283, 3002/1/1. Pr 2, Original File No. 704, Memorandum 350.

13. Jawaharlal Nehru, "Report on Bandung," Statement in Lok Sabha, 30April 1955, as reproduced in Nehru, *Jawaharlal Nehru's Speeches*, vol. 3, *March 1953–August 1957*, 300.

14. Ahmed Sukarno, Conference Opening Address, as reproduced in Kahin, *The Asian-African Conference*, 40.

15. Romulo, *The Meaning of Bandung*, 31.

16. Ibid., 35.

17. Quoted from Sir John Kotelewala's opening address to the Conference, 18 April 1955, as reproduced in Baker et al., *The Facts of the Bandung Conference*, 20.

18. Malik, "A.B.C Sunday Radio Program Transcript. Guest of Honour Charles Malik," Australian Broadcasting Corporation, 5 May 1955, 1, National Archives of Australia, A1838/278, 3002/1 Pr 5.

19. Western responses to Bandung have been the subject of considerable

scholarship, see for instance, Tarling, "'Ah-Ah': Britain and the Bandung Conference"; Waters, "After Decolonisation"; Parker, "Cold War II."

20. Fraser, "An American Dilemma," 121.

21. Ibid., 120.

22. Ibid., 121–22.

23. During the early 1950s, Fath had been one of Nasser's close allies, serving as a propagandist and speechwriter for the new leader. His newspaper, *Al-Misri*, had been a key organ for disseminating the nationalist rhetoric of the new Republican government. But as the authoritarian tendencies of the regime became increasingly apparent, Fath became a vocal critic of Nasser and his emerging dictatorship. *Al-Misri* was promptly suppressed and Fath was forced into exile. For a précis of Fath's experiences with Nasser, see Searle, "L'affaire Nasser (Review)."

24. Mahmoud Aboul Fath, Letter to Bandung Delegates, 13 April 1955, Charles Malik Collection, Box 130, File 7, Correspondence—Asian-African Conference, April 1955.

25. Ali Sastroamidjojo, Conference Introductory Address, as reproduced in Hassan, *Collected Documents from the Asian-African Conference*, 18–19.

26. Asian-African Conference, *Speeches and Communiqués*, passim.

27. Closing Address of Afghanistan, as reproduced in Hassan, *Collected Documents from the Asian-African Conference*, 149.

28. Closing Address of Egypt, as reproduced in ibid., 154.

29. Closing Address of Pakistan, as reproduced in ibid., 173.

30. Opening Address of Thailand, as reproduced in ibid., 109.

31. Final Communiqué, Article C-1, as reproduced in Kahin, *The Asian-African Conference*, 80.

32. Romulo, *The Meaning of Bandung*, 36.

33. Ibid.

34. Ibid., 54. The identification of democratic thought with the West was a tendency that continually frustrated Romulo. In his autobiography, he expressed his disappointment with the prevalence of this thinking in the American media in reporting his speeches from Bandung, commenting that the "American newspapermen thought to honor me by reporting: 'Romulo is pro-American. He is defending America against the Communist charges.' They did me no service by those words. I was not defending America; I was defending democracy." See Romulo, *I Walked with Heroes*, 68–69.

35. Romulo, *The Meaning of Bandung*, 54.

36. Charles Malik, "Talk Given by Dr. Charles Malik at Luncheon," Canberra: Department of External Affairs, Australia, 28 April 1955, 2, National Archives of Australia, A1838/278, 3002/1 Pr 5, File No. 156/3/3.

37. Detail of these debates is given by Malik, ibid., 2. See also K. C. O. Shann, "Report on Asian-African Conference—Bandung," Canberra: Department of External Affairs, United Nations Branch, Australia, 11 May 1955, 5, National Archives of Australia, A4311/1, Item 94/28.

38. Jansen, *Afro-Asia*, 198.

39. Djalal Abdoh, "The Bandung Conference. An Appreciation," Tehran: British Foreign Office, Tehran Embassy, 3 May 1955, 1–2, National Archives UK, Kew, FO 371/116984, 1071/55/55, D2231/336.

40. Roderick W. Parkes, "Some Impressions of the Bandung Conference," Jakarta: British Foreign Office, 28 April 1955, 2, National Archives UK, Kew, FO371/116983, 40 (1071/242/55), D2231/319.

41. Malik, "Talk Given by Dr. Charles Malik at Luncheon," 2.
42. Ibid.
43. Romulo, *The Meaning of Bandung*, 14.
44. Abdoh, "The Bandung Conference: An Appreciation," 1.
45. Wilson, *Zhou: The Story of Zhou Enlai, 1898–1976*.
46. Romulo, *The Meaning of Bandung*, 14.
47. Malik, "Talk Given by Dr. Charles Malik at Luncheon," 2.
48. Parkes, "Some Impressions of the Bandung Conference," 2.
49. Shann, "Report on Asian-African Conference," 5.
50. Malik, "Talk Given by Dr. Charles Malik at Luncheon," 2.
51. Record of interview between Charles Malik of Lebanon and Mr. Zhou Enlai, Prime Minister of the People's Republic of China, on April 25, 1955, in Bandung, Indonesia. Copy of transcript of interview between Zhou Enlai and Charles Malik, 6.30–8.30 pm, Monday, 25 April 1955, Bandung, Indonesia. Transcript is a carbon copy of that presented to John Foster Dulles, 5 May, 1955, and sent to Zhou Enlai, 6 May, 1955, Personal Papers of Charles Malik, Malik Collection, Box 130, Folder 4.
52. Handmer, "Afro-Asian Conference: Zhou Enlai's Report," 4, 6. See also Zhou Enlai, *China and the Asian-African Conference*, 32.
53. Abdoh, "The Bandung Conference: An Appreciation," 2.
54. H. M. Loveday, "ROK Reaction to Bandung Conference," 3, Seoul: Department of External Affairs, Australia, Seoul Delegation, 4 May, 1955, 1, National Archives of Australia, A1838/2, 851/19/1, Memorandum No. 127, Seoul Ref. 9/8.
55. R. G. Casey, Asian-African Conference: Cabinet Submission No. 373, c. May 1955, 3, 4, National Archives of Australia, A1838/2.
56. Ahmed Sukarno, Conference Opening Address, as reproduced in Hassan, *Collected Documents from the Asian-African Conference*, 4–5.
57. Opening Address of China, as reproduced in ibid., 39.
58. Opening Address of Lebanon, as reproduced in ibid., 77.
59. Final Communiqué as reproduced in Kahin, *The Asian-African Conference*, 80.
60. Opening Address of Egypt, as reproduced in Hassan, *Collected Documents from the Asian-African Conference*, 50.
61. Opening Address of Syria, as reproduced in ibid., 106.
62. Opening Address of Afghanistan, as reproduced in ibid., 27.
63. Opening Address of Iran, as reproduced in ibid., 59.
64. For further discussion of the Communism-as-colonialism debate inside the Political Committee see Sir John Kotelawala, *An Asian Prime Minister's Story* (London: Harrap, 1956), 186–88; Malik, *The Problem of Coexistence*, 18–19, 30–31. For contemporary press reports of the incident, see Doty, "Asian-African Talks Continue Bogged on Colonial Issue"; and Durdin, "Bandung Meeting Asked to Assail Red Colonialism."
65. Opening Address of Iran, 59.
66. Opening Address of Iraq, as reproduced in Hassan, *Collected Documents from the Asian-African Conference*, 65.
67. Opening Address of Libya, as reproduced in ibid., 83.
68. Opening Address of Pakistan, as reproduced in ibid., 89.
69. Opening Address of Turkey, as reproduced in ibid., 116.
70. Ibid., 115.
71. Opening Address of Vietnam, as reproduced in ibid., 127.

72. Ibid., 129.
73. Philippine Opening Address, reproduced in Romulo, *The Meaning of Bandung*, 66.
74. Ibid., 67.
75. Ibid., 68.
76. See Romulo, *I Walked with Heroes*, 167.
77. Philippine Opening Address, 75.
78. Ibid., 76.
79. Jamali was especially vehement in his criticism of the atheism of communist ideology, labeling it a "one-side materialistic religion" that "denies God and the spiritual heritage of mankind." Subversion spread by "the agents of this new anti-God religion" extended across the world without exception, provoking hatred and conflict. See the Opening Address of Iraq. By contrast, Thai delegate Prince Wan emphasized the religious diversity of Asia and Africa, and the preeminent role spirituality played in their respective cultures. He argued for the "fundamental importance of moral and spiritual values" as a "common characteristic" of the cultures shared by the delegates, with "moral and spiritual values" a defining component of the Asian and African identity. See the Opening Address of Thailand, as reproduced in Hassan, *Collected Documents from the Asian-African Conference*, 106.
80. Chinese Supplementary Address, as reproduced in ibid., 45.
81. Press Release, Conference Secretariat, as reproduced in Asian-African Conference, *Speeches and Communiqués*.
82. Kotelawala, *An Asian Prime Minister's Story*, 186–87.
83. Kahin, *The Asian-African Conference*, 19–20.
84. Jawaharlal Nehru, "Problems of Dependent Peoples," address in closed session, Political Committee, 22 April 1955. File No. SI/162/9/64-MEA, as reproduced in *Selected Works of Jawaharlal Nehru*, 101–2.
85. Ibid., 103.
86. Romulo, *The Meaning of Bandung*, 56
87. Opening Address of Yemen, as reproduced in Hassan, *Collected Documents from the Asian-African Conference*, 132.
88. Opening Address of Jordan, as reproduced in ibid., 70.
89. Malik, *The Problems of Coexistence*, 17.

Chapter 2. "Transforming the End into the Means": The Third World and the Right to Self-Determination

Epigraphs: "The Process of Liberation," address by President Julius K. Nyerere to Convocation of Ibaden University, Nigeria, 17 November 1976; Verbatim Records of General Assembly Plenary Meeting, 94th session, 13 December 1960, A/PV. 945, para 177.
1. Pomerance, *Self-Determination in Law and Practice*, 1.
2. Cassese, "The Self-Determination of Peoples," 97–98.
3. Franck, "The Emerging Right to Democratic Governance," 55.
4. Simpson, *End of Empire*, 304.
5. Ibid., 305.
6. Young, "African States and the Search for Freedom," 32.
7. Henkin, "The United Nations and Human Rights," 513.
8. Patrick Thornberry has also observed the tension between these two concepts in self-determination. See Thornberry, "The Democratic or Inter-

nal Aspect of Self-Determination," 105. See also Pomerance, *Self-Determination*, 37–47.

9. Humphrey, *A Great Adventure*, 66.

10. Summary Records of the Third Committee, 370th meeting, 19 December 1951, A/C.3/SR. 370, para. 35.

11. Summary Records of the Third Committee, 401st meeting, 24 January 1951, A/C.3/SR. 401, para. 23.

12. Agi, *René Cassin*, 233–35, 244–45.

13. Summary Records of the Third Committee, 311th meeting, 10 November 1950, A/C.3/SR. 311.

14. Humphrey, *A Great Adventure*, 66.

15. Ibid., 129.

16. Ibid. Humphrey did moderate his opinion somewhat as it became clear that the right to self-determination was being interpreted in a conservative manner.

17. This persisted into the 1950s; see Report on the Third Committee of the General Assembly (1952), 3.

18. See, for example, Summary Records of the Third Committee, 180th–225th meetings, 14 April–11 May 1949, A/C.3/SR. 180–225, especially the statements from Jamil Baroody (Saudi Arabia), meetings 180, 193, 198, 218, 225. In a provocative April 1949 address to the Third Committee, Baroody protested against the West's insistence on untrammelled press freedoms: "It has been said that the price of freedom of information had to be paid. The price, for certain small countries, was too high." A/C.3/SR. 198.

19. Cmiel, "Human Rights, Freedom of Information, and the Origins of Third World Solidarity."

20. Humphrey, *On the Edge of Greatness*, vol. 2, 129.

21. Ibid., vol. 1, 222.

22. Ibid., vol. 3, 10.

23. See Summary Records of the Third Committee, 115th–162nd meetings, A/C.3/SR. 115–62.

24. Examples of the affinity between nationalism and individual rights are discussed in Ishay, *The History of Human Rights*, 11–12, 195–96; see also Emerson, *From Empire to Nation*, 223–24; Ghoshal, *Indonesian Politics 1955–59*, 2.

25. A brief précis of the colonial clause issue is given by Normand and Zaidi, *Human Rights at the UN*, 231–33.

26. Cf. Simpson, *End of Empire*, 476–77, 540–41.

27. Summary Records of the Third Committee, 294th meeting, 26 October 1950, A/C.3/SR. 294, para. 38. See also Cassin's earlier statement in defense of the clause in the Commission on Human Rights, Summary Records of the Commission on Human Rights, 129th meeting, 15 June 1949, E/CN. 4/SR. 129.

28. This was a source of considerable anxiety for the British Colonial Office. In October 1949, the Office decided not to publish the Universal Declaration in Gambia, Ghana (Gold Coast), or Sierra Leone because of the gulf between international rhetoric and colonial reality. One memorandum notes that "we can hardly expect to win the confidence of Africans by making statements of 'ultimate aims' while in practice we take steps in precisely the opposite direction." Simpson, *End of Empire*, 458. There was also the inherently antidemocratic aspect to colonialism, highlighted by W. E. B Du Bois in his famous treatise *Colour and Democracy*, 10.

29. Summary Records of the Third Committee, 296th meeting, 27 October 1950, A/C.3/SR. 296, para. 83.

30. Ibid., para. 74.

31. Ibid., para. 77.

32. Summary Records of the Third Committee, 294th meeting, 26 October 1950, A/C.3/SR. 294, para. 17.

33. Simpson, *End of Empire*, 814.

34. The Soviet Union had attempted to include a self-determination provision as early as the Universal Declaration, in an attempt to obstruct its passage. They had also drafted a right to self-determination in their list of amendments to the human rights covenant on 6 November, 1950, A/C.3/L. 96, para. 2.

35. Summary Records of the Third Committee, 302nd meeting, 2 November 1950, A/C.3/SR. 302. The vote was overwhelmingly in favor of removing the colonial clause, with 30 voting to delete it, 11 against, and 8 abstentions. Draft text of amendment is available in UN Document A/C.3/L. 71/Rev. 1. As well as repudiating the colonial clause itself, the Philippine-Syrian amendment explicitly specified the extension of the covenant to colonial territories.

36. UN Document A/C.3/L. 88, 9 November 1950.

37. Summary Records of the Third Committee, 310th meeting, 10 November 1950, A/C.3/SR. 310.

38. Ibid., A/C.3/SR. 311, para. 4.

39. Verbatim Records of the General Assembly Plenary Meeting, 317th session, 4 December 1950, A/PV. 317. Adopted as General Assembly Resolution 421D (V).

40. Particularly outraged was Belgian delegate Fernand Dehousse, who openly impugned the motives of those advocating a right to self-determination. "Certain delegations which had spoke in favour of the self-determination clause did not seem to be sufficiently interested in the solution of the question, but appeared to regard the clause in the negative sense, as a weapon for use against the colonial Powers. . . . Some of the representatives who had expatiated most eloquently on the necessity of introducing various rights into the covenant disregarded the fact that in their own countries certain political parties were forbidden, religious groups were suppressed and the right of habeas corpus was non-existent." Summary Records of the Third Committee, 361st meeting, 7 December 1951, A/C.3/SR. 361, paras. 11–12.

41. Summary Records of the Third Committee, 370th meeting, 19 December 1951, A/C.3/SR. 370, para. 30.

42. Summary Records of the Third Committee, 397th meeting, 21 January 1952, A/C.3/SR. 397, para. 4.

43. Ibid., para. 5.

44. Summary Records of the Third Committee, 401st meeting, 24 January 1952, A/C.3/SR. 401, para. 15.

45. Ibid., para. 45.

46. During the drafting of the new Indonesian constitution, the relative balance between state power and individual freedom was fiercely contested. See Nasution, *The Aspiration for Constitutional Government*.

47. Summary Records of the Third Committee, 447th meeting, 18 November 1952, A/C.3/SR. 447, para. 17.

48. Summary Records of the Third Committee, 454th meeting, 24 November, 1952, A/C.3/SR. 454, para. 25, 32.

49. UN Document A/C.3/L. 296.

50. Summary Records of the Third Committee, 456th meeting, 26 November 1952, A/C.3/SR. 456, para. 76.

51. Summary Records of the Third Committee, 566th meeting, 28 October 1954, A/C.3/SR. 566, para. 35.

52. Summary Records of the Third Committee, 563rd meeting, 25 October 1954, A/C.3/SR. 563, para. 12.

53. Summary Records of the Third Committee, 569th meeting, 1 November 1954, A/C.3/SR. 569, para. 21.

54. Kotelawala, *An Asian Prime Minister's Story*, 186–87.

55. Asian-African Conference Final Communiqué, Article D(1-a). For a general discussion on UN anticolonial activity and Bandung, see El-Ayouty, *The United Nations and Decolonisation*, 55–60, 62–63.

56. Opening Address of Iran, as reproduced in Hassan, *Collected Documents from the Asian-African Conference*, 59.

57. Asian-African Conference Proceedings, as reproduced in ibid. Verified through reference to original proceedings mimeograph, Bandung Conference Secretariat, 1955.

58. Opening Address of Afghanistan, as reproduced in ibid., 25–27.

59. Summary Records of the Commission on Human Rights, 500th meeting, 21 April 1955, E/CN. 4/SR. 500, United States. This included notionally "pro-Western" countries such as the Philippines and Lebanon. The delegate from Pakistan openly rejected it as a "diversionary move," and the Egyptian representative was similarly scornful.

60. Summary Records of the Commission on Human Rights, 500th meeting, 21 April 1955, E/CN. 4/SR. 500, India.

61. Summary Records of the Commission on Human Rights, 502nd meeting, 22 April 1955, E/CN. 4/SR. 502, Philippines.

62. Ibid. But he remained generally positive about the role played by the U.S. in the struggle for self-determination, and recognized the difficulties posed by its ties with the European colonial countries.

63. This tendency was criticized by Roger Baldwin and the International League for the Rights of Man. It was a source of concern even before the Hungarian revolution had been suppressed; see Baldwin, Memorandum to the board of members of the International League for the Rights of Man, Regarding Self-Determination, May 1956, International League for Human Rights Records.

64. Anabtawi, "The Afro-Asian States and the Hungarian Question," 874.

65. Appadorai, *The Domestic Roots of India's Foreign Policy*, 70.

66. Ibid., 875.

67. Ibid., passim.

68. See, for example, Memorandum from Department of State, Washington, D.C., Vote on Self-Determination in Committee Three, 3 December 1952, 320.13/12-352, Decimal File 1950–1954; General Records of the Department of State, RG 59; NACP. Its author reports that "the U.S., however, for more than a year maintained that the resolution should apply not merely to non-self-governing territories but to former sovereign states such as Estonia, Latvia, Lithuania, etc., which have been absorbed by the Soviet Union." The 1952 resolution on self-determination, which the U.S. abstained on, was actually acceptable to the Department of State, which expressed surprise at the delegation's failure to support it. See also Telegram from the Department of State to the Mission at the United Nations, Soviet Item on Colonialism, 1 November 1960,

321.410-2560, Decimal File; General Records of the Department of State, RG 59; NACP; Paper Prepared in the Bureau of International Organization Affairs, The Fourteenth General Assembly and Future United Nations Prospects, Admission of New Members to the United Nations, "Colonial Questions," May 1960. NARA, 301/12–160, in *FRUS*, vol. II, 1958–60.

69. Summary Records of the Third Committee, 823d meeting, 28 November 1957, A/C.3/SR. 823, para. 2.

70. Ibid.

71. Summary Records of the Third Committee, 822nd meeting, 27 November 1957, A/C.3/SR. 826.

72. Ibid., para. 3.

73. Summary Records of the Third Committee, 827th meeting, 3 December 1957, A/C.3/SR. 827, para. 28.

74. Summary Records of the Third Committee, 824th meeting, 29 November 1957, A/C.3/SR. 824, para. 13.

75. Ibid., para. 14.

76. In the two years following Bandung, a considerable expansion of the Third World presence at the UN took place. Nine of the countries at the conference were admitted to the UN between 1955 and 1957: Cambodia, Ceylon, Ghana (Gold Coast), Japan, Jordan, Libya, Laos, Nepal, and Sudan.

77. Summary Records of the Third Committee, 827th meeting, 3 December 1957, A/C.3/SR. 826, para. 4.

78. Although he supported a universal approach to self-determination, Lopez did appear to give priority to independence, and he invoked first Philippine President Manuel Quezon's declaration "that bad government by the people themselves was preferable to the most enlightened government by a foreign power." However, Lopez also recognized that this reasoning "did not solve the humanitarian questions which were the concern of the Committee."

79. Summary Records of the Third Committee, 826th meeting, 2 December 1957, A/C.3/SR. 826, para. 13.

80. This was not surprising given the domestic unpopularity of Kotelawala's performance at Bandung, and his subsequent defeat in the 1956 parliamentary election.

81. Summary Records of the Third Committee, 827th meeting, 3 December 1957, A/C.3/SR. 827, para. 36.

82. Summary Records of the Third Committee, 825th meeting, 2 December 1957, A/C.3/SR. 825, para. 23.

83. Summary Records of the Third Committee, 826th meeting, 2 December 1957, A/C.3/SR. 826, para. 24.

84. Summary Records of the Third Committee, 827th meeting, 3 December 1957, A/C.3/SR. 827, para. 16.

85. Request for the inclusion of an additional item in the agenda of the fifteenth session: item proposed by the USSR, UN Document A/4501, attached letter from Khrushchev, 23 September 1960.

86. Legum, "The Romantic Period, 1939–1970," 25.

87. Draft Declaration on the Granting of Independence to Colonial Countries and Peoples, submitted by the Chairman of the Council of Ministers of the USSR, A/4502, Preamble, Article 3.

88. A/4502, Preamble.

89. Ibid.

90. A/4502, Article 3.

91. The initial sponsors of the Afro-Asian group's draft resolution (UN document A/L. 323) were Afghanistan, Burma, Cambodia, Ceylon, Chad, Ethiopia, Ghana, Guinea, India, Indonesia, Iran, Iraq, Jordan, Lebanon, Liberia, Libya, Morocco, Nepal, Nigeria, Pakistan, Saudi Arabia, Sudan, Togo, Tunisia, Turkey, Cyprus, Mali, and United Arab Republic. A large number of other sponsors emerged in the course of the debate, including Cameroon, Central African Republic, Congo (Brazzaville), Congo (Leopoldville), Dahomey, Federation of Malaya, Gabon, Ivory Coast, Laos, Madagascar, Niger, Philippines, Senegal, Somalia, and Upper Volta (Burkina Faso).

92. Article 1, UN document A/L. 323, adopted as Resolution 1514 (XV), Declaration on the Granting of Independence to Colonial Countries and Peoples, 14 December 1960, http://www.unhchr.ch/html/menu3/b/c_coloni.htm, accessed 12 August 2006.

93. Preamble, article 7, UN document A/L. 323, adopted as Resolution 1514 (XV), Declaration on the Granting of Independence to Colonial Countries and Peoples, 14 December 1960.

94. States referring to Bandung included Cambodia, Iran, Ceylon, Ghana, Ethiopia, Libya, Burma, Liberia, Guatemala, Laos, Sudan, Nepal, Indonesia, Togo, Congo (Brazzaville), Morocco, and Cyprus. African regional conferences in Accra, Monrovia, and Addis Ababa, which endorsed the Bandung decisions, also received prominent mention. In addition to the African and Asian countries, Soviet bloc representatives were also enthusiastic proponents of the Bandung Conference, though they tended to emphasize different aspects of it in their speeches, such as the role of communist China. Of the communist countries, USSR, Poland, and Ukrainian Soviet Socialist Republic referred to Bandung in the general debate, and attempted to position themselves as bearers of the imprecisely defined Bandung Spirit—a difficult task given that representatives from states that attended the conference were pushing a rival text.

95. Verbatim Records of the General Assembly Plenary Meeting, 928th session, 30 November 1960, A/PV. 928, para. 17.

96. Verbatim Records of the General Assembly Plenary Meeting, 935th session, 5 December 1960, A/PV. 935, paras. 68–69. Formerly the leader of the Nepalese parliamentary opposition, Shaha had been one of the founders of Nepal's mission to the UN, and an influential figure in its adoption of a neutralist foreign policy. Once serving as foreign minister, Shaha became deeply disillusioned by the monarchy's sham "Panchayat" democracy, and was jailed for his opposition to it in 1967. He later established the Nepalese office of Amnesty International and the Human Rights Organisation of Nepal. In 1990, he campaigned for a return to parliamentary democracy and the abandonment of the "Panchayat" system. See Thapa, "Nepal's Scholar-Statesman."

97. Verbatim Records of the General Assembly Plenary Meeting, 927th session, 29 November 1960, A/PV. 927, para. 50.

98. Verbatim Records of the General Assembly Plenary Meeting, 926th session, 28 November 1960, A/PV. 926, para. 35. Admittedly, the Shah was hardly the most consistent practitioner of these great principles, and had annulled the results of the September 1960 election. See "The Shah Annuls Iran Elections."

99. Verbatim Records of the General Assembly Plenary Meeting, 940th session, 8 December 1960, A/PV. 940, para. 39.

100. Ibid., para. 42.

101. Verbatim Records of the General Assembly Plenary Meeting, 945th session, 13 December 1960, A/PV. 945, para. 26.

102. Verbatim Records of the General Assembly Plenary Meeting, 926th session, 28 November 1960, A/PV. 926, para. 42.

103. Verbatim Records of the General Assembly Plenary Meeting, 933rd session, 2 December 1960, A/PV. 933, para. 196. Sumulong would later serve as chairperson of the Constitutional Commission, formed in 1986 after the fall of Ferdinand Marcos. He is often cited as the figure who provoked the controversial "shoe-banging" of Soviet Premier Khrushchev, during an earlier General Assembly debate in October 1960.

104. The Laotian government had recently resumed hostilities against Pathet Lao guerrillas. Simmonds, "The Evolution of Foreign Policy in Laos Since Independence," 16–18. For further background on Laotian foreign policy, see Fall, "The International Relations of Laos." For details of the events in 1960, consult "Coup in Laos"; "Civil War Report Imminent in Laos"; "Laos Still in Political Turmoil"; "Laos Threat of Civil War"; "Fighting Reported near Vientiane."

105. Verbatim Records of the General Assembly Plenary Meeting, 933rd session, 2 December 1960, A/PV. 933, para. 237.

106. Verbatim Records of the General Assembly Plenary Meeting, 938th session, 6 December 1960, A/PV. 938, para. 111.

107. Ibid. para. 112.

108. Verbatim Records of the General Assembly Plenary Meeting, 933rd session, 2 December 1960, A/PV. 933, para. 238.

109. Verbatim Records of the General Assembly Plenary Meeting, 935th session, 5 December 1960, A/PV. 935, para. 117.

110. "Emergency in Malaya Declared at an End."

111. Verbatim Records of the General Assembly Plenary Meeting, 938th session, 6 December 1960, A/PV. 938, para. 56.

112. The delegate from Honduras, for instance, expressed mock astonishment that the Soviet Union would even place the question of colonialism on the agenda, remarking "that the nation least morally qualified to propose this item is the Union of Soviet Socialist Republics" and castigating the hypocrisy of Soviet anticolonialism. Verbatim Records of the General Assembly Plenary Meeting, 930th session, 1 December 1960, A/PV. 930, para. 17. See also 929th session, 30 November 1960, A/PV. 929, para. 78; 933rd session, 2 December 1960, A/PV. 933, para. 130, 137.

113. Glendon, "The Forgotten Crucible."

114. Verbatim Records of the General Assembly Plenary Meeting, 930th session, 1 December 1960, A/PV. 930, para. 15.

115. Pessimism about Africa's potential for democracy was also prevalent in the State Department around the time of the 1960 self-determination debate. In January 1960, the National Security Council of the Eisenhower administration had already dismissed the possibility of democratic African governments, and had instead recommended support for friendly authoritarian regimes:
"The US must avoid assuming that the struggle in Africa will be between Western-style democracy and Communism. We must recognize, although we cannot say it publicly, that we need the strong men of Africa on our side. It is important to understand that most of Africa will soon be independent and it would be naïve of the US to hope that Africa will be democratic. The Vice President added that it was difficult to realize the problems faced by Africa without visiting the Continent. Some of the peoples of Africa have been out of the trees only for about fifty years." Memorandum of Discussion at the 432d Meeting

of the National Security Council, 14 January 1960, NARA Whitman File, NSC Records, Eisenhower Library, in *FRUS*, vol. XIV, 1958–60.

American policy in the Congo was conditioned by culturally deterministic ideas of the African people. In an August 1960 meeting on Africa policy, Maurice Stans, advisor on African affairs, argued that "Africans do not understand Western-style ballot box democracy." Accordingly, he asserted that the U.S. "should not assume that Africans would accept our kind of democracy." Any national government would most probably have to be authoritarian, Stans claimed, because "democracy in Africa did not extend beyond the village; beyond the village the people look to the chief of the tribe who is a kind of dictator." He warned that there was "no solution to this problem," and counseled that the State Department "should recognize it in everything that we plan in Africa." Memorandum of Discussion at the 456th Meeting of the National Security Council, National Security Implications of Future Developments Regarding Africa, 18 August 1960, NARA, Eisenhower Library, Whitman File, NSC Records, in ibid.

These kinds of ideas also encouraged U.S. skepticism about the UN democratic initiatives in the Congo. A November 1960 memorandum from the U.S. ambassador to the Congo, Clare Timberlake, was dismissive of UN proposals for democracy. "[The] fact is Congo is years away from more than façade of democracy. I do not believe there is one single Congolese who has more than a theoretical idea of even the most elementary principles of democracy. They obviously cannot practice something they do not understand. This does not insult the many well-intentioned Congolese but does discount there [sic] ability [to] produce anything resembling democratic government until they have been taught. Furthermore, I do not believe democracy can be imposed upon any people overnight any more than it can be injected by hypodermic. Therefore I do not share UN enthusiasm for accelerated parliamentary solution in Congo." Telegram from Embassy in the Congo to the Department of State, 2 November 1960, NARA 770G/11-260, in ibid.

116. Suggested Amendments to draft resolution "Declaration on the Granting of Independence to Colonial Countries and Peoples" introduced on 28 November 1960 (A/L.323.) The original text of the declaration is indicated in parentheses.

Paragraph 4: "[Aware of the increasing conflicts resulting from the denial of or impediments in the way of the freedom of such peoples, which constitute a serious threat to world peace], as well as in once independent nations which have become dependent in law or only in fact."

Paragraph 5: "[Considering the important role of the United Nations in assisting the movement for independence in Trust and Non-Self-Governing Territories],as well as the obligation of the United Nations to assist similar movements in nations which have been forcibly deprived of the exercise of their right to self-determination."

Paragraph 6: "[Recognizing that the peoples of the world ardently desire the end of colonialism in all its] forms and [manifestations]." International League for Human Rights Records.

117. Roger Baldwin, To Chief of the delegation [unnamed] to the General Assembly, Regarding Declaration on Granting of Independence to Colonial Peoples, International League for the Rights of Man, 29 November 1960, International League for Human Rights Records.

118. Memorandum on Self-determination, undated, c. 1960, International League for Human Rights Records.

119. Telegram from the Mission at the United Nations [James Wadsworth] to the Department of State, 4 December 1960 [1 a.m.], NARA 321.4/12-1460, *FRUS*, vol. II, 1958–60. Eisenhower had been called by British Prime Minister Harold Macmillan and persuaded to reverse his initial support for the draft declaration. For further details on the passage of the resolution, see Feron, "U.N. Urges Steps to Free Colonies."

120. The Afro-Asian group's reaction to the U.S. abstention was one of absolute dismay, as Wadsworth relayed in his telegram. "US abstention was greeted by audible gasp of surprise followed by diminishing murmur of whispered comments. Immediately after vote, [Alex] Quaison-Sackey (Ghana) commented 'How could you vote this way? You have no problem with colonies.' Ifeagwu (Nigeria) said he 'couldn't believe it, US abstention was incomprehensible.' He then asked, 'Are you trying to commit political suicide?' Malley (Radio Tunis): 'Felicitations on your vote. Understand Khrushchev is sending medal.' . . . Chelli (Tunisia) said US took [a] very bad position. US might not understand but for 'us, who are your friends, it is sickening to see you in same camp as Portugal.' US claims to be champion of liberty but truth is in vote. US has given ammunition to USSR across board including in Congo discussion. 'Who will believe Mr. Wadsworth after this.' Menemencioglu (Turkey) found US vote 'unbelievable and incomprehensible.' Other comments heard were in accord with general theme specified above. US explanation of vote greeted by absolute silence. We heard several comments to effect that no explanation could salvage position left by vote." Telegram from Mission at the United Nations to the Department of State, Colonial item, 15 December 1960, NARA 321.4/12-1560, in *FRUS*, vol. II, 1958–60.

121. Telegram from Wadsworth, in *FRUS*, vol. II, 1958–60.

122. Memorandum from Secretary of State to the President's Staff Secretary, 8 December 1960. NARA, 321.4/12-860, in *FRUS*, vol. II, 1958–60.

123. Ibid.

124. Raič, "The Emergence and Development of the Principle of Self-Determination," 206, 214; Pomerance, *Self-Determination*, 28.

125. Salmon, "Internal Aspects of the Right to Self-Determination," 258.

126. Roger Baldwin and Jan Papanek, Letter from the International League for the Rights of Man to the Members of the Special Committee on the Situation with Regard to the Implementation of the Declaration on the Granting of Independence to Colonial Countries and Peoples, 5 June 1963, New York; Roger Baldwin and Jan Papanek, Letter from the International League for the Rights of Man to the Sori Coulibaly, Chairman of the Special Committee on the Situation with Regard to the Implementation of the Declaration on the Granting of Independence to Colonial Countries and Peoples, 9 December 1964, New York; Jan Papanek, Letter from the International League for the Rights of Man to Sour Coulibaly, Chairman of the Special Committee on the Situation with Regard to the Implementation of the Declaration on the Granting of Independence to Colonial Countries and Peoples, 5 November 1965, New York; Roger Baldwin, Memorandum to Sidney Lisofsky and Jan Papanek, Regarding Self-Determination and Special Committee of 24, International League for the Rights of Man, 8 June 1964, New York, International League for Human Rights Records.

127. Raič, "The Post-Colonial Era," 226, quoting UN Document A/AC.125/

SR.68, 4 December 1967. See, more generally, Engo, "Peaceful Co-Existence and Friendly Relations Among States."

128. Pomerance, *Self-Determination*, 39, 41.

129. Ibid., 39, notes 216, 217.

130. UN Document A/RES/2131/Rev. 1, Resolution 2131 (XX), Declaration on the Inadmissibility of Intervention in the Domestic Affairs of States and the Protection of Their Independence and Sovereignty, 21 December 1965, reproduced in *American Journal of International Law* 60, no. 3 (1966): 662–64.

131. Ibid., Article 5.

132. Pomerance, *Self-Determination*, 47, note 229.

133. Ibid.

134. See generally, US Mission United Nations, New York, to Secretary of State, Washington DC, UNGA-Legal Committee-Protection of Diplomat-Liberation Movements Exception, 17 November 1973, USUN 4849, para. 2; US Mission United Nations, New York, to Secretary of State, Washington DC, UN Ad Hoc Committee on Terrorism, 31 July 1973, USUN 2733, NARA electronic telegram archive, accessed 25 July 2006.

135. From US Mission United Nations, New York, to Secretary of State, Washington DC, UNGA Ad Hoc Committee on Terrorism, 25 July 1973, USUN 2687, para. 4, NARA electronic telegram archive, accessed 25 July 2006.

Chapter 3. Putting the Stamps Back On: Apartheid, Anticolonialism, and the Accidental Birth of a Universal Right to Petition

Epigraphs: Jamil Baroody, Sub-Division of the Report on the Reorganization of the United Nations, Pertaining to the Division of Human Rights, 25 May 1971, 13–14, 19, UN Chef de Cabinet 1961-1973: Narasimhan, Human Rights—General Correspondence, January 1971–August 1971, S-0198-001-06, UN Archives. Memorandum from Timothy Rothermel to Ihan Lutem, regarding removal of stamps from allegations of human rights violations, New York, 12 December 1974, United Nations Secretary General. 1972–1981: Waldheim, Relations with the United Nations Commissions—economic and social commissions—Human Rights-Chile, s-0913-0024-04, UN Archives.

1. See especially Mertus, *The United Nations and Human Rights*, 162–63; Freeman, *Human Rights: An Interdisciplinary Approach*, 43–44; Vincent, *Human Rights in International Relations*, 76–91, 95. For general histories of the right of petition and the United Nations, see Zuijdwijk, *Petitioning the United Nations*; Stamatopoulou, "The Development of United Nations Mechanisms"; Tardu, "United Nations Response to Gross Violations of Human Rights"; Möller, "Petitioning the United Nations"; Tolley, "The Concealed Crack in the Citadel"; Tolley, *The UN Commission on Human Rights*, 53–54; Tardu and McCarthy, *Human Rights: The International Petition System*; Lillich, "The U.N. and Human Rights Complaints."

2. Lauren, *The Evolution of International Human Rights*, 252.

3. Ibid. See also Tolley, "The Concealed Crack in the Citadel," 429; Zuijdwijk, *Petitioning the United Nations*, 14, 375.

4. For the detail of these procedures, see Commission on Human Rights, Fifth Session, Right of Petition. Guatemala, India and Philippines: Draft Resolution, 13 June 1949, E/CN. 4/316; Commission on Human Rights, Fifth Session, Right of Petition. Lebanon: Amendment to Draft Resolution 316, 18 June 1949, E/CN. 4/347; Commission on Human Rights, Fifth Session, Philippines: Amendment to Article 25, 15 June 1949, E/CN. 4/338. See generally, Commis-

sion on Human Rights, Sixth Session, Comments of Governments on the Draft International Covenant on Human Rights and Measures of Implementation, 29 December 1949, E/CN. 4/353; Commission on Human Rights, Compilation of the Comments of Governments on the Draft International Covenant on Human Rights and on the Proposed Additional Articles, 22 March 1950, E/CN. 4/365.

5. Commission on Human Rights, First Session, Verbatim Record, 16th meeting, 5 February 1947, 87–90, Charles Malik Collection, Library of Congress, Manuscript Reading Room, Box 76, File 1: First Session, Commission on Human Rights—Minutes, 1947.

6. Commission on Human Rights, First Session, Verbatim Record, 16th meeting, 5 February 1947, 86–87, Charles Malik Collection, Box 76, File 1: First Session, Commission on Human Rights—Minutes, 1947.

7. Commission on Human Rights, First Session, Verbatim Record, 2nd meeting, 27 January 1947, 13–20, Charles Malik Collection, Box 76, File 1: First Session, Commission on Human Rights—Minutes, 1947.

8. Ibid., 23; Commission on Human Rights, First Session, Verbatim Record, 9th meeting, 1 February 1947, 51, 81, Charles Malik Collection, Box 76, File 1: First Session, Commission on Human Rights—Minutes, 1947.

9. Commission on Human Rights, First Session, Verbatim Record, 15th meeting, 5 February 1947, 31, Charles Malik Collection, Box 76, File 1: First Session, Commission on Human Rights—Minutes, 1947.

10. Commission on Human Rights, First Session, Summary Record, 4th meeting, 28 January 1947, E/CN. 4/SR. 4, Philippines, noted in Zuijdwijk, *Petitioning the United Nations*, 4.

11. Ibid., 3.

12. Ibid., 4; Anderson, *Eyes Off the Prize*, 96–98.

13. For an account of how the self-denying ordinance eventuated, see Humphrey, *The Great Adventure*, 28. See also Möller, "Petitioning the United Nations," 57–58.

14. ECOSOC Resolution 75(V), 5 August 1947. For the sub-committee on petition report that precipitated the vote to deny the Commission's right to investigate petitions, see Commission on Human Rights, Report of the Subcommittee on the Handling of Communications, 6 February 1947, E/CN. 4/14/Rev. 2. A narrative of the debate is given in Zuijdwijk, *Petitioning the United Nations*, 4–5.

15. For examples of Roosevelt's opinion on petition, see Commission on Human Rights, Verbatim Record, 2nd meeting, 27 January 1947; Radio Transcript, "Today with Mrs. Roosevelt," 14 May 1950, 6, 9, Charles Malik Collection, Box 39, File 8, Correspondence, Roosevelt, Eleanor, 1947–1960; Anderson, *Eyes Off the Prize*, 134.

16. See also the assessment of Normand and Zaidi, *Human Rights at the UN*, 236–37.

17. Humphrey, *On the Edge of Greatness*, vol. 1, 165, 170.

18. Ibid., 170.

19. Ibid., 174.

20. Teltsch, "Private Appeals to the UN Barred," 8.

21. Humphrey, *On the Edge of Greatness*, vol. 2, 206.

22. Ibid., 213.

23. Ibid. See also Möller, "Petitioning the United Nations," 58–59.

24. Humphrey, *A Great Adventure*, 108.

25. For biographical details of Azmi, see Humphrey, *On the Edge of Greatness,* vol. 2, 53.

26. Zuijdwijk, *Petitioning the United Nations,* 11.

27. A triumphant report from the 1953 U.S. delegation, led by pro-segregation South Carolina governor James Byrnes, heralded the failure of both individual petition to the Commission, and the petition article for the covenants. "From the point of view of our relations with other delegations, this was the most satisfactory session of the Third Committee in recent years. . . . The Committee rejected or postponed a number of proposals to which our Delegation was opposed. It rejected a proposal that the Commission on Human Rights review communications from individuals, groups, and non-governmental organizations. This was probably one of the most significant decisions of the session. It deferred any decision on proposals that the Covenants on Human Rights provide for the examination of petitions." Report on the Third Committee (Social, Humanitarian, and Cultural) of the General Assembly, Eighth Session, 15 September–9 December 1953, 17 March 1954, 1, 320.13/3-1754, Decimal File 1950–1954; General Records of the Department of State, RG 59; NACP.

28. Humphrey, *On the Edge of Greatness,* vol. 3, 101. A meeting of the 1955 Commission on Human Rights were devoted to tributes to Azmi's work, see Summary Records of the Commission on Human Rights, 480th meeting, 5 April 1955, E/CN. 4/480. See also Jamil Baroody's personal tribute to Azmi in the Third Committee, Summary Records of the Third Committee, 574th meeting, 4 November 1954, A/C. 3/SR. 574, para. 48.

29. He was also the author of an influential 1960 study on freedom of movement, further discussed in Korey, *NGOs and the Universal Declaration of Human Rights,* 64–65.

30. During the late 1950s, the Philippines stood virtually alone in its activism for amendments to remove the block on studying petitions. See Zuijdwijk, *Petitioning the United Nations,* 10.

31. Summary Records of the Commission on Human Rights, 435th meeting, 16 March 1954, E/CN. 4/SR. 435, Philippines.

32. A comprehensive study of the League's Upper Silesia Treaty and the importance of individual petition is given by Burgess, "The Human Rights Dilemma in Anti-Nazi Protest." Ingles himself was later discredited by his service as deputy foreign minister under the Marcos regime. Under the Marcos, the Philippines was the only state represented on the Sub-Commission that failed to vote for a new communications procedure in 1971. See Carey, "Progress on Human Rights at the United Nations," 108.

33. Summary Records of the Commission on Human Rights, 435th meeting, 16 March 1954, E/CN. 4/SR. 435, Egypt.

34. Humphrey held Dayal in high esteem, praising him as "one of the best debaters in the United Nations." Humphrey, *A Great Adventure,* 231.

35. Dixit, *India-Pakistan in War and Peace,* 138.

36. Summary Records of the Commission on Human Rights, 435th meeting, 16 March 1954, E/CN. 4/SR. 435, India.

37. Summary Record of the Commission on Human Rights, 436th meeting, 16 March 1954, E/CN. 4/SR. 436, India.

38. Quoted in Anderson, *Eyes Off the Prize,* 237.

39. For a detailed account of the session, see ibid., 237–38.

40. Summary Records of the Commission on Human Rights, 436th meeting, 16 March 1954, E/CN. 4/SR. 436, United States.

41. Summary Records of the Commission on Human Rights, 437th meeting, 17 March 1954, E/CN. 4/SR. 437, United Kingdom.

42. Humphrey, *On the Edge of Greatness,* vol. 4, 15, 42.

43. Ibid., 13.

44. Ibid.

45. Summary Records of the Commission on Human Rights, 437th meeting, 17 March 1954, E/CN. 4/SR. 437, United Kingdom.

46. Humphrey, *On the Edge of Greatness*, vol. 4, 42. For Hoare's own reflections on the human rights program, and the 1954 debate on petitions, see Hoare, "The UN Commission on Human Rights."

47. Summary Records of the Commission on Human Rights, 435th meeting, 16 March 1954, E/CN. 4/SR. 435, Ukrainian Soviet Socialist Republic.

48. Summary Records of the Commission on Human Rights, 436th meeting, 16 March 1954, E/CN. 4/SR. 436, Poland.

49. Summary Records of the Commission on Human Rights, 435th meeting, 16 March 1954, E/CN. 4/SR. 435, Pakistan.

50. Summary Records of the Commission on Human Rights, 436th meeting, 16 March 1954, E/CN. 4/SR. 436, Turkey.

51. Lebanon's independent stance on the covenant during Malik's tenure in the Commission had not gone unnoticed in Washington. The U.S. exerted pressure on the Lebanese government to fall into line with the American covenant policy in early 1950, though Malik successfully resisted these moves. See Humphrey, *On the Edge of Greatness,* vol. 2, 36.

52. Summary Records of the Commission on Human Rights, 435th meeting, 16 March 1954, E/CN. 4/SR. 435, Lebanon.

53. See Anderson, *Eyes Off the Prize,* 133, and passim.

54. British Colonial Office figures were appalled by the mere suggestion of an individual right to petition the UN. A March 1948 memorandum from the Governor of Kenya, Sir Philip Mitchell, expressed his outrage at the discussion of petition. "Such a proposal should not be acceded to under any circumstances . . . I can . . . think of nothing more calculated to create dangerous conditions and even a threat to the peace of the world than to confer such a power upon a body such as the United Nations." An April 1948 Colonial Office memorandum argued that the "overriding objective [of British policy] must be to remove so far as possible all teeth from the petition procedure and make it as innocuous as we can." Additional detail on the British objections is provided by Simpson, *End of Empire,* 406, 497.

55. Eric Beckett, a senior advisor in the British Foreign Office, warned that it was "all too likely" that "communist stooges" might inundate the UN Commission with "bogus petitions" relating to the West, while simultaneously "preventing by police method anybody in their own countries from petitioning" (ibid., 41–46, 406, 701). U.S. proximity to the UN exacerbated the State Department perception of these sorts of risks. In January 1947, an official Department of State memorandum noted the "peculiar disadvantage" of hosting the UN inside its borders. "With the seat of the United Nations in this country and with a freer flow of information here than elsewhere the United Nations could be flooded with petitions relating to United States abuses . . . thus giving the impression that the United States was the chief offender against rather than defender of civil liberties." Anderson, *Eyes Off the Prize,* 79. This attitude toward individual petition persisted among some Western countries into the 1960s. It was given as one of the reasons for Australian skepticism on the implementation procedures

proposed for the Convention on the Elimination of All Forms of Racial Discrimination. A telegram briefing Canberra on the developing Western enthusiasm for petition was unconvinced of its merits. "Any advantages," the delegation warned, will "have to be weighted against the likelihood that strong implementation procedures will bite more severely in the case of Western than of other countries." From Australian Mission, United Nations, New York, to Department of External Affairs, Canberra, Human Rights: Implementation Proposals, 12 November 1965, UN1777, National Archives of Australia, A1838, 929/5/6 Part 3, 1965.

56. State Department opposition to petition is apparent in a February 1953 memorandum from Assistant Secretary Hickerson to Secretary of State John Foster Dulles. "Recommendations . . . Oppose the inclusion of provisions in the Covenants to authorize the proposed Human Rights Committee to receive or consider complaints or petitions from organizations or individuals concerning alleged violations of the Covenants. If such provisions are included, the United States should urge that they be set forth in a separate protocol or protocols." Memorandum by the Assistant Secretary of State for United Nations Affairs (Hickerson) to the Secretary of State, Washington, American Foreign Policy and the Promotion of Human Rights Through the United Nations, 9 February 1953, Hickerson-Murphy-Key files, lot 58 D 33. Reproduced in *FRUS*, vol. III, *1952–1954, United Nations Affairs.*

57. Heffernan, "A Comparative View."

58. Möller, "Petitioning the United Nations," 59.

59. Humphrey, *A Great Adventure*, 28. The Commission on the Status of Women had also passed an equivalent self-denying ordinance with respect to complaints, codified in ECOSOC Resolution 76(V).

60. Created under the terms of Resolution 1654; also discussed in Tolley, "The Concealed Crack in the Citadel," 246.

61. Authorized by General Assembly Resolution 1761, "The Policies of *apartheid* of the Government of the Republic of South Africa," 6 November 1962, Article 5.

62. The striking double-standard between the practice of the special committees and that of the Commission was criticized at length by U.S. expert on the Sub-Commission on Discrimination, Carey, "The United Nations' Double Standard."

63. See Summary Record of the Special Committee on the Policies of Apartheid of the Government of the Republic of South Africa, 2nd meeting, 5 April 1963, UN Document A/AC.115/SR. 2. See also 3rd meeting, 5 April 1963 (Cable from Pan-Africanist Congress), 11th meeting, 10 May 1963 (Hearing of Petitioners), 13th meeting, 6 June 1963 (Hearing of Petitioners).

64. See generally Verbatim Records of the Special Committee on the Situation with Regard to the Implementation of the Declaration on the Granting of Independence to Colonial Countries and Peoples, 739th–895th meetings, 21 April 1970–2 February 1973, UN Document A/AC. 109/PV. 739–895. See especially Special commemorative meeting in honour of the late Secretary-General of the Partido Africano da Independencia da Guiné e Cabo Verde, Dr. Amilcar Cabral, A/AC. 109/PV. 895; Tributes on the occasion of the one hundredth anniversary of the birth of Vladimir Illyich Lenin, A/AC. 109/PV. 739–40.

65. Memorandum from Timothy Rothermel to Ihan Lütem.

66. Finger, "A New Approach to Colonial Problems at the United Nations," 145.

67. Ibid., 144.

68. International Convention on the Elimination of All Forms of Racial Discrimination, General Assembly Resolution 2106 (XX), 21 December 1965, http://www.unhchr.ch/html/menu3/b/d_icerd.htm, accessed 10 August 2006.

69. See, for example, Summary Records of the Third Committee, 1293rd meeting, 5 October 1965, A/C. 3/SR. 1293, USSR.

70. International Convention on the Elimination of All Forms of Racial Discrimination; see especially Article 5(d), (e).

71. From Department of External Affairs, Canberra, to Australian Mission, United Nations, New York, Human Rights—Implementation (Your 1851), 19 November 1965, 2123, National Archives of Australia, A1838, 929/5/6 PART 3, 1965.

72. M. R. Booker, First Assistant Secretary, Second Division, External Affairs, to the Minister, External Affairs, Convention on Racial Discrimination—Implementation Clauses, 23 November 1965, 929/5/6, para. 5, National Archives of Australia, A1838, 929/5/6 PART 3, 1965.

73. From Australian Mission, United Nations, New York, to Department of External Affairs, Canberra, Racial Discrimination, 16 November 1965, UN1820, National Archives of Australia, A1838, 929/5/6 PART 3, 1965.

74. From New Zealand UN Delegation, New York, to Department of External Affairs, Wellington (682), Racial Discrimination Convention, 27 October 1965, para. 2, National Archives of Australia, A1838, 929/5/6 PART 3, 1965. The author of the telegram was critical of this approach, seemingly more concerned with maintaining the appearance of consensus than the completion of a meaningful Convention. "[The] Western Group does not repeat not, however, seem to have taken into consideration of the implications of pushing strong implementation to the limit. The Americans seem to be more interested in embarrassing the Eastern Europeans in discussion in the Committee than in achieving a Convention to which the Eastern Europeans could adhere."

75. J. H. A. Hoyle to the Secretary of Department of External Affairs, Draft International Convention on the Elimination of all Forms of Racial Discrimination, Implementation Debate, 15 December 1965, Memorandum 1529/65, File 103/6 (3) 213/5/4, National Archives of Australia, A432, 1964/3071 Part 2, 1965–67. Hoyle reported on the emergence of Lamptey's leadership in the implementation debate. "A somewhat disparate group of Afro-Asian powers also spoke up on behalf of significant implementation measures and they found their most eloquent spokesman in the representative of Ghana (Lamptey) who, to our knowledge, largely advocated this approach because of murmurs that he had heard that the Afro-Asian group as a whole did not believe in implementation which would breach national sovereignty. Whatever his motivation, he was effective and took the leading role in the formulation of the various drafts that were table in the Committee."

76. Australian Mission, Racial Discrimination, 16 November 1965, UN1820.

77. Banton, *International Action Against Racial Discrimination*, 249. See also Lamptey's arguments on the need for broad acceptability of the Convention, Summary Records of the Third Committee, 1306th meeting, 15 October 1965, UN Document A/C. 3/SR. 1306, para. 9.

78. Humphrey privately reported that the Ghanaian delegation might have been provoked into taking the leading role after being insulted by the Soviets, who questioned their independence. In his diary entry for 25 November 1965,

Humphrey wrote: "I wonder what has motivated the Ghanaian delegation, which is taking the initiative. Preoccupation with their image? Someone told me a story yesterday which may or may not be true. It seems that a member of the Soviet mission approached one [of] the Ghanaians and reproached him for unwittingly acting in the interests of the U.S.A. This so infuriated the Ghanaians that they decided to really push their proposal." See Humphrey, *On the Edge of Greatness*, vol. 4, 149–50.

79. L. J. Lawrey to the Secretary of Department of External Affairs, Article XV (Consideration of Petitions from Dependant Territories), 17 December 1965, Memorandum 1530/65, File 213/5/4, 103/6(3), para.8, National Archives of Australia, A432, 1964/3071 PART 2, 1965–67.

80. Summary Records of the Third Committee, 1364th meeting, 3 December 1965, A/C. 3/SR. 1364, para. 16.

81. Ibid., para. 13. This statement "made a very considerable impression" according to the Australian delegation, which identified it as a "high point" in the debate. See L. J. Lawrey, Article XV, 17 December 1965, para. 6.

82. Summary Records of the Third Committee, 1357th meeting, 29 November 1965, A/C. 3/SR. 1357, paras. 38–39.

83. The tensions between these two delegates were reported by the Australian delegation, see J. H. A. Hoyle to Secretary of Department of External Affairs, Draft International Convention on the Elimination of all Forms of Racial Discrimination Implementation, 17 December 1965, Memorandum 1531/65, File 213/5/4, para. 4, National Archives of Australia, A432, 1964/3071 Part 2, 1965–67. Further incidents of conflict between Lamptey and Waldron-Ramsey are catalogued in L. J. Lowery to the Secretary of Department of External Affairs, Article XV (Consideration of Petitions from Dependant Territories), Memorandum 1530/65, File 213/5/4, 15 December 1965, paras. 2, 3, 8, 10, National Archives of Australia, A432, 1964/3071 PART 2, 1965–67.

84. L. J. Lawrey, Article XV, 17 December 1965.

85. A memorandum of conversation between U.S. Ambassador Charles Yost and UN Human Rights Division Director Marc Schreiber records Schreiber's frustration with some of Waldron-Ramsey's alleged behavior. "Schreiber believes that 6-man [committee] has outlived [its] usefulness and is merely [an] instrument for personal gratification of certain members. UN paid first class airfare for Waldron Ramsey from London to New York for Ad Hoc [committee] which he attended for 'one minute.'" See U.S. Mission, United Nations, New York, to Secretary of State, Human Rights—Conversation with Marc Schreiber, 27 January 1971, USUN 0023, Subject Numeric Files 1970–73, Social-ECOSOC; General Records of the Department of State, RG59; NACP. According Jamil Baroody, this sort of practice was not uncommon among those assigned to the special committees. Various representatives, he advised the Secretary-General, had "sought appointments to seminars for taking a trip to a new country and in order to have a good time, sometimes not even discreetly or circumspectly." See Baroody, *Pertaining to the Division of Human Rights*, 10.

86. Summary Records of the Third Committee, 1345th meeting, 17 November 1965, A/C. 3/SR. 1345, para. 39.

87. ibid., para. 42.

88. Summary Records of the Third Committee, 1349th meeting, 19 November 1965, A/C. 3/SR. 1349, para. 39.

89. New Zealand UN Delegation, Racial Discrimination Convention, 27 October 1965. The New Zealand delegation related its appraisal of the general

disposition of the Afro-Asian members toward the implementation. "Attempts to discuss implementation clauses seriously with other delegations have not [repeat] not so far been very fruitful. Afro-Asian and Latin American attitudes on substance of implementation clauses have not yet crystallized. Many of them in fact seem to be without instructions although a number have expressed unhappiness or are said to be unhappy about complaints procedure, either on their own account or because they know the Eastern Europeans will not [repeat] not buy it."

90. Summary Records of the Third Committee, 1346th meeting, 17 November 1965, A/C. 3/SR. 1346, para.18. Pant was a senior member of the Congress Party, and the son of Govind Ballabh Pant, once the Chief Minister of Uttar Pradesh, a province with large Urdu and Muslim minorities. India also had the immense liability presented by its discriminatory caste system.

91. Ibid. Chandra Pant was not liked by the Australian delegation, which complained to Canberra of "[the] usual irritating preaching which characterized most of his delegation's interventions." See J. H. A. Hoyle to the Secretary of Department of External Affairs, Draft International Convention on the Elimination of all Forms of Racial Discrimination, 13 December 1965, Memorandum 1519/65, File 213/5/4, National Archives of Australia, A432, 1964/3071 PART 2, 1965–67.

92. Summary Records of the Third Committee, 1346th meeting, 17 November 1965, A/C. 3/SR. 1346, para. 18.

93. General Assembly Resolution: Treatment of Indians in the Union of South Africa, 8 December 1946, A/RES/44 (I); Letter dated 12 July 1948 from the representative of India to the Secretary-General concerning the treatment of Indians in South Africa, 16 July 1948, A/577, reproduced in United Nations, *The United Nations and Apartheid*, 221–22.

94. Summary Records of the Third Committee, 1347th meeting, 18 November 1965, A/C. 3/SR. 1347, para. 8.

95. ibid., para. 7.

96. For details of Baathist repression of the Kurds, see Edgar O'Ballance, *The Kurdish Struggle, 1920–1994* (Basingstoke: Macmillan, 1996).

97. In this instance, John Humphrey's diary relates how bureaucratic "stupidity," and a "badly drafted" document produced "a complete white-washing" of the Iraqi government. Humphrey, *On the Edge of Greatness*, vol. 4, 153.

98. Humphrey, "The UN Charter and the Universal Declaration," 56. Humphrey's diary entry for 3 December 1965 also reflected his confidence in the precedent of the Convention: "I am highly pleased with developments in the Third Committee which has now adopted what should be a fairly effective system for the implementation of the Convention on the Elimination of All forms of Racial Discrimination. This is important in itself but it also establishes a precedent and a model for the Covenants." See Humphrey, *On the Edge of Greatness*, vol. 4, 151.

99. Humphrey himself later commented on the profound differences between action on racial discrimination, and that on civil and political rights more generally. See Humphrey, *A Great Adventure*, 331–34.

100. Smith, *Rebels in Law*, 304.

101. Summary Records of the Third Committee, 1399th meeting, 19 October 1966, A/C. 3/SR. 1399, para. 3.

102. Summary Records of the Third Committee, 1401st meeting, 21 October 1966, A/C. 3/SR. 401, para. 20.

103. For further reflections on this, see Quentin-Baxter, "International Protection of Human Rights," 135–36.

104. Summary Records of the Third Committee, 1439th meeting, 30 November 1966, A/C. 3/SR. 1439, para. 41.

105. Summary Records of the Third Committee, 1455th meeting, 12 December 1966, A/C. 3/SR. 1455, para. 59.

106. Ibid., para. 58.

107. Summary Records of the Third Committee, 1420th meeting, 11 November 1966, A/C. 3/SR. 1420, para. 41.

108. Meredith, *The State of Africa*, 272.

109. Summary Records of the Third Committee, 1429th meeting, 21 November 1966, A/C. 3/SR. 1429, para. 6.

110. Meredith, *The State of Africa*, 486–88.

111. "General Mobutu Takes Over." For a comprehensive general history of Mobutu's rule, see Wrong, *In the Footsteps of Mr. Kurtz.*

112. Summary Records of the Third Committee, 1440th meeting, 30 November 1966, A/C. 3/SR. 1440, para. 19.

113. Summary Records of the Third Committee, 1455th meeting, 12 December 1966, A/C. 3/SR. 1455, para. 20.

114. Meredith, *The State of Africa*, 222.

115. Summary Records of the Third Committee, 1455th meeting, 12 December 1966, A/C. 3/SR. 1455, para. 20.

116. For further detail see "Clashes in Upper Volta After Strikers Defy Ban"; "Army Succeeds in Upper Volta Take-Over"; "Upper Volta Head in Full Control."

117. Summary Records of the Third Committee, 1456th meeting, 12 December 1966, A/C. 3/SR. 1456, para. 27.

118. See generally Diamond, *Class, Ethnicity and Democracy in Nigeria*; Ogbondah, *Military Regimes and the Press in Nigeria*; Oladimeji and Mundt, *Politics in Nigeria.*

119. Summary Records of the Third Committee, 1438th meeting, 29 November 1966, A/C. 3/SR. 1438, para. 2, 7.

120. Ibid., para. 2.

121. Ibid., para. 7.

122. The voting record is as follows: *For the removal and placement in optional protocol*: Poland, Romania, Rwanda, Saudi Arabia, Senegal, Sudan, Syria, Thailand, Togo, Uganda, Ukrainian Soviet Socialist Republic, USSR, UAR, Tanzania, Upper Volta, Yugoslavia, Zambia, Afghanistan, Algeria, Bulgaria, Byelorussian Soviet Socialist Republic, Cameroon, Cuba, Czechoslovakia, Ethiopia, Guinea, Guyana, Hungary, India, Indonesia, Iran, Iraq, Japan, Jordan, Kuwait, Lebanon, Liberia, Mali, Mauritania, Mongolia, Morocco; *Against*: Panama, Philippines, Spain, Switzerland, Trinidad, UK, U.S., Uruguay, Venezuela, Argentina, Australia, Austria, Belgium, Bolivia, Canada, Ceylon, Chile, Columbia, Costa Rica, Denmark, Dominican Republic, Ecuador, El Salvador, Finland, France, Ghana, Guatemala, Honduras, Iceland, Ireland, Italy, Ivory Coast, Jamaica, Luxembourg, Mexico, Netherlands, New Zealand, Nigeria, Norway ; *Abstaining*: Portugal, Sierra Leone, Tunisia, Turkey, Brazil, Chad, Taiwan, Zaire, Cyprus, Gabon, Grenada, Israel, Liberia, Malawi, Malaya, Pakistan. The Optional Protocol was approved 41 to 39 with 16 abstentions; see Summary Records of the Third Committee, 1440th meeting, 30 November 1966, A/C. 3/SR. 1440.

123. Speech of Peter Smithers (UK) to Special Political Committee, 5 April

1961, A/SPC/SR. 242, as reproduced in United Nations, *The United Nations and Apartheid*, 248.

124. A detailed explanation of the shift is given in a memorandum addressed to the External Affairs Department in Canberra in May 1966. "Ministers have authorized a modification of the British Government's policy in regard to the effect to be given to Articles 2(7), 55 and 56 of the United Nations Charter so far as activities of the Organization in the field of human rights are concerned . . . The British Government has, however, now decided to accept that Article 55 and 56 of the Charter impose on member governments of the United Nations a positive obligation to pursue a policy designed to promote respect for and observance of human rights. . . . A breach of the obligations contained in these two Articles would therefore occur when a member of state patently failed to promote human rights and in that respect failed or refused to cooperate with the Organization. The South African Government's policy over apartheid is a clear breach of obligation according to this interpretation. It would be open to us also to maintain that the continual failure by Communist Governments to promote many of the rights and freedoms contained in the Universal Declaration of Human Rights . . . constituted a breach of this obligation. . . . The present decision does not involve the abandonment of the position previously taken in relation to Article 2(7) but the adoption of a more generous interpretation of Articles 55 and 56. . . . This change of policy will bring the United Kingdom into line with a number of other States and will place the policy of this country on a firmer legal basis, notably in respect of apartheid. . . . We do not intend to make a special announcement on this matter." See Memorandum [from British High Commissioner] regarding Human Rights Policies at the United Nations, 13 May 1966, National Archives of Australia, A1838, 929/5/6 Part 1, 1964–65.

125. Marc Schreiber, Director of Division of Human Rights, to C. V. Narasimhan, UN Chef de Cabinet, 20 May 1966, UN Chef de Cabinet, 1961–1973: Narasimhan, Human Rights—General Correspondence. S-0198-002-001, UN Archives.

126. For details of the Human Rights Commission's new geographical composition, and the reforms proposed by U.S. Ambassador Clyde Ferguson, see Tolley, *The UN Commission*, 53–54.

127. New Zealand delegation [Robert Q. Quentin-Baxter], Geneva to Department of External Affairs, Wellington, Violations Item, 11 March 1967, National Archives of Australia, A1838, 929/10/4, 1966–67.

128. Privately, the New Zealand Government gave precisely this reason for its reluctance to support the Commission's reform. "We remain unconvinced," wrote the New Zealand External Affairs office, "that a more active Commission will not [repeat] not in practice look and sound very like a joint meeting of the Committee of 24 and the Special Committee on *Apartheid*." Prime Minister, Secretary of External Affairs, Departmental of External Affairs, Wellington, to Geneva, Human Rights Commission: Your 86, 2 March 1967, para.3, National Archives of Australia, A1838, 929/10/4, 1966–67.

129. New Zealand UN delegation [Quentin-Baxter], Geneva, to Department of External Affairs, Wellington, Human Rights Commission, 28 February 1967, para.4, National Archives of Australia, A1838, 929/10/4, 1966–67.

130. Ibid., para.5.

131. Ibid., para.4.

132. Ibid., para.3.

133. Ibid., para.4.

134. Jha was not well regarded by U.S. Ambassador William Buffum, who described the Indian Ambassador in an unflattering confidential profile to the State Department. "He never hesitates to sound forth in a strong tone on a patriotic, even jingo Indian line . . . Jha, who is one of several First Secretaries, is number six on the Indian Mission to the UN totem pole, is ambitious, a pusher and an operator, hardworking, fairly shrewd, not overly bright . . . He works hard at selective entreating where he exudes a hearty, bluff non-Indian exterior. One must not be taken in by this attitude." Department of State to USUN New York, Human Rights Working Group of Experts on South Africa and Middle East, 15 July 1969, USUN 2377, File 5/1/69, Social, Central Foreign Policy Files 1967–1969; General Records of the Department of State, RG59; NACP.

135. Provisional Summary Records of the Social Committee of the Economic and Social Council, 567th meeting, 22 May 1967, E/AC. 7/SR. 567, India.

136. Ibid., (USSR), for Waldron-Ramsey, see 569th meeting, 23 May 1967, E/AC. 7/SR. 569, Tanzania.

137. Provisional Summary Records of the Social Committee of the Economic and Social Council, 570th meeting, 25 May 1967, E/AC. 7/SR. 570, USSR.

138. "We have never had a better chairman than Salvador Lopez," wrote Humphrey in his entry for 10 April 1965. *On the Edge of Greatness*, vol. 4, 94. See also Letter from John Humphrey to C. V. Narasimhan, Agenda of the 21st session of the Commission on Human Rights, Geneva, 26 March 1965, UN Chef de Cabinet, 1961–1973: Narasimhan, Human Rights: High Commissioner for Human Rights, S-0198-0003-07, UN Archives. Humphrey also praised his work on Freedom of Information, a role where "he did such a good job governments were frightened."

139. Provisional Summary Records of the Social Committee of the Economic and Social Council, 567th meeting, 22 May 1967, E/AC. 7/SR. 567, Philippines.

140. The vote was 15 (for)-3 (against)-6 (abstentions). Provisional Summary Records of the Social Committee of the Economic and Social Council, 571st meeting, 25 May 1967, E/AC. 7/SR. 571.

141. Ibid., (USSR).

142. Provisional Summary Record of the Economic and Social Council, 1479th meeting, 6 June 1967, E/SR. 1479, India.

143. Ibid., USSR.

144. Ibid., Philippines.

145. Ibid., Dahomey.

146. Ibid., United Kingdom.

147. ECOSOC Resolution 1235 (XLII), Violations of Human Rights and Fundamental Freedoms, Including Policies of Racial Discrimination and Segregation and of *Apartheid* in All Countries, With Particular Reference to Colonial and Other Dependent Countries and Territories, 6 June 1967, reproduced in Hamalengwa, Flinterman, and Dankwa, *The International Law of Human Rights in Africa*, 377–78.

148. Ibid.

149. The U.S. delegation report was more ambivalent regarding the outcome of the meeting, though it remained basically positive about the future implications of the communication procedure. See US Mission Geneva to Department of State, Report on the 20th Session of the Subcommission on Discrimination and Minorities, 25 September–13 October 1967, 15 October 1967, SOC 14, File

9/1/67, Social, Central Foreign Policy Files 1967–1969; General Records of the Department of State, RG59; NACP.

150. US Mission Geneva to Secretary of State, info to US Mission United Nations New York. Subcommission on Discrimination and Minorities, 11 October 1967, Geneva 1166, SOC 14, File 9/1/67, Social, Central Foreign Policy Files 1967–1969; General Records of the Department of State, RG59; NACP.

151. Carey, *UN Protection of Civil and Political Rights*, 88.

152. Humphrey, "The United Nations Sub-Commission on the Prevention of Discrimination," 866.

153. See Ganji, *Defying the Iranian Revolution*, passim. See also U.S. Ambassador Armin Meyer's description of Ganji as a "bright, able . . . intellectual gadfly." US Mission Tehran to US Mission Geneva, info to U.S. Mission United Nations New York, Secretary of State, *Apartheid Human Rights Commission*, 21 March 1967, Tehran 3706, Social, Central Foreign Policy Files 1967–1969; General Records of the Department of State, RG59; NACP. Ganj was also a principal author of an important report on Economic and Social Rights, see Manouchehr Ganji and United Nations Commission on Human Rights, The Realization of Economic, Social, and Cultural Rights : Problems, Policies, Progress, UN Document E/CN. 4/1108/Rev. 1, E/CN. 4/1131/Rev. 1 (New York: United Nations, 1975).

154. Summary Records of the Commission on Human Rights, 965th meeting, 20 February 1968, E/CN. 4/SR. 965.

155. Ibid., United States.

156. Ibid., USSR.

157. Ibid., Nigeria.

158. Summary Records of the Commission on Human Rights, 968th meeting, 23 February 1968, E/CN. 4/SR. 968, Tanzania.

159. Clark, "Human Rights Strategies of the 1960s", 324, citing Report on the Twenty-Fourth Session, 5 February–12 March 1968, notes 76, 60.

160. Summary Records of the Commission on Human Rights, 968th meeting, 23 February 1968, E/CN. 4/SR. 968,(Morocco.

161. Ibid., United Kingdom.

162. Ibid., Austria.

163. Summary Records of the Commission on Human Rights, 969th meeting, 23 February 1968, E/CN. 4/SR. 969, Tanzania.

164. Summary Records of the Commission on Human Rights, 970th meeting, 26 February 1968, E/CN. 4/SR. 970, USSR.

165. Ibid., Ukrainian SSR. Nedbailo was an experienced representative, having represented the Ukrainian Soviet Socialist Republic in the Commission intermittently since 1958. Later in 1968, he led his country's delegation to the First International Conference on Human Rights in Tehran. In December 1968, he was awarded the UN Human Rights Prize along with rather more prestigious figures such as Eleanor Roosevelt, René Cassin, and Albert Luthuli, though by comparison his achievements in the field were modest. The UN Awards included at least one representative from every major political bloc. For further biography on Nedbailo, see Assembly President Announces Winners of First United Nations Human Rights Prizes, 2 December 1968, UN Document GA/3836/HR/209, UN Chef de Cabinet, 1961–1973: Narasimhan, Human Rights—General Correspondence, S-0198-001-04, UN Archives.

166. Summary Records of the Commission on Human Rights, 970th meeting, 26 February 1968, E/CN. 4/SR. 970, Greece.

167. Summary Records of the Commission on Human Rights, 972nd meeting, 27 February 1968, E/CN. 4/SR. 972, Haiti. One of the first Haitian delegates to the Commission on Human Rights, Herard Roy, had actually been one of the few to support individual petition in the early 1950s. See Summary Records of the Third Committee, 370th meeting, 19 December 1951, A/C. 3/SR. 370, paras. 26–27.

168. Ibid. Iran.

169. Ibid., Senegal. Ciss proposed an expansion of the Sub-Commission with African members, and a broadening of its mandate, as a means for resolving the clash of opinions on petition. A Sub-Commission with Africans would presumably place greater emphasis on *apartheid*, though formally all petitions would be eligible for discussion and study.

170. Summary Records of the UN Sub-Commission on the Prevention of Discrimination, 538th meeting, 10 October 1968, E/CN. 4/Sub. 2/SR. 538, Abu Rannat.

171. For a contrary view on the results of the events of the debate, see Korey, *NGOs and the Universal Declaration of Human Rights*, 67–70.

172. US Mission Geneva to US Mission Lagos, To [Clyde] Ferguson from [Rita] Hauser, 17 March 1969, Geneva 00841, SOC 14, Social, Central Foreign Policy Files 1967–1969; General Records of the Department of State, RG59; NACP.

173. Tolley, *The UN Commission*, 164. The Sub-Commission on the Prevention of Discrimination was supposedly a body filled with experts that did not represent their home states, and served instead in an independent capacity. Their independence was conspicuous in the cases of some Third World and Western members, who sometimes contradicted the positions of their official state delegates in the main Commission on Human Rights. However, those from the Soviet bloc invariably voted in accordance with state policy—and were, from time to time, the same delegate changing seats.

174. Summary Records of the UN Sub-Commission on the Prevention of Discrimination, 571st meeting, 5 September 1968, E/CN. 4/Sub. 2/SR. 571 (Waldron-Ramsey).

175. Nikiema's response to Waldron-Ramsey was quoted with approval by the U.S. delegation telegram on the session, see US Mission United Nations New York to Secretary of State Washington DC, Human Rights—Sub-Commission on Discrimination State for Ambassador Ferguson, 8 September 1969, USUN 2917, SOC 14—3 ECOSOC, Social, Central Foreign Policy Files 1967–1969; General Records of the Department of State, RG59; NACP. Nikiema's conduct during the session demonstrated impeccable independence, with extensive discussion of his own country's failings in the judicial field. See, for example, Summary Records of the UN Sub-Commission on the Prevention of Discrimination, 563rd meeting, 29 August 1968, E/CN. 4/Sub. 2/SR. 563 (Nikiema). See also US Mission United Nations New York to Secretary of State Washington DC, Human Rights—Sub-Commission on Discrimination State for Ambassador Ferguson, 15 September 1969, USUN 3028, SOC 14—3 ECOSOC, Social, Central Foreign Policy Files 1967–1969; General Records of the Department of State, RG59; NACP. A further testament to Nikiema's character was delivered at the 1970 Sub-Commission meeting, where he was singled out for special criticism by Soviet delegation. See US Mission United Nations New York to Secretary of State Washington DC, info US Mission Kampala, *Human Rights*—Sub-Commission on Discrimination—Summary Second Week, 25 August 1970, USUN 1743,

Subject Numeric Files 1970–73, Social; General Records of the Department of State, RG59; NACP.

176. US Mission United Nations New York to Secretary of State Washington DC, Human Rights—Sub-Commission on Discrimination—Summary Last Week, 1 September 1970, USUN 1773, Subject Numeric Files 1970–73, Social; General Records of the Department of State, RG59; NACP.

177. Ibid., para.7.

178. Ibid., para.8.

179. Carey, "Progress on Human Rights at the United Nations," 108.

180. Quentin-Baxter, "The United Nations Human Rights Commission," 573. The article was drafted c. 1969.

Chapter 4. "It Is Very Fitting": Celebrating Freedom in the Shah's Iran, the First World Conference on Human Rights, Tehran 1968

Some of this research has been previously published in Burke, "From Individual Rights to National Development: The First UN International Conference on Human Rights, Tehran 1968," *Journal of World History* 19, 3 (September 2008): 275–96.

Epigraphs: Verbatim text of address by His Imperial Majesty the Shahinsha Aryamehr, International Conference on Human Rights, 3, UN Secretary-General, 1961–1971: U Thant, Trip to Tehran, Iran, International Conference in Human Rights, 20–23 April 1968. S-0883-018-08, UN Archives, 1st Plenary Meeting, 22 April 1968, A/CONF. 32/SR. 1, Conference President Ashraf.

1. Official Records of the International Human Rights Conference, Tehran, 27th Plenary Meeting, 13 May 1968, A/CONF.32/SR. 27, Holy See.

2. United Nations, Regarding International Human Rights Conference, Tehran, 23 April 1968, ZY225, UNIC Rome, 6, UN Secretary-General, 1961–1971: U Thant, Trip to Tehran, Iran, International Conference in Human Rights, 20–23 April 1968, S-0883-018-08, UN Archives.

3. Espiritu, *Five Faces of Exile*, 40.

4. There are a limited number of academic works that refer to the conference; see Moskowitz, *International Concern with Human Rights*, 13–23; Robertson, *Crimes Against Humanity*, 32; Cranston, *What Are Human Rights?*, 76; Suter, *An International Law of Guerilla Warfare*, 28–35.

5. International Commission of Jurists, United Nations Conference on Human Rights: Report by Miss Muireann McHugh, Barrister-at-Law, approved by Mr. Sean McBride, Secretary-General, S.2021, 22. Excerpts reproduced in Moskowitz, *International Concern with Human Rights*, 179–80.

6. *ICJ Tehran Report*, 21–22, cited in ibid., 179–80.

7. Bruno Bitker, Report on Tehran Conference, Department of State Bulletin, 2 September, 1968, 257. Excerpts reproduced in Moskowitz, *International Concern with Human Rights*, 179.

8. At the time, the conference was perceived as a major international event. It attracted telegrams of congratulation from the pope, the premier of the USSR, and the president of the United States. Senior State Department officials gave serious consideration to sending Vice President Humphrey as leader the U.S. contingent. Ambassador David Popper, a diplomat with a keen interest in human rights, thought the conference was something well beyond the standard international diplomatic gathering. In a confidential memorandum to the White House, Popper warned that "we can no longer think of the Tehran

Human Rights Conference as a routine affair to be staffed out of International Organization together with a few experts." See Memorandum from International Organizations—David H. Popper to OIC Mr. Parelman, UN Human Rights Conference, Tehran—April 22–May 13, 29 January 1968. See also US Mission United Nations, New York, to Department of State, info US Mission Tehran, 8 March 1968, USUN 4063, SOC 1/1/67, Central Foreign Policy Files 1967–1969; General Records of the Department of State, RG59; NACP.

9. Quentin-Baxter, "International Protection of Human Rights," 141.

10. Ibid., 141–42.

11. Moskowitz, *International Concern with Human Rights*, 13–14.

12. Tolley, *The U.N. Commission on Human Rights*, 54.

13. M. J. Peterson, *The General Assembly in World Politics* (Boston: Allen and Unwin, 1986), 13.

14. See for example the statement of Adib Dauody, 5th Plenary Meeting, A/CONF. 32/SR. 5, Syria. See also U Thant's speech, which reminded the delegates that one of Bandung's major accomplishments was its recognition of the Universal Declaration, see Address by Secretary-General in Commemoration of Twentieth Anniversary of Adoption of Universal Declaration of Human Rights, at International Conference on Human Rights, Tehran, 22 April, Advance Text, 19 April 1968, UN Document SG/SM/932/HR/135, 1. UN Chef de Cabinet, 1961–1973: Narasimhan. Social Matters 1/1/1963–31/12/1973. S-0198-001. UN Archives

15. 10th Meeting, First Committee, 28 April 1968, A/CONF. 32/C. 1/SR. 10, Iran.

16. 5th Plenary Meeting, 24 April 1968, A/CONF/SR. 5, Syria.

17. 22nd Plenary Meeting, 7 May 1968, A/CONF/SR. 22, Syria. The "connection" between Zionism and Nazism became an increasingly popular theme in Arab rhetoric, see Summary Records of the Third Committee, 1697th, 1700th, and 1701st meetings, 10–13 November 1969, A/C.3/SR. 1697, para. 9 (Iraq), A/C.3/SR. 1700, paras. 20 (UAR), 68 (Iraq), A/C.3/SR. 1701, paras. 23–24 (Kuwait).

18. Sastroamidjojo and Penders, *Milestones on My Journey*, 289.

19. As demonstrated in the collection of press reports collected in *Asian-African Conference: Views and News*; on Indonesian press freedom in this period generally, see Ghoshal, *Indonesian Politics 1955–59*), 5–6.

20. Sastroamidjojo, *Milestones on My Journey* 288.

21. Ibid., 303.

22. In a letter to Badr Tyabji, ambassador to Indonesia, Nehru placed bathroom facilities high on the list of concerns to be raised with the Indonesian government. "Above all, one fact should be remembered, and this is usually forgotten in Indonesia. This fact is an adequate provision of bath rooms and lavatories etc. . . . I am writing about what might be considered trivial matters. But these trivial matters upset people and frayed tempers are no good when we consider important problems." To B. F. H. B. Tyabji, 20 February 1955, New Dehli, reproduced in Nehru, *Selected Works*, 2nd ser., vol. 28, 100.

23. Ganji, *Defying the Iranian Revolution*, xxv.

24. Department of External Affairs, Canberra, United Nations Human Rights Commission—Conference on Human Rights—Teheran April to May 1968, National Archives of Australia, A1838 929/1/5, Part 4.

25. For example, in 1971, when the Shah celebrated the founding of Persia, visitors arrived to special tents with two marble bathrooms per tent. See Wil-

liam Shawcross, *The Shah's Last Ride: The Story of the Exile, Misadventures and Death of the Emperor* (London: Pan Books, 1989), 41.

26. Ibid., 160–63, 198–201.

27. Ganji, *Defying the Iranian Revolution*, xxi–ii, citing Alam, *The Shah and I.*

28. Thant, Address by Secretary-General (note 14). See also Press Statement by Secretary-General on Departure from Tehran, 23 April 1968, UN Document SG/T/198. UN Secretary-General. 1961–1971: U Thant. Trip to Tehran, Iran, International Conference in Human Rights, 20–23 April 1968. S-0883-018-08. UN Archives. For details of Thant's decision to reject human rights petitions presented to UN offices, see Press Release from Secretary-General, 22 December 1969, UN Document SG/SM/1200.

29. Note for the Secretary-General on the Opening of the International Conference on Human Rights, 22 April 1968, 1. See also Note for the Secretary-General, Proposed Program for the Opening Meeting of the International Conference on Human Rights, Monday, 22 April 1968. UN Secretary-General, 1961–1971: U Thant, Trip to Tehran, Iran, International Conference in Human Rights, 20–23 April 1968. S-0883-018-08, UN Archives.

30. Though this is not confirmed, it appears that the willingness of the Shah to bear the costs of UN conferences held in Tehran played a determining role in its eventual selection ahead of the initial favorites Nice and Vienna or poorer, but more liberal, African and Asian cities. See Letter from Marc Schreiber, Director of Human Rights Division, to C. V. Narasimhan, UN Chef de Cabinet, New York, 15 July 1966, 4. UN Chef de Cabinet. 1961–1973: Narasimhan, Human Rights—General Correspondence. S-0198-002-01, UN Archives; and Letter from John Humphrey, Director of Human Rights Division, to Georges Peissel, Director of Language and Meetings Service, Regarding Eighteenth Session of the Commission on the Status of Women, 7 July 1964. See also Letter from John Humphrey, Director of Human Rights Division, to C. V. Narasimhan, Regarding Success of Eighteenth Session of the Commission on the Status of Women, 25 March 1965. UN Chef de Cabinet, 1961–1973: Narasimhan, Status of Women, S-0271-004-19, UN Archives.

31. Ganji, *Defying the Iranian Revolution*, xxi, citing Alam, *The Shah and I.*

32. Keddie and Yann, *Roots of Revolution*, 179.

33. Ganji, *Defying the Iranian Revolution*, xxvii, citing Fitzgerald.

34. These comments were made in a conversation with academic Ehsan Naraghi on 23 November 1978, when the Shah issued a tirade against criticism on the regime's human rights record:

"Don't you think that the countries which keep harping on human rights are only using their campaign as a shield to hide their real objectives—of which exploitative contracts are only one example—and that they in fact want to establish their hegemony throughout the world? Do you really think they mean what they say? Is it not just a tactic to bring those countries into line which have not submitted to their policies and which have tried to maintain their independence? I have my doubts about their sincerity." See Naraghi, *From Palace to Prison*, 76.

35. Verbatim text of address by His Imperial Majesty the Shahinsha Aryamehr.

36. Ibid. The speech strongly resembles passages in Mohammed Reza Pahlavi's book, and some of the phrases are close to identical. See Pahlavi, *The White Revolution*, 21, 170–71.

37. See ibid.

38. Department of State Telegram, Secretary of State, action to U.S. Delegation (UN), information to Mission (Tehran) 1 December 1970, USUN 3411, para 4, Subject Numeric Files 1970–73, Social; General Records of the Department of State, RG59; NACP. See also Department of State Telegram, Mission (Tehran) to Secretary of State, 3 December 1970, Tehran 5190, Subject Numeric Files 1970–73, Social; General Records of the Department of State, RG59; NACP.

39. Ashraf's presidency may have been prearranged with the hosts. Before the start of the conference, Director of the Human Rights Division Marc Schreiber advised the Secretary-General that Ashraf would "in all likelihood be elected president after several nominating speeches," and the conference adhered closely to his prediction, see Marc Schreiber, *Regarding arrangements for visit to Tehran*, UNTHN 102. UN Secretary-General. 1961–1971: U Thant. Trip to Tehran, Iran, International Conference in Human Rights, 20–23 April 1968, S-0883-018-08, UN Archives.

40. 1st Plenary Meeting, 22 April 1968, A/CONF. 32/SR. 1, Conference President Ashraf.

41. Pahlavi, *Faces in a Mirror*, 174.

42. Ibid., xii. Queen Farah Pahlavi's response to the criticisms of the Shah's human rights record reiterated Ashraf's basic argument: "This attack on the king was quite unjustified. How long did it take France to find the calm waters of democracy after 1789? Nearly a century. And Iran was asked to move straight out of the Middle Ages into the democratic refinement of contemporary Europe." Farah Pahlavi, *An Enduring Love* (New York: Miramax, 2004), 234.

43. Pahlavi, *Faces in a Mirror*, 173–74. See also Pahlavi, "A Talk with Princess Ashraf of Iran."

44. Pahlavi, *Faces in a Mirror*, 173–74. Ashraf's speech at the Mexico City Conference is reproduced in Appendix 1 of her memoir. For her reflection on the meeting in general, see 193.

45. 18th Plenary Meeting, 4 May 1968, A/CONF.32/SR. 18, Greece.

46. 14th Plenary Meeting, 30 April 1968, A/CONF. 32/SR. 14, Mauritania.

47. Ibid. Similar claims were at the center of debate twenty-five years later, at the second UN World Conference on Human Rights in Vienna (1993).

48. Iran was, by the early 1970s, viewed as something of a model for the other Third World states. A 1971 article by Professor Peter Avery (Cambridge) published in *UNESCO Courier*, proclaimed Iran's new status: "Now Iran again commands international respect. It both can and does play a positive role in world affairs. As a member of the United Nations it set the pace for other developing countries, and has become the obvious milieu for international conventions for the discussion of such topics as nutrition, agricultural development, illiteracy, the rights of women. It is thus once more the centre where ideas and techniques may be pooled, to meet the problems of the less technologically advanced Orient with the experience and skills of the more technologically advanced Occident, Iran acting as the catalyst." Avery, "Iran: Cultural Crossroads for 2,500 Years," 9.

49. 4th Plenary Meeting, 24 April 1968, A/CONF. 32/SR. 4, Philippines.

50. Espiritu, *Five Faces*, 40.

51. 14th Plenary Meeting, 30 April 1968, A/CONF. 32/SR. 14, Pakistan. See also General Ayub Khan's attitudes on the relationship between democracy, rights, and development, Ayub Khan, *Friends Not Masters*), ix, 90, 92, 101, 103, 179–80, 187, 189, 192–93, 204–7, 215, 218. Ayub Khan argued that development

had to precede democracy. "Past experience had shown that the western type of parliamentary democracy could not be imposed on the people of Pakistan. There were certain basic requirements in the western system which were lacking here. . . . In the absence of these prerequisites, people could not be expected to exercise their right of vote in the context of broad national policies. It is too much to expect a man, sick and illiterate, and worried about his next meal, to think in terms of national policies." (207–8).

52. 18th Plenary Meeting, 4 May 1968, A/CONF. 32/SR. 18, Argentina.

53. Radji, *In the Service of the Peacock Throne*, 84.

54. 4th Plenary Meeting, 24 April 1968, A/CONF. 32/SR. 4, Iran.

55. 5th Plenary Meeting, 24 April 1968, A/CONF. 32/SR. 5, Ethiopia. Later in 1968, Selassie issued a breathtakingly hypocritical press release on the importance of human rights and constitutionalism to celebrate the anniversary of the Universal Declaration. See Message from Haile Selassie I, Emperor of Ethiopia, on Observance of International Year for Human Rights, 17 December 1968, UN Document HRD/72. UN Under-Secretary-General for Special Political Affairs. 1965-1971: Rolz-Bennett. General Subject Files, Human Rights—General Correspondence, S-0084-0003-01, UN Archives.

56. United Nations Conference on Human Rights, Proclamation of Teheran, 13 May 1968, A/CONF. 32/41.

57. Though there were some honorably consistent exceptions, notably Tanzanian leader Julius Nyerere, who recognized Biafran independence on 13 April 1968.

58. US Mission Tehran to Secretary of State, info to US Mission United Nations, New York, Human Rights Conference: Arab Tactics, 1 May 1968, Tehran 4467, File 5/1/68, SOC 14-3, Central Foreign Policy Files 1967–1969; General Records of the Department of State, RG59; NACP. Meyer noted that the Arab bloc's hard negotiating style risked alienating their other Afro-Asian allies, and observed that they were "hurting themselves by tactics which clearly obnoxious even to those countries which felt compelled to jump on bandwagon." For further background on Meyer and his diplomatic experience in Iran, see Meyer, *Quiet Diplomacy*.

59. US Mission Tehran to Secretary of State, info to various, Human Rights and Middle East: Voting Tendencies, 9 May 1968, Tehran 4624, File 4/1/68, SOC 14-3, Central Foreign Policy Files 1967–1969; General Records of the Department of State, RG59; NACP.

60. US Mission Tehran to Secretary of State, info US Mission United Nations New York, Tel Aviv, Amman, Beirut, Canberra, Human Rights Conference—Middle East, Supplemental, 26 April 1968, Tehran 4371, File 4/1/68, SOC 14-3, Central Foreign Policy Files 1967–1969; General Records of the Department of State, RG59; NACP.

61. 5th Plenary Meeting, 24 April 1968, A/CONF. 32/SR. 5, Syria.

62. 14th Plenary Meeting, 30 April 1968, A/CONF. 32/SR. 14, Saudi Arabia.

63. 17th Plenary Meeting, 2 May 1968, A/CONF. 32/SR. 17, Kuwait.

64. This developed into an official doctrine of the Non-Aligned Movement, see "Declaration on the Struggle for National Liberation," issued at the National Fourth Conference of Heads of State or Government of Non-Aligned Countries, Algiers, September 5–9, 1973, reproduced in *Documents of the Gatherings of Non-Aligned Countries, 1961–1978*, 104.

65. 9th Plenary Meeting, 27 April 1968, A/CONF. 32/SR. 9, Algeria. The

State Department thought Yazid "friendly" and "approachable." For biographical details on Algerian delegation to Tehran, see US Mission Algiers to Secretary of State, info US Mission Tehran, UN Conference on Human Rights, 18 April 1968, Algiers 01510, File 4/1/68, SOC 14-3, Central Foreign Policy Files 1967–1969; General Records of the Department of State, RG59; NACP.

66. 9th Plenary Meeting, 27 April 1968, A/CONF. 32/SR. 9, Algeria.

67. 5th Meeting, First Committee, 2 May 1968, A/CONF. 32/C. 1/SR. 5, Mauritania.

68. 8th Meeting, First Committee, 27 April 1968, A/CONF. 32/C. 1/SR. 8, Uganda.

69. 11th Plenary Meeting, 29 April 1968, A/CONF. 32/SR. 11, Cuba. Cuba was the most outspoken and consistent proponent of the claim that the freedom fighter was the ultimate human rights worker. See, for instance, the remarks of Fernandez de Cossio Rodríguez to the Third Committee: "The peoples of the Portuguese colonies, in taking arms against foreign oppression, had chosen the right way of achieving national liberation and full human dignity. In the view of his delegation, the greatest contribution which could be made by Governments striving sincerely for respect for human rights in colonial and dependent Territories was to give the maximum moral and material support to those peoples in their struggle." Summary Records of the Third Committee, 1380th meeting, 3 October 1966, para 44.

70. Laliam background in US Mission Algiers, UN Conference on Human Rights.

71. 3rd Meeting, Second Committee, 29 April 1968, A/CONF. 32/C. 2/SR. 3, Algeria.

72. Roosevelt was recognized for her contribution to the Universal Declaration as part of the twentieth anniversary celebrations, being posthumously awarded the UN Human Rights Medal. See Assembly President Announces Winners of First United Nations Human Rights Prizes, 2 December 1968, UN Document GA/3836/HR/209. UN Chef de Cabinet. 1961–1973: Narasimhan, Human Rights—General Correspondence, S-0198-0002-09, UN Archives.

73. Meyer had an astute sense of the new UN mindset. This perverse logic was later codified in the early 1970s, when the UN determined that its sole metric of social harmony was the presence or absence of protest. See Moynihan, August 1972 cable, reproduced in Buckley, *United Nations Journal,* 258.

74. US Mission Tehran to Secretary of State, info US Mission United Nations, New York, Re: Washington Demonstration and Tehran, 6 March 1968, Tehran 3631, para. 2, File 1/1/68, SOC 14-3, Central Foreign Policy Files 1967–1969; General Records of the Department of State, RG59; NACP.

75. Department of State info US Mission Tehran, US Mission United Nations, New York, For Ambassador Meyer from Popper, State 126411, 7 March 1968, File 1/1/68, SOC 14-3, Central Foreign Policy Files 1967–1969; General Records of the Department of State, RG59; NACP.

76. There appeared to be a substantial difference in approach between the permanent UN diplomatic staff and Secretary of State Rusk. The U.S. delegation in New York originally advocated a minimal presence, or "partial boycott," of the conference, only to be rebuked by Rusk. "We very much doubt that suggestion of truncated US representation at Tehran Human Rights Conference would work to our advantage. As reftel states, conference will certainly be an overall political exercise heavily centered on apartheid and attacks on so-called colonialism. Our experience in human rights seminars in past and in other UN

organs where these matters are considered is that forthright explanation and defence of US position is normally more helpful, and certainly more satisfying to our friends, than a partial boycott would be. Latter would, we fear, only intensify problem of winning greatest possible support for our point of view." Secretary of State, Dean Rusk, Department of State to USUN New York, info US Mission Teheran, Commission on Human Rights, 15 March 1968, State 130541, File 4/1/68, SOC 14, Central Foreign Policy Files 1967–1969; General Records of the Department of State, RG59; NACP.

77. 4th Plenary Meeting, 24 April 1968, A/CONF. 32/SR. 4, United States. Meyer noted that the "statement received extraordinary applause and much congratulatory comment: demand for copies far outran anticipation. Wilkins had already proved an outstanding figure at [the] conference. He handled magnificently unexpected request by Uganda delegate for moment silence in tribute to Martin Luther King." See US Mission Tehran to Secretary of State, info US Mission United Nations New York, Dept. pass to White House, Human Rights Conference, attention International Organizations, Averill Harriman, 25 April 1968, Tehran 4344, File 4/1/68, SOC 14-3, Central Foreign Policy Files 1967–1969; General Records of the Department of State, RG59; NACP.

78. Wilkins's own memoir gives only the most fleeting reference to the conference, see Wilkins and Mathews, *Standing Fast*, 341.

79. US Mission Tehran, Human Rights Conference [25 April], para 4.

80. Memorandum for the Secretary of State from Joseph J. Sisco, International Organizations, Appointment with Roy Wilkins After His Return From UN Human Rights Conference—Action Memorandum, S/S 6456, File 4/1/68, SOC 14-3, Central Foreign Policy Files 1967–1969; General Records of the Department of State, RG59; NACP. Sisco's memorandum offered the highest praise for Wilkins's success in Tehran: "His opening statement for the United States on April 24 met with wide acclaim and will substantially assist our Delegation in projecting a balanced picture of the racial outlook in the United States and American objectives at the Conference. In light of Mr. Wilkins' contribution, I feel that it would be advantageous domestically and internationally for him to meet with the President. . . . We have informal indications that this proposal would be well received in the White House." See also Memorandum for the President from Dean Rusk. Proposed Meeting With Roy Wilkins Executive Director NAACP, 26 April 1968, File 4/1/68, SOC 14-3, Central Foreign Policy Files 1967–1969; General Records of the Department of State, RG59; NACP.

81. Ambassador Meyer, US Mission Tehran to Secretary of State, info US Mission United Nations New York, Dept. pass to White House, Human Rights Conference, attention IO, Harriman, 25 April 1968, Tehran 4344, File 4/1/68, SOC 14-3, Central Foreign Policy Files 1967–1969; General Records of the Department of State, RG59; NACP. See also Ambassador Meyer's summary of the first week of the conference, in which Wilkins's presence was seen to have protected the US from the criticism it was expecting: "Much of what has been said here so far has been predictable. Major change from anticipated scenario, from our standpoint, has been virtually complete absence of criticism of US over its racial problems and policies. We attribute this to Wilkins' statement and presence. Needless to say, it greatly facilitates our task. We believe impact of Wilkins' activities will continue to be felt throughout conference." US Mission Tehran to Secretary of State, info US Mission United Nations New York, Canberra, Human Rights Conference—Summary, First Week, 26 April 1968,

Tehran 4370, File 4/1/68, SOC 14-3, Central Foreign Policy Files 1967–1969; General Records of the Department of State, RG59; NACP.

82. Moynihan and Weaver, *A Dangerous Place*, 175.

83. Moynihan's generally low opinion of US human rights diplomatic personnel was encapsulated in his infamous August 1972 cable to Secretary of State Kissinger, reproduced in Buckley, *United Nations Journal*, 259. See also Moynihan, "The Politics of Human Rights," 22; Moynihan, "The United States in Opposition," passim.

84. 3rd Plenary Meeting, 23 April 1968, A/CONF. 32/SR. 3, France.

85. Ibid.

86. See, generally, Plenary Meetings, A/CONF.32/SR.1-14, statements from the United Kingdom, Federal Republic of Germany, Italy, and United States. The UK was especially vulnerable following Conservative MP Enoch Powell's highly inflammatory statements on race relations only three days before the conference opened. Powell's speech would be remembered as the "Rivers of blood" address, and produced his dismissal from Edward Heath's shadow cabinet. See Lewis, "A Top Tory Fears Black Dominance." Its major initiative in the preparatory Western Europe and Others caucus had been a resolution on racism; see Department of External Affairs, cable from Australian delegation to the United Nations, New York, UN—Human Rights Conference, 29 February 1968, U. 338, para 2.

87. Veteran UN representative Robert Q. Quentin-Baxter (New Zealand) singled out Bystricky's speech as one of the few meaningful contributions made to human rights by the conference. "At the Teheran Conference, one of the most impressive statements was that made in the general debate by the leader of the Czechoslovak delegation. He was himself a man of distinction, the rector of Charles University in Prague, and he spoke reflectively of the benefits, particularly in the economic and social fields, which the people of Czechoslovakia had derived from communism. He went on to say, however, that these benefits had perhaps been pursued too singlemindedly, so that some reforms were necessary. The present government of Czechoslovakia was pledged to make these reforms, and especially to promote freedom of expression. This, he said, was his country's gift to International Human Rights Year." See Quentin-Baxter, "International Protection of Human Rights," 144.

88. 12th Plenary Meeting, 29 April, A/CONF. 32/SR. 12, Czechoslovakia. Quotes are taken from the summary record, for the verbatim transcript of the Czechoslovakian address, see US Mission Tehran to Secretary of State, UN Human Rights Conference in Tehran, Enclosure, Czech Speech, Verbatim, 1 May 1968, Airgram.

89. Ibid. A later Czech speech on the importance of self-determination was arguably more provocative. Alternate delegate Kosta outlined the Czechoslovak position on self-determination in the conference First Committee a little over a week later on 6 May during a debate on the obligatory reaffirmation of the right to self-determination. Kosta explained that "his government's policy towards countries of the Third World was to aid them in achieving their independence. At the same time, the right of self-determination was universal and applied also to European countries. . . . From his country's experiences, he could draw a conclusion relevant to the work of the Committee, namely that only in a democratic climate was it possible to ensure the implementation of human rights and particularly the right to self-determination." His arguments were somewhat prescient given the flagrant violation of that right only three months later

with the Warsaw Pact invasion of Czechoslovakia. There was scant support for Dubček from those who applauded at Tehran. At the UN Third Committee session, attempts to get a resolution condemning Soviet violation of Czechoslovakian self-determination were abandoned as hopeless before a draft text was even introduced. See Memorandum from [James Russell] Wiggins, US Mission New York to Secretary of State, info US Mission Prague, Czech Res.—Comite III Human Rights, 27 November 1968, 8118 USUN. See also US Mission New York to Secretary of State, info US Mission Moscow, Prague, Czech—Comite III Human Rights, 21 November 1968, 7971 USUN; US Mission Prague to Secretary of State, info US Mission Moscow, USUN, Czech—Comite III—Human Rights, 21 November 1968, 4271 Prague, Social, Central Foreign Policy Files 1967–1969; General Records of the Department of State, RG59; NACP. A marginally more successful attempt to focus attention on the invasion of Czechoslovakia was made in the October 1968 session of the Sub-Commission, see 541st and 542nd meetings, 14 October, UN Document E/CN. 4/Sub. 2/SR. 541–42.

90. Department of State Telegram, Tehran, Human Rights Conference: Czech Speech, 29 April 1968, 04428 Tehran, File SOC 14 UN, Central Foreign Policy Files 1967–1969; General Records of the Department of State, RG59; NACP. The delegation commented that the speech "was remarkably liberal in tone and as far as we know goes farther than anything the Czechs have yet said in an intergovernmental forum . . . we suggest good play." Its delivery "caused a minor sensation."

91. Department of State Telegram, Tehran, Human Rights Conference—Vietnam, 29 April 1968, 04426 Tehran, para 3, File SOC 14 UN, Central Foreign Policy Files 1967–1969; General Records of the Department of State, RG59; NACP.

92. Western planning for the conference had been essentially defensive, predicated on the assumption of Afro-Asian dominance. See generally, the deliberations of the Western and Others Caucusing Group, as reported in Department of State to USUN New York, info US Mission Teheran, US Mission London, Tehran Human Rights Conference, WEO Caucus, 4 March 1968, State 124480, SOC 14; US Mission United Nations New York to Department of State, info US Mission Teheran, info US Mission London, 24 February 1968, USUN 3913, Social, Central Foreign Policy Files 1967–1969; General Records of the Department of State, RG59; NACP. See also the draft instructions to the Australian delegation, Department of External Affairs, Draft Instructions to the Australian Delegation to the International Conference on Human Rights Tehran, 22 April–13 May 1968, passim, National Archives of Australia, United Nations Human Rights Commission—Conference on Human Rights—Teheran April to May 1968, A1838 929/1/5, Part 4; Letter from Senator Thomas J. Dodd to Dean Rusk regarding tactics at Human Rights Conference in Tehran. April 5 1968. See also, Response to letter from Senator Thomas J. Dodd regarding tactics at Human Rights Conference in Tehran. May 8 1968. William B. Macomber, Assistant Secretary for Congressional Relations, File 5/1/68 SOC 14, Central Foreign Policy Files 1967–1969; General Records of the Department of State, RG59; NACP.

93. US Mission Tehran, Summary of First Week.

94. Department of State to US Mission Tehran, Human Rights Conference—Final Proclamation, 9 May 1968, 161440, File 5/1/68 SOC 14-3, Central Foreign Policy Files 1967–1969; General Records of the Department of State, RG59; NACP.

95. See for example, 1968 Session of the Commission on Human Rights, 965th to 972nd meetings, 20–27 February, E/CN. 4/SR. 965-972. Haiti had been named in the Commission as early as 1963, see 740th meeting, 12 March, E/CN. 4/SR. 740. Haitian diplomatic protests to the Secretariat were relatively unsophisticated. In a response to a letter sent to the UN claiming the existence of gross human rights violations, Duvalier's Permanent Representative to the UN, Carlet Auguste replied with the conclusions of his own investigation. "I am pleased to say," wrote Auguste, "that life in Haiti is calmer than ever. Everyone goes about their business, great or small, in complete freedom and safety." There appears to have been no further correspondence from the Secretariat regarding the matter. See Carlet Auguste, Permanent Representative of the Republic of Haiti to United Nations, 610, to U Thant, Secretary General, United Nations, New York, 6 August 1966, UN Chef de Cabinet, 1961–1973: Narasimhan. Human Rights—General Correspondence, S-0198-002-01, UN Archives.

96. 9th Plenary Meeting, 27 April 1968, A/CONF. 32/SR. 9, Haiti.

97. Ferguson, *Papa Doc, Baby Doc*, 54. Duvalier's President-for-Life office had been endorsed by a referendum, but the ballots only had a "yes" option available. For further detail on Papa Doc, see his autobiography, Duvalier, *Memoirs of a Third World Leader.*

98. Ibid., 49. The prayer's text was as follows: "Our Doc, who art in the National Palace for life, hallowed be Thy name by present and future generations. Thy will be done in Port-au-Prince as it is in the provinces. Gives us this day our new Haiti and forgive not the trespasses of those anti-patriots who daily spit upon our country."

99. US Tehran, Summary of First Week, para 3.

100. US Mission Tehran to Secretary of State, info to US Mission United Nations, New York, Human Rights Conference: Third Round, 9 May 1968, Tehran 4649, para 2, File 5/1/68 SOC 14-3, Central Foreign Policy Files 1967–1969; General Records of the Department of State, RG59; NACP.

101. US Mission Tehran to Secretary of State, info to US Mission United Nations New York, Moscow, Human Rights Conference—Proclamation, 9 May 1968, Tehran 4648, para. 1, File 5/1/68 SOC 14-3, Central Foreign Policy Files 1967–1969; General Records of the Department of State, RG59; NACP.

102. Tanzanian representative Wambura best exemplified this hard-line style, and was highly dismissive of the value of consensus for the Final Proclamation. "He attached more importance to the text itself than to the number of votes it had obtained. If oppressors and oppressed were agreed on a proposal, it could be assumed that the latter was of meagre substance. In his opinion, it would have been better if the Proclamation had not been adopted unanimously, but had better reflected the progress that the Conference had brought about in that connexion." 27th Plenary Meeting, 13 May 1968, A/CONF. 32/SR. 27, Tanzania.

103. US Mission Tehran to Secretary of State, info US Mission United Nations, New York, Human Rights Conference: Proclamation, 10 May 1968, Tehran 4656, File 5/1/68 SOC 14-3, Central Foreign Policy Files 1967–1969; General Records of the Department of State, RG59; NACP.

104. US Mission Tehran to Secretary of State, info to US Mission United Nations New York, Moscow, Human Rights Conference: Russian Moderation, April 1968, Tehran 4398, File 4/1/68 SOC 14-3; and US Mission Tehran to Secretary of State, info to US Mission United Nations New York, Moscow, Human

Rights Conference: Friendly Noises from Soviets, 6 May 1968, Tehran 4543, File 5/1/68 SOC 14-3, Central Foreign Policy Files 1967–1969; General Records of the Department of State, RG59; NACP.

105. Such an arrangement was inherently advantageous to the communist bloc given that the Afro-Asian states were doing much to attack the West by themselves, though there was at least one instance of the Soviets being attacked by an African state that it was, in fact, arming at the time (Nigeria). See 12th Meeting, Second Committee, 8 May 1968, A/CONF. 32/C. 2/SR. 12.

106. US Mission Tehran to Secretary of State, Human Rights Conference— Vietnam, 28 April 1978, Tehran 4402, File 4/1/68 SOC 14-3, Central Foreign Policy Files 1967–1969; General Records of the Department of State, RG59; NACP.

107. US Mission Tehran to Secretary of State, info to US Mission United Nations New York, Moscow, Human Rights Conference—Soviet Statement, 2 May 1968, Tehran 4480, File 5/1/68 SOC 14-3, Central Foreign Policy Files 1967–1969; General Records of the Department of State, RG59; NACP. Ambassador Meyer speculated on the tensions between Moscow and the delegation in his report to Secretary Rusk on the Soviet statement: "We think it likely Sov[iet] del[egation] here engaged in some tug-of-warring with Moscow re Tchikvadze speech. . . . We heard Tchikvadze had been instructed by Moscow to step up his attacks on US, and Ostrovsky told us speech was going through repeated drafts. Still later Ambassador here told Amb[assador] Meyer he was urging mild approach despite Moscow's instructions. Delivery of speech was several times delayed as Sov[iet]s moved themselves downward on speakers' list. Excuse for final postponement was that Tchikvadze was not well, though few hours later he attended Fo[reig]n minister's dinner party." See also Meyer's report of a conversation with Soviet delegate Yerofeyev, and his reference to rumors from the UK delegation that there were instructions to escalate from Moscow. Human Rights Conference: Russian Moderation, para 3.

108. US Tehran, Human Rights Conference: Friendly Noises from Soviets.

109. Soviet tactics were highly reactive, which made for embarrassing last-minute reversals of vote when their delegation had misread the Afro-Asian position. For one such instance, see US Mission Tehran to Secretary of State, info US Mission United Nations, New York, Human Rights Conference, 9 May 1968, Tehran 4646, File 5/1/68 SOC 14-3, Central Foreign Policy Files 1967–1969; General Records of the Department of State, RG59; NACP.

110. Ibid.

111. US Mission Tehran to Secretary of State, info to US Mission United Nations New York, Moscow, Human Rights Conference: Final Act, 6 May 1968, Tehran 4567, File 5/1/68 SOC 14-3, Central Foreign Policy Files 1967–1969; General Records of the Department of State, RG59; NACP.

112. US Mission Tehran to Secretary of State, info to US Mission United Nations, New York, Human Rights Conference—Second Roundup, Sections 1 and 2, 2 May 1968, Tehran 4507-1, 2, File 5/1/68 SOC 14-3, Central Foreign Policy Files 1967–1969; General Records of the Department of State, RG59; NACP.

113. Statement by Chairman of Commission on Human Rights, Ibrahima Boye, on 20th Anniversary of Declaration of Human Rights, 9 December 1968, UN Document GA/3845/HRD/50, 4.

114. Nwankwo and Ifejika, *The Making of a Nation*, 266.

115. Friendly, "Boycott Cuts Vote in Dahomey."

116. Brady, "Nasser Is Backed by 99.9% of the Vote."

117. Roger Baldwin and Jan Papanek, Appeal to the United Nations (U Thant) from The International League for the Rights of Man, United Nations Human Rights Commission—Conference on Human Rights Tehran—April 1968, National Archives of Australia, A1838, 929/1/5.

118. The sterile bureaucratic language of Humphrey's letter is striking, though perhaps unsurprising given the number of such cases and his inability to intervene in any form. "The Shah's confirmation of the death sentences is apparently expected tomorrow, April 27. We are, of course, dealing with these communications under resolution 728 F (XXVIII) of the Economic and Social Council in the usual way." John Humphrey, Director of Division of Human Rights, memorandum to Mr. José Rolz-Bennett, 26 April 1966, SO 215/1 IRAN, UN Chef de Cabinet, 1961–1973: Narasimhan, Human Rights—General Correspondence, S-0198-002-01, UN Archives.

119. Confidential Marc Schreiber, Director, Division of Human Rights, Note for the Secretary-General on the twenty-fifth session of the Commission on Human Rights, 9 April 1969, para. 2. UN Under-Secretary-General for Special Political Affairs, 1965–1971: Rolz-Bennett, General Subject Files, Human Rights—General Correspondence, S-0084-0003-02, UN Archives.

120. This is well illustrated by the agendas of the 1973 and 1974 sessions of the Commission on Human Rights. See Summary Records of the Commission on Human Rights, E/CN. 4/SR. 1180–1216, 26 February–19 March, E/CN. 4/SR, 1243–1267, 4, 1 February 1974.

Chapter 5. "According to Their Own Norms of Civilization": The Rise of Cultural Relativism and the Decline of Human Rights

Epigraphs: Pollis and Schwab, "Human Rights: A Western Construct with Limited Applicability," 1; Summary Records of the Third Committee, 296th meeting, 27 October 1950, A/C. 3/SR. 296, para 6.

1. American Anthropological Association, Statement on Human Rights, 543. For further background on the AAA statement see Washburn, "Cultural Relativism, Human Rights, and the AAA."

2. Commission on Human Rights, First Session, Verbatim Record, 15th meeting, 5 February 1947, 53, Charles Malik Collection, Box 76, File 1: First Session, Commission on Human Rights—Minutes, 1947.

3. Pollis and Schwab, "Human Rights: A Western Construct with Limited Applicability," 1.

4. Steward, "Comments on the Statement on Human Rights."

5. Shivji, *The Concept of Human Rights in Africa*, 3.

6. Mutua, *Human Rights: A Political and Cultural Critique*, 155.

7. Harris-Short, "International Human Rights Law," 174.

8. For some of the more sophisticated elaborations of cultural relativism, and the importance of cross-culturalism in human rights scholarship, see Ibawoh, "Cultural Relativism and Human Rights"; Freeman, "Human Rights and Real Cultures"; Wilson, *Human Rights, Culture and Context*; Pollis, "Towards a New Universalism"; Perry, "Are Human Rights Universal?"; An-Na'im, *Human Rights in Cross-Cultural Perspective*. The best examples of universalist arguments can be found in Donnelly, *The Concept of Human Rights*; Donnelly, "Human Rights, Democracy, and Development"; Donnelly, *International Human Rights*; Donnelly, *Universal Human Rights in Theory and Practice*; Donnelly and Howard, *Interna-*

tional Handbook of Human Rights; Howard, "The Dilemma of Human Rights in Sub-Saharan Africa"; Howard, "The Full-Belly Thesis."

9. See also the colonial transformation of traditional authority and customary law under Lugard's idea of indirect rule, discussed in Chanock, *Law, Custom, and Social Order* and Mamdani, *Citizen and Subject*.

10. Summary Records of the Third Committee, 294th meeting, 26 October 1950, A/C. 3/SR. 294, para. 38.

11. Summary Records of the Third Committee, 292nd meeting, 25 October 1950, A/C. 3/SR. 292, para. 5.

12. Humphrey, *On the Edge of Greatness*, vol. 1, 88.

13. Ibid., vol. 3, 93.

14. Fereydoun Hoveyda, Signed, Sealed & Delivered, 12 August 2005, http://www.iranian.com/ FereydounHoveyda/2005/August/UDHR/, accessed 10 November 2005.

15. Summary Records of the Third Committee, 621st meeting, 2 October 1954, A/C. 3/SR. 621, paras 37–39.

16. Summary Records of the Third Committee, 43rd meeting (32nd session), November 1977, A/C. 3/32/SR. 43, para. 38.

17. The conflict between colonial and Cold War imperatives is discussed extensively in Simpson, *Human Rights and the End of Empire*.

18. Summary Records of the Third Committee, 292nd meeting, 25 October 1950, A/C. 3/SR. 292, para. 5.

19. Summary Records of the Third Committee, 294th meeting, 27 October 1950, A/C. 3/SR. 294, para. 37.

20. Ibid., paras. 37–38.

21. Humphrey, *On the Edge of Greatness*, vol. 1, 124.

22. Ibid.,

23. Simpson, *Human Rights and the End of Empire*, 531.

24. Humphrey, *On the Edge of Greatness*, vol. 1, 125.

25. Summary Records of the Third Committee, 295th meeting, 27 October 1950, A/C. 3/SR. 295, para. 25.

26. Ibid., para. 23.

27. Ibid., para. 24.

28. Humphrey, *On the Edge of Greatness*, vol. 4, 136. See also U.S. State Department, Report on the Third Committee of the General Assembly, September–December 1953, 22, 320.13/3-1754, Decimal File 1950–1954; General Records of the Department of State, RG 59; NACP. At the 1953 session of the Fourth Committee, Menon would become so hostile that, at least according to U.S. observers, her own delegation almost disowned her. See U.S. State Department, Indian Attitudes and Policies at the Eighth Session of the General Assembly, 1953, 2–3, 320.13/3-1754, Decimal File 1950–1954, General Records of the Department of State, RG 59; NACP.

29. Summary Records of the Third Committee, 296th meeting, 27 October 1950, A/C. 3/SR. 296.

30. Summary Records of the Third Committee, 313th meeting, 13 November 1950, A/C. 3/SR. 313, paras. 11–15; see also Waltz, "Universal Human Rights."

31. U.S. State Department, Report on the Third Committee of the General Assembly, October–December 1952, 17, 320.1/1-752, 320.14/12-253, Decimal File 1950–1954, General Records of the Department of State, RG 59; NACP. See also U.S. State Department, Memorandum of Conversation: Iraqi Views on the US, 9 October 1953, 320.12-253, Decimal File 1950–1954; General Records

of the Department of State, RG 59; NACP. This memorandum relates an argument between Vijaya Lakshmi Pandit, Afnan, and Mary Lord. According to Pandit, Afnan was "a very difficult person."

32. Tripp, *A History of Iraq*, 114–18.

33. Ibid., 114.

34. Marr, *The Modern History of Iraq*, 73.

35. Summary Records of the Third Committee, 296th meeting, 27 October 1950, A/C. 3/SR. 296, para. 6.

36. For detail of Indonesian human rights debates of the early 1950s, see Nasution, *The Aspiration for Constitutional Government*.

37. Summary Records of the Third Committee, 296th meeting, 27 October 1950, A/C. 3/SR. 296, para. 45.

38. Blasier, "Chile: A Communist Battleground."

39. Summary Records of the Third Committee, 296th meeting, 27 October 1950, A/C. 3/SR. 296, para. 69.

40. Ibid., para. 72.

41. Humphrey, *On the Edge of Greatness*, vol. 2, 53. *Al-Misri* was the newspaper owned by Senator Mahmoud Aboul Fath, suppressed under Nasser. In 1950, Fath was also part of the Egyptian UN delegation. See Chapter 1 for further details on Fath, *Al-Misri*, and human rights.

42. Ibid., vol. 3, 98.

43. Humphrey, *On the Edge of Greatness*, vol. 3, 101.

44. U.S. State Department, 1953 Report on the Third Committee, 22.

45. U.S. State Department, 1952 Report on the Third Committee, 17.

46. Summary Records of the Third Committee, 296th meeting, 27 October 1950, A/C. 3/SR. 296, para. 81.

47. Humphrey, *On the Edge of Greatness*, vol. 1, 128.

48. See Convention on the Political Rights of Women, GA Resolution 640 (VII), 20 December 1952, Articles 1–3. This is compared to the sixteen substantive articles in the Convention on the Elimination of All Forms of Discrimination against Women (CEDAW), GA Resolution 34/180, 18 December 1979, Articles 1–16. The majority of the CEDAW articles are significantly more detailed.

49. Those on nondiscrimination on the basis of sex (a subset of nondiscrimination set out in Article 2) and the right to participate in government (Article 21, sub-articles 1, 2).

50. Hessel also appeared ambivalent about the vigorous pursuit of women's rights more generally. In an interview for the UN Oral History Project, he commented that "When we set up . . . a Commission on the Condition of Women. . . . That was in the early 1950s, or even late 1940s . . . there were some rather terrible women sitting on that commission and we were rather afraid of their enthusiasm and their emphasis . . . I have never been a feminist in the way that I feel that one has absolutely to fight because women are so underprivileged. . . . The fight for gender seems to me a bit of an alibi . . . always gender, gender, gender. So you see, on that I am not as staunch a defender of gender as I should be. . . . It is a proper fight. It is good that this fight continues. If it is not too vocal and too offensive, I think it is proper." Weiss, *UN Voices*, 253–54.

51. Summary Records of the Third Committee, 476th meeting, 13 December 1952, A/C. 3/SR. 476, para. 46.

52. Vidal-Naquet, *Torture, Cancer of Democracy*.

53. Summary Records of the Third Committee, 478th meeting, 15 December 1952, A/C. 3/SR. 478, para. 24.

54. Elkins, *Britain's Gulag.*

55. Summary Records of the Third Committee, 478th meeting, 15 December 1952, A/C. 3/SR. 478, para. 46.

56. See Population Registration Act, No. 30, 1950 as reproduced in Brookes, *Apartheid.*

57. Official Report of the Native Education Commission 1949–51, cited in Christie and Collins, "Bantu Education," 175.

58. Ibid., 176.

59. The rhetoric surrounding the Bantustan policy, for example, was replete with pseudocultural relativist language. "South Africa is a multinational country, made up of a nation of European descent . . . and a number of Bantu nations differing from one another in language, culture, traditions and everything else that determines national identities, each with its own undeniable right to separate nationhood in its own territory. Taking into account the history, culture and circumstances of each of the nations in South Africa, it is the objective of the South African Government to provide every individual with a chance of unlimited development within his own nation and, wherever possible, in his own national homeland. . . . South Africa's policy is therefore the reverse of domination and repression . . . the South African Government subscribes fully to the human rights provisions of the United Charter, and strives to promote and encourage respect for such rights, taking into account the particular circumstances existing in South Africa." UN General Assembly, The Policies of Apartheid of the Government of the Republic of South Africa, Letter 9 April 1968 from the Permanent Representative of South Africa to the UN addressed to the Secretary-General, UN Document A/7125 1968. UN Chef de Cabinet. 1961–1973: Narasimhan. Human Rights—General Correspondence. S-0198-002-02. UN Archives.

60. Summary Records of the Third Committee, 479th meeting, 16 December 1952, A/C. 3/SR. 479, para. 22.

61. Ibid., para. 57.

62. Nashat, "Women in Pre-Revolutionary Iran," 29.

63. Summary Records of the Third Committee, 477th meeting, 15 December 1952, A/C. 3/SR. 477, paras. 44–47.

64. Ibid., paras. 47, 49.

65. For further detail on the 1958 Personal Status Code, see Farouk-Sluglett, "Liberation or Repression?"

66. U.S. State Department, 1952 Report on the Third Committee, 17. She was also a friend of Eleanor Roosevelt.

67. Summary Records of the Third Committee, 478th meeting, 15 December 1952, A/C.3/SR. 478, paras 3, 8, 9.

68. Ibid., para. 4.

69. Patel, *Socio-Economic Political Status,* 177.

70. Ibid., 176–79.

71. Ibid., 13–15.

72. U.S. State Department, 1952 Report on the Third Committee, 19. The U.S. delegation noted that Bernardino played "an outstanding role" in the passage of the convention, and "obviously had all the Latin American votes in her pocket for this item."

73. U.S. State Department, 1953 Report on the Third Committee, 25.

74. Summary Records of the Third Committee, 479th meeting, 16 December 1952, A/C. 3/SR. 479, para. 26.

75. The Asian and African states present all voted for the Convention, as did the Latin American countries. The roll call vote was as follows. In favor (36): Argentina, Australia, Belgium, Bolivia, Brazil, Burma, Canada, Chile, China, Cuba, Denmark, Dominican Republic, Ecuador, Ethiopia, France, Greece, Guatemala, Haiti, India, Indonesia, Israel, Mexico, Netherlands, New Zealand, Norway, Pakistan, Panama, Peru, Philippines, Sweden, Syria, Thailand, Turkey, United Kingdom, United States of America. Afghanistan voted in favor after consultation with its government. Abstaining (11): Byelorussian SSR, Czechoslovakia, Egypt, Iran, Iraq, Poland, Saudi Arabia, Ukrainian SSR, Union of South Africa, USSR, Yemen.

76. Rasanayagam, *Afghanistan: A Modern History*, 25–26.

77. Report on the Third Committee of the General Assembly, 18. The U.S. author commended him for his patience.

78. Jain, *Women, Development, and the UN*, 20.

79. Jayawardena, *Feminism and Nationalism in the Third World*.

80. The draft text initially proposed (A/C. 3/L. 457) was sponsored by Argentina, Cuba, Dominican Republic, Egypt, Greece, Guatemala, Iraq, Peru, Venezuela, and Yugoslavia.

81. Resolution 843 (IX), preamble.

82. Hussein, "Crossroads for Women at the UN"; see also Sami, "Hot Line to Washington."

83. Hussein, "Crossroads for Women at the UN," 8.

84. Sami, "Hot Line to Washington."

85. Summary Records of the Third Committee, 621st meeting, 15 December 1954, A/C. 3/SR. 621, para. 5; see also Hussein, "The Role of Women in Social Reform in Egypt."

86. Summary Records of the Third Committee, 621st meeting, 15 December 1954, A/C. 3/SR. 621, para. 10.

87. Sullivan, *Women in Egyptian Public Life*, 33.

88. Summary Records of the Third Committee, 621st meeting, 15 December 1954, A/C.3/SR. 621, para. 44.

89. Ibid., para. 24.

90. Davies, *Defender of the Old Guard*, 181.

91. Jain, *Developing Power*, 25.

92. Ibid., 24.

93. Ibid., 27–29.

94. Summary Records of the Third Committee, 1062nd meeting, 4 October 1961, A/C. 3/SR. 1062, para. 19.

95. Ibid, para. 18.

96. Summary Records of the Third Committee, 1063rd meeting, 4 October 1961, A/C. 3/SR. 1063, para. 10.

97. Ibid., para. 42.

98. Ibid., para. 46.

99. Ibid., paras. 48, 49.

100. Ibid., para. 49.

101. For the text of the South African objection, see Summary Records of the Third Committee, 1065th meeting, 5 October 1961, A/C. 3/SR. 1065, paras. 10–15; for that given by Pakistan, see 1066th meeting, 6 October 1961, A/C. 3/SR. 1066, paras. 15–18. Indonesia also suggested that the text was more appro-

priately incorporated into a recommendation, as opposed to a binding convention, on the grounds that "attitudes and customs with respect to marriage were
a manifestation of the identity and characteristic way of life of a people and as
such should not be subject to regulation by a convention." For the full reserva-
tion see 1064th meeting, 4 October 1961, A/C. 3/SR. 1064, para. 4.

102. For the debate on how to address customary and traditional discrimination, as opposed to legislative discrimination, see Summary Records of the
Third Committee, 5–13 October 1967, 1473rd to 1483rd meetings, A/C. 3/
SR. 1473–83. African, Asian, and Arab delegations adopted a sophisticated
approach to the question, and a range of conflicting propositions were put
forward.

103. Summary Records of the Third Committee, 1476th meeting, 9 October
1967, A/C. 3/SR. 1476, para. 35

104. Declaration on the Elimination of Discrimination against Women, General Assembly Resolution 2263(XXII), 7 November 1967, http://www.UNHigh
Commissioner.ch/html/menu3/b/21.htm.

105. Ibid. See also Jain, *Developing Power*, 45–48.

106. See for example, Baroody's remarks of 18 October 1950 that "the draft
eighteen articles did not sufficiently reflect the various cultural patterns of
Member States," A/C.3 /SR. 288, para. 28; his April 1949 comments on foreign
news correspondents, A/C. 3/SR. 193, 115; and his reservations regarding the
World Conference of the International Women's Year, 1 December 1975, A/C.
3/SR. 2173, paras. 2–7.

107. Summary Records of the Third Committee, 1443rd meeting, 1 December 1966, A/C. 3/SR. 1443.

108. For more on Baroody's influential dissents, see the case of the South
African delegations credentials, discussed in Buckley, *United Nations Journal*,
111–16.

109. See generally Schwab, *Africa: A Continent Self-Destructs*; Meredith, *The
State of Africa*.

110. For direct reports of the nature of Amin's regime, see Amnesty International, *Human Rights in Uganda* and Allen, *Days of Judgment*. For general
studies of the Amin regime and its consequences, see Avirgan and Honey, *War
in Uganda*; Omara-Otunnu, *Politics and the Military in Uganda*; Smith, *Ghosts of
Kampala*.

111. Casper, *Fragile Democracies*; Celoza, *Ferdinand Marcos and the Philippines*;
Rosenberg, *Marcos and Martial Law in the Philippines*.

112. Keddie and Yann, *Roots of Revolution*, 179. See also the shah's disparaging comments about democracy and freedom of thought in Ganji, *Defying the
Iranian Revolution*, xxi–xxii, xxvi.

113. Keddie and Yann, *Roots of Revolution*, 179.

114. Marr, *Modern Iraq*, 151.

115. Rasanayagam, *Afghanistan*, 38–58. See also Ewans, *Afghanistan: A New
History*, 120–27.

116. Al-Rasheed, *A History of Saudi Arabia*.

117. Buckley, *United Nations Journal*, 122–30.

118. Ibid., 117–21.

119. Gold, *Tower of Babble*, 37–38.

120. Department of State Telegram, Embassy (Mexico City) to Secretary of
State, 9 December 1970, Mexico 6669, para. 1, Subject Numeric Files 1970–73,
Social-ECOSOC; General Records of the Department of State, RG59; NACP.

121. Clark, *A United Nations High Commissioner for Human Rights.*

122. Proposals for a High Commissioner were reintroduced to the human rights program in 1965, having first been raised in 1950 by Uruguay, with various precursors discussed in the late 1940s. In the 1960s, 1970s, and early 1980s, it was a regular item on the agenda. For details of the creation of the High Commissioner, see Clapham, "Creating the High Commissioner for Human Rights."

123. Korey, *Curious Grapevine*, 56–60; see also Humphrey, *On the Edge of Greatness*, vol. 4, passim.

124. Ibid., 58.

125. See Macdonald, "The United Nations High Commissioner for Human Rights."

126. This was especially so because of the command the Arab delegations appeared to have on many African votes. See Buckley, *United Nations Journal*, 51–52.

127. Ibid., 99.

128. Summary Records of the Third Committee, 1727th meeting, 5 December 1969, A/C. 3/SR. 1727, para. 31.

129. Summary Records of the Third Committee, 43rd meeting (32nd session), 10 November 1977, A/C. 3/32/SR. 43, para. 38.

130. "Jamil the Irrepressible," *Time*, 13 December 1971, 21.

131. Buckley, *United Nations Journal*, 68–69.

132. Ibid., 201. See also the 1953 private meeting where C. A. Meade (UK) and Mary Lord (U.S.) sought to avoid the final two agenda items and eagerly assented when Baroody's requested "a long time to discuss" earlier proposals without "being hurried." The tactic was christened "a silent filibuster"; see U.S. State Department, Memorandum of Conversation: Self-Determination, 30 October 1953, 1, 320.12-253, Decimal File 1950–1954; General Records of the Department of State, RG 59; NACP.

133. "Dispute Delays UN Action."

134. Buckley, *United Nations Journal*, 111–16.

135. Ibid., 191.

136. Ibid., 84. Buckley was rebuked by his superior John Scali for raising a point of order while Baroody was speaking.

137. Department of State Telegram, US Delegation (UN) action for Mission (Jeddah), Baroody at UN, 11 November 1970, UN 22-2 SAUD XRPOLARAB-DSK/UN, Subject Numeric Files 1970–73, Social—UN, General Records of the Department of State, RG59; NACP.

138. Buckley, *United Nations Journal*, 69–70.

139. Summary Records of the Third Committee, 1726th meeting, 5 December 1969, A/C. 3/SR. 1726, para. 40, see also para. 37 for further elaboration of this argument.

140. Summary Records of the Third Committee, 1730th meeting, 9 December 1969, A/C. 3/SR. 1730, para. 22. See also Syria, A/C. 3/SR. 1731, para. 3.

141. For the text, including attempts to stop Baroody's speech, see Summary Records of the Third Committee, 1808th meeting, 1970, A/C. 3/SR. 1808.

142. Summary Records of the Third Committee, 1809th meeting, 3 December 1970, A/C. 3/SR. 1809, para. 3, 8.

143. Department of State Telegram, US Delegation (UN) to Secretary of State, 21 December 1970, USUN A-2109, Subject Numeric Files 1970–73, Social—SOC 14; General Records of the Department of State, RG59; NACP.

144. Summary Records of the Third Committee, 1812th meeting, 7 December 1970, A/C. 3/SR. 1812, para. 4.

145. Ibid., para. 3.

146. Ibid., para. 11.

147. See, for example, USSR: A/C. 3/SR.1809, para. 36, 45, 48, 50 and A/C. 3/SR. 1812 para. 31; Ukrainian SSR: A/C. 3/SR. 1810, para. 18.

148. Summary Records of the Third Committee, 1809th meeting, 4 December 1970, A/C. 3/SR. 1809, para. 18.

149. Ibid., para. 24.

150. Summary Records of the Third Committee, 1899th meeting, 1971, A/C. 3/SR. 1899, para. 22.

151. Summary Records of the Third Committee, 2047th meeting, 3 December 1973, A/C. 3/SR. 2047, para. 74.

152. Dresch, *A History of Modern Yemen*, 121–22.

153. Summary Records of the Third Committee, 2049th meeting, 4 December 1973, A/C. 3/SR. 2049, para. 44.

154. Donnelly, "Recent Trends in UN Human Rights Activity."

155. See also Gregor, *Italian Fascism and Developmental Dictatorship.*

156. For an overview of the place of modernization in the Cold War context, see Engerman, *Staging Growth*; Gilman, *Mandarins of the Future*; Latham, *Modernization as Ideology*; and Simpson, *Economists with Guns.*

157. Summary Records of the Third Committee, 43d meeting (32nd session), 10 November 1977, A/C. 3/32/SR. 43, para. 38.

158. Ibid., para. 34.

159. Ibid., paras. 33, 38.

160. See Pollis, "A Western Construct."

161. Department of State Telegram, Secretary of State action to US Delegation (UN), information to Mission (Tehran) 1 December 1970, USUN 3411, para. 4. See also Department of State Telegram, Mission (Tehran) to Secretary of State, 3 December 1970, Tehran 5190, Subject Numeric Files 1970–73, Social—SOC 14 UN; General Records of the Department of State, RG59; NACP.

162. Summary Records of the Third Committee, 43rd meeting (32nd session), 10 November 1977, A/C. 3/32/SR. 43, para. 26.

163. The term "trade-off" refers to the putative "trade" in favor of economic rights at the expense of civil ones. See also Lee Kuan Yew, *From Third World to First.*

164. Summary Records of the Third Committee, 50th meeting (32nd session), 17 November 1977, A/C.3/32/SR. 50, para. 24.

165. Ibid., para. 26.

166. "Leaders to Meet After Mali Coup"; "Officers in Mali Claim Seizure of Power"; Moorhead, "Prisoners of Conscience."

167. Summary Records of the Third Committee, 50th meeting (32nd session), 17 November 1977, A/C.3/32/SR. 50, para. 74.

168. Korey, *The Curious Grapevine*, 92. Benin, along with Somalia and Cuba, played an important lobbying role for the USSR during the notorious 1975 "Zionism as Racism" resolution. See also Moynihan, "Big Red Lie."

169. Summary Records of the Third Committee, 22 November 1977, 54th meeting (32nd session), A/C. 3/32/SR. 54, para. 30.

170. Summary Records of the Third Committee, 68th meeting (32nd session), 5 December 1977, A/C. 3/32/SR. 68, para. 14. See also A/C. 3/32/SR. 52, para. 77.

171. Ibid., para. 15.

172. Summary Records of the Third Committee, 59th meeting (33rd session), 28 November 1978, A/C. 3/33/SR. 59, para. 12. See also (1979), A/C. 3/34/SR. 25, para. 10.

173. Summary Records of the Third Committee, 28th meeting (34th session), 26 October 1979, A/C. 3/34/SR. 28, para. 19.

174. Senegal had actually undergone a significant liberalization in 1976, with the introduction of two opposition parties. See Fatton, *The Making of a Liberal Democracy.*

175. See Summary Records of the Third Committee, 28th meeting (34th session), 26 October 1979, A/C. 3/34/SR. 28, paras 29–33 ; A/C. 3/34/SR. 33, paras 40–44. The speeches also functioned, in part, as justification for the Tanzanian intervention, but the sincerity of the sentiments, especially in the first address, seems beyond question. Prior to Amin's seizure of power, Uganda had been one of the few states to support the High Commissioner when it was discussed at the 1968 World Conference on Human Rights in Tehran.

176. Allen, *Days of Judgment,* passim.

177. Ambah, "Idi Amin, Brutal Former Dictator of Uganda, Dies at 80."

178. Summary Records of the Third Committee, 28th meeting (34th session), 26 October 1979, A/C. 3/34/SR. 28, para. 31

179. Ibid., para. 32.

180. Summary Records of the Third Committee, 33rd meeting (34th session), 1 November 1979, A/C. 3/34/SR. 33, para. 42. A further endorsement was given in 1980, see 59th meeting (35th session), 18 November 1980, A/C. 3/35/SR. 59, para. 37.

181. Ibid., para. 44.

182. Meredith, *The State of Africa,* 238.

183. The cultural relativist influence was unmistakable in both the Tunis Declaration (Africa) and the Bangkok Declaration (Asia). The Tunis Declaration cautioned that "no ready-made model can be prescribed at the universal level since the historical and cultural realities of each nation and the traditions, standards and values of each people cannot be disregarded." Article 5, Final Declaration of the Regional Meeting for Africa of the World Conference on Human Rights, 2–6 November 1992, A/CONF.157/AFRM/14, A/CONF.157/PC/57, 2; Final Declaration of the Regional Meeting for Asia of the World Conference on Human Rights, March 29–April 3 1993, A/CONF.157/ ASRM/8, A/CONF.157/PC/59, 5. See also the statements of various East Asian governments in the "Asian Values" debate of the 1990s: Kausikan, "Asia's Different Standard"; Barr, "Lee Kuan Yew and the 'Asian Values' Debate"; "Malaysian Premier Declares U.N. Rights Charter Out of Date."

184. Final Declaration of the Regional Meeting for Asia, 5.

185. See also Korey, *Curious Grapevine,* 273–306; Kent, *China, the United Nations, and Human Rights,* 170–93.

186. Interview with Haile Mengistu Mariam in Orizio, *Talk of the Devil,* 160–61.

187. Mayer, "Shifting Grounds for Challenging the Authority of International Human Rights Law."

188. See, for example, Afshari, *Human Rights in Iran.*

189. Interview with Sudanese leaders Al-Turabi and Al-Attabani, African Studies Center, University of Pennsylvania, 1994, http://www.africa.upenn.edu/Hornet/horn_sdn.html, accessed 11 January 2005.

190. Chinese Foreign Ministry, White Paper.

191. Korey, *Curious Grapevine*, 488.

192. This much has been conceded by one of the academic pioneers of cultural relativism, Adamantia Pollis; see "Cultural Relativism Revisited."

193. See Maluka, *The Myth of Constitutionalism in Pakistan*.

194. See, for example, his use of Islamism in explaining the structure of the new government. Mohammad Zia-ul-Haq, Introduction of Islamic Laws; President Addresses Shariah Seminar; President Ends Political Uncertainty; The President on Pakistan's Ideological Basis; President Reviews National Issues.

195. Weiss, "The Transformation of the Women's Movement in Pakistan." See also Weiss, *Islamic Reassertion in Pakistan*.

196. Weiss, "The Transformation of the Women's Movement in Pakistan." 101.

197. Ibid., 99.

198. This was clearly a primary impulse behind the anthropological discourse of cultural relativism, pioneered by Franz Boas, Ruth Benedict, and Melville Herskovits. See Benedict, *Patterns of Culture*; Caffrey, *Ruth Benedict: Stranger in This Land*; Modell, *Ruth Benedict, Patterns of a Life*; Boas, *The Mind of Primitive Man*.

Conclusion

Epigraph: Senghor, *On African Socialism*, 87.

1. Summary Records of the Commission on Human Rights, 129th meeting, 15 June 1949, E/CN.4/SR. 129.

2. Humphrey, *On the Edge of Greatness*, vol. 2, 288.

3. Summary Records of the Commission on Human Rights, 129th meeting, 15 June 1949, E/CN.4/SR. 129.

4. NSC memorandum 432nd meeting, in *FRUS*, vol. XIV.

5. NSC memorandum 465th meeting, in ibid.

6. Report on the Third Committee of the General Assembly (1952), 20.

7. Moynihan and Weaver, *A Dangerous Place*.

Bibliography

Archives and Document Collections

Charles Malik Collection, Library of Congress, Manuscript Reading Room, Washington, D.C.
National Archives and Records Administration (II), College Park, Maryland (NACP).
National Archives of Australia, Canberra.
Records of the International League for the Rights of Man (ILRM).
United Nations Archives, New York City.
Official Records of the General Assembly, 1947–1980.
Summary Records of the Commission on Human Rights, 1949–1974.
Summary Records of the Economic and Social Council, 1967–1970.
Summary Records of the International Conference on Human Rights, Tehran, April–May 1968.
Summary Records of the Sixth Committee, 1972.
Summary Records of the Social Committee of the Economic and Social Council, 1966–1967.
Summary Record of the Special Committee on the Policies of Apartheid of the Government of the Republic of South Africa, 1963.
Verbatim Records of the Special Committee on the Situation with Regard to the Implementation of the Declaration on the Granting of Independence to Colonial Countries and Peoples, 1970–1973.
Summary Records of the Sub-Commission on the Prevention of Discrimination and the Protection of Minorities, 1966–1970.
Summary Records of the Third Committee, 1948–1980.
Verbatim Records of the General Assembly Plenary, 1960.

United Nations Documents and Conventions

Alternative Approaches and Ways and Means Within the United Nations System for Improving the Effective Enjoyment of Human Rights and Fundamental Freedoms. GA Res. A/RES/32/130 (XXXII), 16 December 1977.
Division for the Advancement of Women. Declarations, Reservations, and Objections to CEDAW, 2005. http://www.un.org/womenwatch/daw/cedaw/reservations-country.htm, accessed 10 July 2005.
Office of the High Commissioner of Human Rights. Membership of the Commission on Human Rights, 2006. http://www.unhchr.ch/html/menu2/2/chrmem.htm, accessed 2 January 2006.

Convention on the Elimination of All Forms of Discrimination against Women. GA Res. 34/180, 18 December 1979.

Convention on the Political Rights of Women. GA Res. 640 (VII), 20 December 1952.

Declaration on the Elimination of Discrimination against Women. GA Res. 2263 (XXII), 7 November 1967.

Declaration on the Granting of Independence to Colonial Countries and Peoples. GA Res. 1514 (XV), 14 December 1960.

Declaration on the Inadmissibility of Intervention in the Domestic Affairs of States and the Protection of their Independence and Sovereignty. GA Res. 2131 (XX), 21 December 1965.

Declaration on Principles of International Law Concerning Friendly Relations and Co-Operation Among States in Accordance with the Charter of the United Nations. GA Res. 2625 (XXV), 24 October 1970.

International Covenant on Civil and Political Rights. GA Res. 2200A (XXI), 16 December 1966.

International Covenant on Economic, Social and Cultural Rights. GA Res. 2200A (XXI), 16 December 1966.

International Convention on the Elimination of All Forms of Racial Discrimination. GA Res.2106 (XX), 21 December 1965.

Principles Which Should Guide Members in Determining whether or not an Obligation Exists to Transmit the Information Called for Under Article 73(e) of the Charter. GA Res. 1541 (XV), 15 December 1960.

The Situation with Regard to the Implementation of the Declaration on the Granting of Independence to Colonial Countries and Peoples. GA Res. 1654 (XVI), 27 November 1961.

Status of Women in Private Law: Customs, Ancient Laws, and Practices Affecting the Human Dignity of Women. GA Res. 843 (IX), 17 December 1954.

Universal Declaration of Human Rights. GA Res. 217 (III), 10 December 1948.

ECOSOC. Procedure for Dealing with Communications Relating to Violations of Human Rights and Fundamental Freedoms. ECOSOC Res. 1503(XLVIII), 27 May 1970.

———. Violations of Human Rights and Fundamental Freedoms, Including Policies of Racial Discrimination and Segregation and of *Apartheid* in all Countries, With Particular Reference to Colonial and Other Dependent Countries and Territories. ECOSOC Res. 1235 (XLII), 6 June 1967.

UN Conference on Human Rights. Proclamation of Teheran, 13 May 1968. A/CONF. 32/41. Also in *American Journal of International Law* 63, no. 3 (1969): 674–77.

Other Documents

Final Declaration of the Regional Meeting for Africa of the World Conference on Human Rights, 2–6 November 1992. A/CONF.157/AFRM/14, A/CONF.157/PC/57.

Final Declaration of the Regional Meeting for Asia of the World Conference on Human Rights, 29 March–3 April 1993. A/CONF.157/ASRM/8, A/CONF.157/PC/59

Printed Sources

Abdul Rahman Pazhwak (Afghanistan) Elected President of the Twenty-First Session of the General Assembly. United Nations, New York, 2005, http://www.UN.org/ga/55/president/bio21.htm, accessed 14 December 2005.

Abdulgani, Roselan Hadji. *Bandung Spirit: Moving on the Tide of History*. Prapantja: Badan Penerbit, 1964.

Abdullah, Saiful Azhar. "UN Charter Review: Malaysia to Convince Friends." *New Straits Times*, 31 July 1997, 1.

Abel, Elie. "U.S. Forebodings Eased by the Trend in Bandung." *New York Times*, 23 April 1955, A1, A2.

Adams, Bert N. "Uganda Before, During, and After Amin." In *African Nationalism and Independence*, ed. Timothy K. Welliver. New York: Garland, 1993. 153–63.

Adelman, Kenneth. "The Recourse to Authenticity and Negritude in Zaire." *Journal of Modern African Studies* 13, no. 1 (1975): 134–39.

Afkhami, Mahnaz. "Women in Post-Revolutionary Iran: A Feminist Perspective." In *In the Eye of the Storm: Women in Post-Revolutionary Iran*, ed. Mahnaz Afkhami and Erika Friedl. London: I.B. Tauris, 1994. 5–18.

Afshar, Haleh, ed. *Women and Politics in the Third World*. Women and Politics. London: Routledge, 1996.

Afshari, Reza. "An Essay on Islamic Cultural Relativism in the Discourse of Human Rights." *Human Rights Quarterly* 16, no. 2 (1994): 235–76.

———. "On Historiography of Human Rights: Reflections on Paul Gordon Lauren's *The Evolution of International Human Rights: Visions Seen*." *Human Rights Quarterly* 29, no. 1 (2007): 1–67.

———. *Human Rights in Iran: The Abuse of Cultural Relativism*. Philadelphia: University of Pennsylvania Press, 2001.

"After Bandung." *New York Times*, 25 April 1955, A22.

Agi, Marc. *René Cassin, fantassin des Droits de l' homme*. Paris: Plon, 1979.

Alam, Asadollah. *The Shah and I*. Ed. Alinaghi Alikhani London: I.B. Tauris, 1991.

Alatas, Farid. *Democracy and Authoritarianism in Indonesia and Malaysia: The Rise of the Post-Colonial State*. New York: St. Martin's, 1997.

Alden, Robert. "Key Men at the Bandung Parley." *New York Times*, 24 April 1955, E5.

———. "Powell Bids U.S. Bar Colonialism." *New York Times*, 23 April 1955, A2.

Allen, Peter. *Days of Judgment: A Judge in Idi Amin' s Uganda*. London: William Kimber, 1987.

Al-Rasheed, Madawi. *A History of Saudi Arabia*. Cambridge: Cambridge University Press, 2002.

al-Sharqi, Amal. "The Emancipation of Iraqi Women." In *Iraq, the Contemporary State*, ed. Tim Niblock. New York: St. Martin's, 1982. 74–87.

Alston, Philip. *The United Nations and Human Rights: A Critical Appraisal*. Oxford: Oxford University Press, 1992.

———. "The UN's Human Rights Record: From San Francisco to Vienna and Beyond." *Human Rights Quarterly* 16, no. 2 (1994): 375–90.

Ambah, Faiza Saleh. "Idi Amin, Brutal Former Dictator of Uganda, Dies at 80." *Associated Press*, Jeddah, Saudi Arabia, 16 August 2003.

American Anthropological Association. "Statement on Human Rights." *American Anthropologist* 49 (1947).

Amnesty International. *Human Rights in Uganda: Report*. London: Amnesty International, 1978.

An-Na'im, Abdullahi Ahmed. *Human Rights Under African Constitutions: Realizing the Promise for Ourselves*. Philadelphia: University of Pennsylvania Press, 2003.

———. "Religious Minorities Under Islamic Law and the Limits of Cultural Relativism." *Human Rights Quarterly* 9, no. 1 (1987): 1–18.

Anabtawi, Samir. "The Afro-Asian States and the Hungarian Question." *International Organization* 17, no. 4 (1963): 872–900.

Anderson, Carol. *Eyes Off the Prize: The United Nations and the African American Struggle for Human Rights, 1944–1955*. Cambridge: Cambridge University Press, 2003.

Anderson, David. *Histories of the Hanged: Britain's Dirty War in Kenya and the End of Empire*. London: Weidenfeld & Nicolson, 2005.

Appadorai, Angadipuram. *The Domestic Roots of India's Foreign Policy, 1947–1972*. Delhi: Oxford University Press, 1981.

Appadurai, Arjun. *Essays in Indian Politics and Foreign Policy*. Delhi: Vikas, 1971.

"Appraising Bandung." *New York Times*, 24 April 1955, A10.

"Army Succeeds in Upper Volta Take-Over: Former President Speaks of Complete Harmony." *The Times*, 5 January 1966, 9.

Arzt, Donna E. "The Application of International Human Rights Law in Islamic States." *Human Rights Quarterly* 12, no. 2 (1990): 202–30.

Asante, Samuel K. B. "Towards the Future in Ghana." *African Affairs* 57, no. 226 (1958): 52–57.

Asian-African Conference. *Bandung, Indonesia, 18th–24th April 1955, Speeches and Communiqués*. Jakarta: Ministry of Information, Republic of Indonesia, May 1955.

———. *Asian-African Conference: Views and News*. Jakarta: National Committee for the Commemoration of the Thirtieth Anniversary of the Asian-African Conference, 1985.

"At the Asian-African Conference: The Setting and Some Key Figures." *New York Times*, 24 April 1955, A1.

Avery, Peter. "Iran: Cultural Crossroads for 2,500 Years." *UNESCO Courier* 24 (October 1971): 4–9.

Avirgan, Tony, and Martha Honey. *War in Uganda: The Legacy of Idi Amin*. Westport, Conn.: L. Hill, 1982.

Ayub Khan, Mohammed. *Friends Not Masters: A Political Autobiography*. London: Oxford University Press, 1967.

Baah, Richard Amoako. *Human Rights in Africa: The Conflict of Implementation*. Lanham, Md.: University Press of America, 2000.

Baker, D. W. *The Facts of the Bandung Conference: Selections of Conference Documents*. Sydney: Australia-China Society, 1955.

Ballinger, R. B. "UN Action on Human Rights in South Africa." In *The International Protection of Human Rights*, ed. Evan Luard. London: Thames & Hudson, 1967. 248–85.

Banton, Michael. *International Action Against Racial Discrimination*. London: Oxford University Press, 1996.

Barr, M. D. "Lee Kuan Yew and the 'Asian Values' Debate." *Asian Studies Review* 24, no. 3 (2000): 309–34.

Beck, Lois, and Guity Nashat. *Women in Iran from 1800 to the Islamic Republic*. Urbana: University of Illinois Press, 2004.

Beckett, Paul, and Crawford Young. *Dilemmas of Democracy in Nigeria*. Rochester: University of Rochester, 1997.

Bell, Daniel. *East Meets West: Human Rights and Democracy in East Asia*. Princeton, N.J.: Princeton University Press, 2000.

———. *Towards Illiberal Democracy in Pacific Asia*. Houndmills: Macmillan, 1995.

Benedict, Ruth. *Patterns of Culture*. Boston: Houghton Mifflin, 1989.

Berween, Mohamed. "International Bills of Human Rights: An Islamic Critique." *International Journal of Human Rights* 7, no. 4 (2003): 129–42.

Bielefeldt, Heiner. "'Western' Versus 'Islamic' Human Rights Conceptions?: A Critique of Cultural Essentialism in the Discussion on Human Rights." *Political Theory* 28, no. 1 (2000): 90–121.

Blasier, S. Cole. "Chile: A Communist Battleground." *Political Science Quarterly* 65, no. 3 (1950): 353–75.

Boas, Franz. *The Mind of Primitive Man*. New York: Macmillan, 1945.

Boekle, Henning. "Western States, the UN Commission on Human Rights, and the '1235 Procedure': The 'Question of Bias' Revisited." *Netherlands Quarterly of Human Rights* 13, no. 4 (1995): 367–402.

Bossuyt, Marc. *Guide to the travaux préparatoires of the International Covenant on Civil and Political Rights*. Dordrecht: Nijhoff, 1987.

Bourchier, David, and John Legge. *Democracy in Indonesia: 1950s and 1990s*. Clayton: Monash University, Centre for Southeast Asian Studies, 1994.

Boven, Theo C. van, and Hans Thoolen. *People Matter: Views on International Human Rights Policy*. Amsterdam: Meulenhoff, 1982.

Brady, Thomas F. "Nasser Is Backed by 99.9% of the Vote." *New York Times*, 4 May 1968, A15.

Bragança, Aquino de, and Immanuel Wallerstein. *The African Liberation Reader*. London: Zed Press, 1982.

Braillard, Philippe, and Mohammad Reza Djalili. *The Third World and International Relations*. London: Pinter, 1986.

Brookes, Edgar H. *Apartheid: A Documentary Study of Modern South Africa*. London: Routledge & Kegan Paul, 1969.

Buckley, William F. *United Nations Journal: A Delegate's Odyssey*. New York: Putnam, 1974.

Bunch, Charlotte. "Women's Rights as Human Rights: Toward a Re-Vision of Human Rights." *Human Rights Quarterly* 12, no. 4 (1990): 486–98.

Bunting, Brian Percy. *Moses Kotane, South African Revolutionary: A Political Biography*. London: Inkululeko Publications, 1975.

Burgess, Greg. "The Human Rights Dilemma in Anti-Nazi Protest: The Bernheim Petition, Minorities Protection, and the 1933 Sessions of the League of Nations." *CERC Working Paper Series* 2 (2002): 1–56.

Burke, Roland. "'The Compelling Dialogue of Freedom': Human Rights at the 1955 Bandung Conference." *Human Rights Quarterly* 28, no. 4 (November 2006): 947–65.

———. "From Individual Rights to National Development: The First UN International Conference on Human Rights, Tehran 1968." *Journal of World History* 19, no. 3 (September 2008): 275–96.

Burton, Antoinette, Augusto Espiritu, and Fanon Che Wilkins. "Introduction: The Fate of Nationalisms in the Age of Bandung." *Radical History Review* 2006, no. 95 (2006): 145–48.

Caffrey, Margaret M. *Ruth Benedict: Stranger in This Land*. Austin: University of Texas Press, 1989.

Carey, John. "Progress on Human Rights at the United Nations." *American Journal of International Law* 66, no. 1 (1972): 107–9.

———. *UN Protection of Civil and Political Rights*. Syracuse, N.Y.: Syracuse University Press, 1970.

———. "The United Nations Double Standard on Human Rights Complaints." *American Journal of International Law* 60, no. 4 (1966): 792–803.

Carey, John, and Thomas Franck. *The Legal Aspects of the United Nations Action in the Congo: Background Papers and Proceedings*. New York: Oceana, 1963.

Casper, Gretchen. *Fragile Democracies: The Legacies of Authoritarian Rule*. Pittsburgh: University of Pittsburgh Press, 1995.

Cassese, Antonio. *Human Rights in a Changing World*. Cambridge: Polity, 1990.

———. "The Self-Determination of Peoples." In *The International Bill of Rights: The Covenant on Civil and Political Rights*, ed. Louis Henkin. New York: Columbia University Press, 1981. 92–113.

———. *Self-Determination of Peoples: A Legal Reappraisal*. Hersch Lauterpacht Memorial Lecture Series. Cambridge: Cambridge University Press, 1995.

Celoza, Albert F. *Ferdinand Marcos and the Philippines: The Political Economy of Authoritarianism*. Westport, Conn.: Praeger, 1997.

Cerna, Christina M. "Universality of Human Rights and Cultural Diversity: Implementation of Human Rights in Difference Socio-Cultural Contexts." *Human Rights Quarterly* 16, no. 4 (1994): 740–52.

Chaliand, Gerard. *Revolution in the Third World: Myths and Prospects*. New York: Viking Press, 1977.

Chanock, Martin. *Law, Custom, and Social Order: The Colonial Experience in Malawi and Zambia*. Cambridge: Cambridge University Press, 1985.

Charlesworth, Hilary. "The Mid-Life Crisis of the Universal Declaration of Human Rights." *Washington and Lee Law Review* 55 (1998): 781–96.

"Chilean and Saudi Delegates Shout and Shove Each Other at U.N." *New York Times*, 4 October 1973, A2.

Chopra, Pran. *Contemporary Pakistan: New Aims and Images*: New Delhi: Vikas, 1983.

Christie, Pamela, and Colin Collins. "Bantu Education: Apartheid Ideology and Labour Reproduction." In *Apartheid and Education: The Education of Black South Africans*, ed. Peter Kallaway. Johannesburg: Ravan Press, 1984.

"Civil War Report Imminent in Laos." *The Times*, 18 August 1960, 8.

Clapham, Andrew. "Creating the High Commissioner for Human Rights: The Outside Story." *European Journal of International Law* 5 (1994): 556–68.

Clark, Roger Stenson. "Human Rights Strategies of the 1960s Within the United Nations: A Tribute to the Late Kamleshwar Das." *Human Rights Quarterly* 21, no. 2 (1999): 308–41.

———. *A United Nations High Commissioner for Human Rights*. The Hague: Nijhoff, 1972.

"Clashes in Upper Volta After Strikers Defy Ban." *The Times*, 4 January 1966, 7.

Cmiel, Kenneth. "Human Rights, Freedom of Information, and the Origins of Third World Solidarity." In *Truth Claims: Representation and Human Rights*, ed. Mark Bradley and Patrice Petro. New Brunswick, N.J.: Rutgers University Press, 2002. 107–30.

Cobbah, Josiah. "African Values and the Human Rights Debate: An African Perspective." *Human Rights Quarterly* 9, no. 3 (1987): 309–31.

Cohen, Ronald. "Human Rights and Cultural Relativism: The Need for a New Approach." *American Anthropologist* 91, no. 4 (1989): 1014–17.

Cook, Rebecca J. "Women's International Human Rights Law: The Way Forward." *Human Rights Quarterly* 15, no. 2 (1993): 230–61.

Cowan, Jane K., Richard Wilson, and Marie-Benedicte Dembour. *Culture and Rights: Anthropological Perspectives.* New York: Cambridge University Press, 2001.

"Coup in Laos." *The Times,* 23 August 1960, 9.

Cranston, Maurice. *What Are Human Rights?* London: Bodley Head, 1973.

Crowder, Michael. "Whose Dream Was It Anyway? Twenty-Five Years of African Independence." In *African Nationalism and Independence,* ed. Timothy K. Welliver. New York: Garland, 1993. 339–56.

Das, Kamleshwar. "Some Reflections on Implementing Human Rights." In *Human Rights: Thirty Years After the Universal Declaration: Commemorative Volume on the Occasion of the Thirtieth Anniversary of the Universal Declaration of Human Rights,* ed. B. G. Ramcharan. The Hague: Nijhoff, 1979. 131–57.

Davies, Richard O. *Defender of the Old Guard: John Bricker and American Politics.* Columbus: Ohio State University Press, 1993.

Dayal, Rajeshwar. *Mission for Hammarskjöld: The Congo Crisis.* Delhi: Oxford University Press, 1976.

Decalo, Samuel. *Psychoses of Power: African Personal Dictatorships.* Boulder, Colo.: Westview Press, 1989.

Desmond, Cosmas. *Persecution East and West: Human Rights, Political Prisoners and Amnesty.* Harmondsworth: Penguin, 1983.

Diamond, Larry Jay. *Class, Ethnicity and Democracy in Nigeria: The Failure of the First Republic.* Basingsoke: Macmillan, 1988.

"Dispute Delays UN Action." *New York Times,* 7 December 1971, A3.

Dixit, J. N. *India-Pakistan in War & Peace.* London: Routledge, 2002.

Documents of the Gatherings of Non-Aligned Countries, 1961–1978. Belgrade: Jugoslovenska stvarnost Medjunarodna politika, 1978.

Donnelly, Jack. *The Concept of Human Rights.* London: Croom Helm, 1985.

———. "Cultural Relativism and Universal Human Rights." *Human Rights Quarterly* 6, no. 4 (1984): 400–419.

———. "Human Rights at the United Nations 1955–85: The Question of Bias." *International Studies Quarterly* 32, no. 3 (1988): 275–303.

———. "Human Rights, Democracy, and Development." *Human Rights Quarterly* 21, no. 3 (1999): 608–32.

———. "The Human Rights Priorities of the UN: A Rejoinder to Alston." *Human Rights Quarterly* 37, no. 3 (1983): 547–50.

———. *International Human Rights.* 2nd ed. Boulder, Colo.: Westview Press, 1998.

———. "Recent Trends in UN Human Rights Activity: Description and Polemic." *International Organization* 35, no. 4 (1981): 633–55.

———. *Universal Human Rights in Theory and Practice.* 2nd ed. Ithaca, N.Y.: Cornell University Press, 2002.

Donnelly, Jack, and Rhoda E. Howard. *International Handbook of Human Rights.* New York: Greenwood Press, 1987.

Doty, Robert C. "Asian-African Talks Continue Bogged on Colonial Issue." *New York Times,* 23 April 1955, A1.

Dresch, Paul. *A History of Modern Yemen.* Cambridge: Cambridge University Press, 2000.

Du Bois, W. E. B. *Colour and Democracy: Colonies and Peace.* New York: Harcourt Brace, 1945.

Durdin, Tillman. "Bandung Meeting Asked to Assail Red Colonialism." *New York Times,* 22 April 1955, A1, A2.

———. "U.S. Finds Support Among Afro-Asians. Outspoken Defense of Our Policies Comes as Surprise at Bandung." *New York Times,* 25 April 1955, E5.

El-Ayouty, Yassin. "Africa's 'Burning Issues' and United Nations Action." *Issue: A Journal of Opinion* 2, no. 3 (1972): 44–48.

———. "Legitimization of National Liberation: The United Nations and Southern Africa." In *Africa and International Organization,* ed. Yassin El-Ayouty and Hugh C. Brooks. The Hague: Nijhoff, 1974. 209–29.

———. *The United Nations and Decolonisation: The Role of Afro-Asia.* The Hague: Nijhoff, 1971.

Elkins, Caroline. *Britain's Gulag: The Brutal End of Empire in Kenya.* London: Jonathan Cape, 2005.

"Emergency in Malaya Declared at an End." *The Times,* 1 August 1960, 5.

Emerson, Rupert. "Colonialism, Political Development, and the UN." *International Organization* 19, no. 3 (1965): 484–503.

———. "The Fate of Human Rights in the Third World." *World Politics* 27, no. 2 (1975): 201–26.

———. *From Empire to Nation: The Rise of Self-Assertion of Asian and African Peoples.* Boston: Beacon Press, 1962.

Engerman, David. *Staging Growth: Modernization, Development, and the Global Cold War.* Culture, Politics, and the Cold War. Amherst: University of Massachusetts Press, 2003.

Englehart, Neil A. "Rights and Culture in the Asian Values Argument: The Rise and Fall of Confucian Ethics in Singapore." *Human Rights Quarterly* 22, no. 2 (2000): 548–68.

Engo, Paul Bamela. "Peaceful Co-Existence and Friendly Relations Among States: The African Contribution to the Progressive Development of Principles of International Law." In *Africa and International Organization,* ed. Yassin El-Ayouty and Hugh C. Brooks. The Hague: Nijhoff, 1974. 31–47.

Espiritu, Augusto Fauni. *Five Faces of Exile: The Nation and Filipino American Intellectuals.* Stanford, Calif.: Stanford University Press, 2005.

———. "'To Carry Water on Both Shoulders': Carlos P. Romulo, American Empire, and the Meaning of Bandung." *Radical History Review* 95 (2006): 173-90.

Evans, Tony. "International Human Rights Law as Power/Knowledge." *Human Rights Quarterly* 27 (2005): 1046–68.

———. "Introduction: Power, Hegemony and the Universalization of Human Rights." In *Human Rights Fifty Years On: A Reappraisal,* ed. Tony Evans. Manchester: Manchester University Press, 1998. 2-23.

———. *The Politics of Human Rights: A Global Perspective.* Human Security in the Global Economy. Sterling, Va.: Pluto Press, 2001.

Ewans, Martin. *Afghanistan: A New History.* 2nd ed. London: Routledge Curzon, 2002.

"Excerpts from Remarks Pro and Con on Zionism." *New York Times,* 12 November 1975, A16.

Eze, Osita C., and Nigerian Institute of International Affairs. *Human Rights in Africa: Some Selected Problems.* Lagos: Nigerian Institute of International Affairs with Macmillan Nigeria, 1984.

Fall, Bernard. "The International Relations of Laos." *Pacific Affairs* 30, no. 1 (1957): 22-34.

Farer, Tom J. "The UN and Human Rights: More Than a Whimper, Less Than a Roar." In *United Nations, Divided World: The UN's Roles in International Relations,* ed. Adam Roberts and Benedict Kingsbury. Oxford: Oxford University Press, 1993. 95–138.

Farouk-Sluglett, Marion. "Liberation or Repression? Pan-Arab Nationalism and the Women's Liberation Movement in Iraq." In *Iraq: Power and Society,* ed. Derek Hopwood, Habib Ishow, and Thomas Koszinowski. Reading: Ithaca Press for St. Antony's College Oxford, 1993. 51–74.

Fatton, Robert. *The Making of a Liberal Democracy: Senegal's Passive Revolution, 1975–1985.* Boulder, Colo.: Lynn Rienner, 1987.

Fegley, Randall. "The U.N. Human Rights Commission: The Equatorial Guinea Case." *Human Rights Quarterly* 3, no. 1 (1981): 34–47.

Feith, Herbert. *The Decline of Constitutional Democracy in Indonesia.* Ithaca, N.Y.: Cornell University Press, 1962.

Feron, James. "U.N. Urges Steps to Free Colonies." *New York Times,* 15 December 1960, A1, A15.

Ferguson, J. A. "The Third World." In *Foreign Policy and Human Rights: Issues and Responses,* ed. R. J. Vincent. Cambridge: Cambridge University Press, 1986. 203–26.

Ferguson, James. *Papa Doc, Baby Doc: Haiti and the Duvaliers.* New York: Blackwell, 1988.

"A Fighting Irishman." *Time,* 26 January 1976.

"Fighting Reported near Vientiane." *The Times,* 9 December 1960, 12.

Finger, Seymour M. *American Ambassadors at the UN: People, Politics, and Bureaucracy in Making Foreign Policy.* New York: Holmes & Meier, 1988.

———. "A New Approach to Colonial Problems at the United Nations." *International Organization* 26, no. 1 (1972): 143–53.

Fisher, Humphrey J. "Elections and Coups in Sierra Leone, 1967." *Journal of Modern African Studies* 7, no. 4 (1969): 611–36.

Foltz, William J. "Developmentalism, Revolution, and Freedom in the Arab East: The Cases of Egypt, Syria, and Iraq." In *The Idea of Freedom in Asia and Africa,* ed. Robert H. Taylor. Stanford, Calif.: Stanford University Press, 2002. 62–96.

Forbis, William H. *Fall of the Peacock Throne: The Story of Iran.* New York: Harper & Row, 1980.

Forsythe, David P. "The United Nations and Human Rights, 1945–1985." *Political Science Quarterly* 100, no. 2 (1985): 249–69.

Franck, Thomas. "Of Gnats and Camels: Is There a Double Standard at the United Nations?" *American Journal of International Law* 78, no. 4 (1984): 811–33.

———. *Nation Against Nation: What Happened to the U.N. Dream and What the U.S. Can Do About It.* New York: Oxford University Press, 1985.

———. "The Emerging Right to Democratic Governance." *American Journal of International Law* 86, no. 1 (1992): 46–91.

———. "Democracy as a Human Right." In *Human Rights: An Agenda for the Next Century,* ed. Louis Henkin and John Lawrence Hargrove. Washington, D.C.: American Society of International Law, 1994. 73–101.

Fraser, Arvonne S., and Irene Tinker. *Developing Power: How Women Transformed International Development.* New York: Feminist Press at the City University of New York, 2004.

Fraser, Cary. "An American Dilemma: Race and Realpolitik in the American Response to the Bandung Conference, 1955." In *Window on Freedom: Race, Civil Rights and Foreign Affairs, 1945–1988*, ed. Brenda Gayle Plummer. Chapel Hill: University of North Carolina Press, 2003.

Freeman, Marsha A., and Arvonne S Fraser. "Women's Human Rights: Making the Theory a Reality." In *Human Rights: An Agenda for the Next Century*, ed. Louis Henkin and John Lawrence Hargrove. Washington, D.C.: American Society of International Law, 1994. 103–35.

Freeman, Michael. *Human Rights: An Interdisciplinary Approach*. Key Concepts. Cambridge: Blackwell, 2002.

———. "Human Rights and Real Cultures: Towards a Dialogue on 'Asian Values'." *Netherlands Quarterly of Human Rights* 16, no. 1 (1998): 25–39.

———."The Philosophical Foundations of Human Rights." *Human Rights Quarterly* 16, no. 3 (1994): 491–514.

———. "Putting Law in Its Place: An Interdisciplinary Evaluation of National Amnesty Laws." In *The Legalization of Human Rights: Multidisciplinary Perspectives on Human Rights and Human Rights Law*, ed. Saladin Meckled-Garca and Baak Cali. New York: Routledge, 2006. 49–64.

Friendly, Alfred, Jr. "Boycott Cuts Vote in Dahomey: Military Rulers' Plan to Shift to Civilian Regime Balked." *New York Times*, 7 May 1968, A10.

Galtung, Johan. *Human Rights in Another Key*. Cambridge: Polity Press, 1994.

———. "The Third World and Human Rights in the Post-1989 World Order." In *Human Rights Fifty Years On: A Reappraisal*, ed. Tony Evans. Manchester: Manchester University Press, 1998. 211–31.

Ganji, Manouchehr. *Defying the Iranian Revolution: From a Minister to the Shah to a Leader of Resistance*. Westport, Conn.: Praeger, 2002.

———. *The Realization of Economic, Social, and Cultural Rights: Problems, Policies, Progress*. E/CN. 4/1108/Rev. 1, E/CN. 4/1131/Rev. 1. New York: United Nations, 1975.

"General Mobutu Takes Over." *The Times*, 26 November 1965, 12.

"The General Picks a New Cabinet." *Times*, 20 January 1966, 8.

Ghoshal, Baladas. *Indonesian Politics 1955–59: The Emergence of Guided Democracy*. New Dehli: Bagchi, 1981.

Gillette, Michael L. "Morris Abram Oral History Interview." Ed. Morris Abram. Austin, Tex.: Lyndon Baines Johnson Library, 1984.

Gilman, Nils. *Mandarins of the Future: Modernization Theory in Cold War America*. Baltimore: Johns Hopkins University Press, 2003.

Glendon, Mary Ann. "The Forgotten Crucible: The Latin American Influence on the Universal Human Rights Idea." *Harvard Human Rights Journal* 16 (2003): 27–39.

———. "Foundations of Human Rights: The Unfinished Business." *American Journal of Jurisprudence* 44 (1999): 1–14.

———. *A World Made New: Eleanor Roosevelt and the Universal Declaration of Human Rights*. New York: Random House, 2001.

Glevin, James L. "Ideas of Freedom in Modern India." In *The Idea of Freedom in Asia and Africa*, ed. Robert H. Taylor. Stanford, Calif.: Stanford University Press, 2002. 97–142.

Gold, Dore. *Tower of Babble: How the United Nations Has Fueled Global Chaos*. New York: Crown Forum, 2004.

Graham, David E. "The 1974 Diplomatic Conference on the Law of War: A Victory for Political Causes and a Return to the 'Just War' Concept of the Eleventh Century." *Washington and Lee Law Review* 32 (1975): 25–63.

Gregor, A. James. "African Socialism, Socialism and Fascism: An Appraisal." *Review of Politics* 29, no. 3 (1967): 324–53.

———. *Italian Fascism and Developmental Dictatorship.* Princeton, N.J.: Princeton University Press, 1979.

Gros Espiell, Héctor. "The Evolving Concept of Human Rights: Western, Socialist and Third World Approaches." In *Human Rights: Thirty Years After the Universal Declaration: Commemorative Volume on the Occasion of the Thirtieth Anniversary of the Universal Declaration of Human Rights,* ed. B. G. Ramcharan. The Hague: Nijhoff, 1979. 41–65.

———. "The Right to Development as a Human Right." *Texas International Law Journal* 16 (1981): 189–205.

Guest, Iain. *Behind the Disappearances: Argentina's Dirty War Against Human Rights and the United Nations.* Philadelphia: University of Pennsylvania Press, 1990.

Haas, Ernst B. "The Attempt to Terminate Colonialism: Acceptance of the United Nations Trusteeship System." In *The United Nations Political System,* ed. David A. Kay. New York: Wiley, 1967. 281–301.

Hamalengwa, Munyonzew, C. Flinterman, and E. V. O. Dankwa. *The International Law of Human Rights in Africa: Basic Documents and Annotated Bibliography.* Boston: Nijhoff, 1988.

Hannum, Hurst. *Autonomy, Sovereignty, and Self-Determination: The Accommodation of Conflicting Rights.* Philadelphia: University of Pennsylvania Press, 1990.

———. "The Right to Self-Determination in the Twenty-First Century." *Washington and Lee Law Review* 55 (1998): 773–80.

Haragopal, G., and K. Balagopal. "Africa: Democratic Theory and Democratic Struggles." In *People's Rights: Social Movements and the State in the Third World,* ed. Manoranjan Mohanty, Partha N. Mukherji, and Olle Trnquist, 353–71. Thousand Oaks, Calif.: Sage, 1997. 353–71.

Harris-Short, Sonia. "International Human Rights Law: Imperialist, Inept and Ineffective? Cultural Relativism and the UN Convention on the Rights of the Child." *Human Rights Quarterly* 25, no. 2 (2003): 130–81.

Hassan, Faud, and Centre for the Study of Asian-African and Developing Countries. *Collected Documents from the Asian-African Conference: April 18–24, 1955.* Jakarta: Agency for Research and Development, Department of Foreign Affairs, 1983.

Haynes, Jeffrey. "Human Rights." In *Third World Politics: A Concise Introduction,* ed. Jeffrey Haynes. Cambridge, Mass.: Blackwell, 1996. 119–45.

Heffernan, Liz. "A Comparative View of Individual Petition Procedures Under the European Convention on Human Rights and the International Covenant on Civil and Political Rights." *Human Rights Quarterly* 19, no. 1 (1997): 78–112.

Henkin, Louis. *The Age of Rights.* New York: Columbia University Press, 1990.

———. "Human Rights from Dumbarton Oaks." In *The Dumbarton Oaks Conversations and the United Nations, 1944–1994,* ed. Angeliki E. Laiou and Ernest R. May. Washington, D.C.: Dumbarton Oaks Research Library and Collection, distributed by Harvard University Press, 1998. 97–104.

———. *The International Bill of Rights: The Covenant on Civil and Political Rights.* New York: Columbia University Press, 1981.

———. "The United Nations and Human Rights." *International Organization* 19, no. 3 (1965): 504–17.

————. "The United Nations and Its Supporters: A Self-Examination." In *The United Nations Political System*, ed. David A. Kay. New York: Wiley, 1967. 365–89.

Hoare, Sir Samuel. "The UN Commission on Human Rights." In *The International Protection of Human Rights*, ed. Evan Luard. London: Thames & Hudson, 1967. 59–98.

Hosken, Fran P. "Toward a Definition of Women's Human Rights." *Human Rights Quarterly* 3, no. 2 (1981): 1–10.

Hovet, Thomas, Jr. *Africa in the United Nations*. Evanston, Ill.: Northwestern University Press, 1963.

————. "Effect of the African Group of States on the Behaviour of the United Nations." In *Africa and International Organization*, ed. Yassin El-Ayouty and Hugh C. Brooks. The Hague: Nijhoff, 1974. 11–17.

Hoveyda, Fereydoun. "Democracy and Islam." *American Foreign Policy Interests* 26 (2004).

————. *The Fall of the Shah*. London: Weidenfeld & Nicolson, 1980.

————. "Not Without the United Nations." *American Foreign Policy Interests* 25 (2003): 169–75.

————. Signed, Sealed & Delivered. 12 August, 2005. http://www.iranian.com/FereydounHoveyda/2005/August/UDHR/, accessed 10 November 2005.

————. "The Universal Declaration and 50 Years of Human Rights." *Transnational Law and Contemporary Problems* 8 (1998): 430.

Howard, Rhoda E. "Cultural Absolutism and the Nostalgia for Community." *Human Rights Quarterly* 15, no. 2 (1993): 315–38.

————. "Evaluating Human Rights in Africa: Some Problems of Implicit Comparisons." *Human Rights Quarterly* 6, no. 2 (1984): 160–79.

————. "The Full-Belly Thesis: Should Economic Rights Take Priority over Civil and Political Rights? Evidence from Sub-Saharan Africa." *Human Rights Quarterly* 5, no. 4 (1983): 467–90.

————. "Human Rights and Personal Law: Women in Sub-Saharan Africa." *Issue: A Journal of Opinion* 12, no. 1–2 (1982): 45–52.

————. "Occidentalism, Human Rights, and the Obligations of Western Scholars." *Canadian Journal of African Studies* 29, no. 1 (1995): 110–26.

Huband, Mark. *Warriors of the Prophet: The Struggle for Islam*. Boulder, Colo.: Westview Press, 1999.

Humphrey, John P. *Human Rights & the United Nations: A Great Adventure*. Dobbs Ferry, N.Y.: Transnational Publishers, 1984.

————. "The UN Charter and the Universal Declaration of Human Rights." In *The International Protection of Human Rights*, ed. Evan Luard. London: Thames & Hudson, 1967. 39–58.

————. "The United Nations Sub-Commission on the Prevention of Discrimination and the Protection of Minorities." *American Journal of International Law* 62, no. 4 (1968): 869–88.

————. "The Universal Declaration of Human Rights: Its History, Impact and Juridical Character." In *Human Rights: Thirty Years After the Universal Declaration: Commemorative Volume on the Occasion of the Thirtieth Anniversary of the Universal Declaration of Human Rights*, ed. B. G. Ramcharan. The Hague: Nijhoff, 1979. 21–37.

Humphrey, John P., A. J. Hobbins, and Louisa Piatti. *On the Edge of Greatness: The Diaries of John Humphrey, First Director of the United Nations Division of Human Rights*. Montreal: McGill University Libraries, 1994.

Huntington, Samuel P. *Political Order in Changing Societies.* New Haven, Conn.: Yale University Press, 1968.

Hussein, Aziza. "Crossroads for Women at the UN." In *Developing Power: How Women Transformed International Development,* ed. Arvonne S. Fraser and Irene Tinker. New York: Feminist Press at the City University of New York, 2004. 4–13.

———. "The Role of Women in Social Reform in Egypt." *Middle East Journal* 7, no. 4 (1954): 440–50.

Ibawoh, Bonny. "Cultural Relativism and Human Rights: Reconsidering the Africanist Discourse." *Netherlands Quarterly of Human Rights* 19, no. 1 (2001): 43–62.

Ingham, Kenneth. *Obote: A Political Biography.* New York: Routledge, 1994.

Ishay, Micheline. *The History of Human Rights: From Ancient Times to the Globalization Era.* Berkeley: University of California Press, 2003.

Jackson, Richard L. *The Non-Aligned, the UN, and the Superpowers.* New York: Praeger, 1983.

Jacobson, Harold Karan. "The United Nations and Colonialism: A Tentative Appraisal." In *The United Nations Political System,* ed. David A. Kay. New York: Wiley, 1967. 302–26.

"Jamil the Irrepressible." *Time,* 13 December 1971, 20–21.

Jain, Devaki. *Women, Development, and the UN: A Sixty-Year Quest for Equality and Justice.* United Nations Intellectual History Project. Bloomington: Indiana University Press, 2005.

Jansen, Godfrey H. *Afro-Asia and Non-Alignment.* London: Faber, 1966.

Jayawardena, Kumari. *Feminism and Nationalism in the Third World.* Third World Books. London: Zed Books, 1986.

Johnson, R. W. "Sekou Toure and the Guinean Revolution." In *African Nationalism and Independence,* ed. Timothy K. Welliver. New York: Garland, 1993. 350–65.

Kahin, George McTurnan. *The Asian-African Conference. Bandung, Indonesia, April 1955.* Ithaca, N.Y.: Cornell University Press, 1956.

Kapur, Ratna. "Revisioning the Role of Law in Women's Human Rights Struggles." In *The Legalization of Human Rights: Multidisciplinary Perspectives on Human Rights and Human Rights Law,* ed. Saladin Meckled-Garca and Baak Cali. New York: Routledge, 2006. 101–16.

Kausikan, Bilahari. "Asian Values and Human Rights: An Alternative View." In *Democracy in East Asia,* ed. Larry Jay Diamond and Marc F. Plattner. Baltimore: Johns Hopkins University Press, 1998. 17–27.

———. "Asia's Different Standard." *Foreign Policy* 92 (Fall 1993): 24–31

Kay, David A. "The Impact of African States on the United Nations." *International Organization* 23, no. 1 (1969): 20–47.

———. "The Politics of Decolonisation: The New Nations and the United Nations Political Process." *International Organization* 21, no. 4 (1967): 786–811.

———. *The United Nations Political System.* New York: Wiley, 1967.

Keddie, Nikki R., and Richard Yann. *Roots of Revolution: An Interpretive History of Modern Iran.* New Haven, Conn.: Yale University Press, 1981.

Kent, Ann E. *China, the United Nations, and Human Rights: The Limits of Compliance.* Philadelphia: University of Pennsylvania Press, 1999.

Kia, Mana. "Negotiating Women' s Rights: Activism, Class, and Modernization in Pahlavi Iran." *Comparative Studies of South Asia, Africa and the Middle East* 25, no. 1 (2005): 227–44.

Kimche, David. *The Afro-Asian Movement; Ideology and Foreign Policy of the Third World.* New York: Halsted Press, 1973.

Kipper, Judith, and Harold H. Saunders. *The Middle East in Global Perspective.* Boulder, Colo.: Westview Press, 1991.

Korany, Bahgat. "Coming of Age against Global Odds: The Third World and Its Collective Decision-Making." In *How Foreign Policy Decisions Are Made in the Third World. A Comparative Analysis,* ed. Bahgat Korany. Boulder, Colo.: Westview Press, 1986. 1–38.

Korey, William. *NGOs and the Universal Declaration of Human Rights: A Curious Grapevine.* New York: St. Martin's 1998.

———. "The U.N.'s Double Standard on Human Rights." *Washington Post,* 22 May 1977, 1.

Kotelawala, John Lionel. *An Asian Prime Minister's Story.* London: Harrap, 1956.

Lackner, Helen. *A House Built on Sand: A Political Economy of Saudi Arabia.* London: Ithaca Press, 1978.

"Laos Still in Political Turmoil." *The Times,* 2 September 1960, 8.

"Laos Threat of Civil War: Cabinet Opposed by Rival Prince, Martial Law Imposed." *The Times,* 12 September 1960, 10.

Latham, Michael. *Modernization as Ideology: American Social Science and "Nation-Building" in the Kennedy Era.* Chapel Hill: University of North Carolina Press, 2000.

Lauren, Paul Gordon. *The Evolution of International Human Rights: Visions Seen.* 2nd ed. Philadelphia: University of Pennsylvania Press, 2003.

———. *Power and Prejudice: The Politics and Diplomacy of Racial Discrimination.* 2nd ed. Boulder, Colo.: Westview Press, 1996.

"Leader of the Coup Named as President of Dahomey." *The Times,* 28 October 1972, 7.

"Leaders to Meet After Mali Coup." *The Times,* 22 November 1968, 7.

Lee Kuan Yew. *From Third World to First: The Singapore Story, 1965–2000.* New York: HarperCollins, 2000.

Legge, J. D. "Indonesia Since Independence." In Legge, *Indonesia,* 2nd ed. Sydney: Prentice-Hall, 1977. 146–76.

———, ed. *Sukarno: A Political Biography.* Sydney: Allen and Unwin, 1972.

Legum, Colin. *Pan-Africanism: A Short Political Guide.* London: Pall Mall Press, 1962.

———. "The Romantic Period, 1939–1970." In *Africa Since Independence,* ed. Colin Legum,. Bloomington: Indiana University Press, 1999. 1–29.

Leith-Ross, Sylvia, and Michael Crowder. *Stepping-Stones: Memoirs of Colonial Nigeria 1907–1960.* London: Owen, 1983.

Lewis, Anthony. "A Top Tory Fears Black Dominance: Powell Seeks Measures to Help Repatriate Britain's Colored Immigrants." *New York Times,* 20 April 1968, A1.

Lewis, Norman. "Human Rights, Law and Democracy in an Unfree World." In *Human Rights Fifty Years On: A Reappraisal,* ed. Tony Evans. Manchester: Manchester University Press, 1998. 77–104.

Lillich, Richard B. "The U.N. and Human Rights Complaints: U Thant as Strict Constructionist." *American Journal of International Law* 64, no. 3 (1970): 610–14.

Lindholt, Lone. *Questioning the Universality of Human Rights: The African Charter on Human and Peoples' Rights in Botswana, Malawi, and Mozambique.* Aldershot: Ashgate, 1997.

Louis, Pierre A. "'Obscure Despotism' and Human Rights in Togo." *Columbia Human Rights Law Review* 23 (1991–1992): 133–65.

Luard, Evan. "Promotion of Human Rights by UN Political Bodies." In *The International Protection of Human Rights*, ed. Evan Luard. London: Thames & Hudson, 1967. 132–59.

Lubis, T. Mulya, Gramedia Pustaka Utama PT., and Society for Political and Economic Studies (Lembaga Penelitian Pendidikan dan Penerangan Ekonomi dan Sosial). *In Search of Human Rights: Legal-Political Dilemmas of Indonesia's New Order, 1966–1990.* Jakarta: PT Gramedia Pustaka Utama; SPES Foundation, 1993.

Macdonald, R. St. J. "The United Nations High Commissioner for Human Rights." *Canadian Yearbook of Internation al Law* (1967): 84–117.

MacFarlane, S. Neil. *Superpower Rivalry & 3rd World Radicalism: The Idea of National Liberation.* London: Croom Helm, 1985.

Mackie, Jamie. *Bandung 1955: Non-Alignment and Afro-Asian Solidarity.* Singapore: Didier Millet, 2005.

"Mahathir Warns of Superpowers' Scare-Tactics on Human Rights Review." *Agence France Presse,* 31 July 1997.

Makiya, Kanan. *Republic of Fear: The Politics of Modern Iraq.* Berkeley: University of California Press, 1989.

"Malaysian Premier Declares U.N. Rights Charter Out of Date," *Deutsche Presse-Agentur,* 28 July 1997.

"Mali Embassy Seized." *The Times,* 25 March 1980, 6.

Malik, Charles. *The Problem of Coexistence: Mars Lectures, 1955.* Evanston, Ill.: Northwestern University Press.

Malley, Robert. *The Call from Algeria: Third Worldism, Revolution, and the Turn to Islam.* Berkeley: University of California Press, 1996.

Maluka, Zulfikar Khalid. *The Myth of Constitutionalism in Pakistan.* New York: Oxford University Press, 1995.

Mamdani, Mahmood. "Africa: Democratic Theory and Democratic Struggles." In *People's Rights: Social Movements and the State in the Third World*, ed. Manoranjan Mohanty, Partha N. Mukherji and Olle Trnquist. Thousand Oaks, Calif.: Sage, 1997. 83–97.

———. *Citizen and Subject: Contemporary Africa and the Legacy of Late Colonialism.* Princeton, N.J.: Princeton University Press, 1996.

Marks, Stephen P. "From the 'Single Confused Page' to the 'Decalogue for Six Billion Persons': The Roots of the Universal Declaration of Human Rights in the French Revolution." *Human Rights Quarterly* 20, no. 3 (1998): 459–514.

Marr, Phebe. *The Modern History of Iraq.* 2nd ed. Boulder, Colo.: Westview Press, 2004.

Martin, David. *General Amin.* London: Faber, 1974.

Mayer, Ann Elizabeth. "Shifting Grounds for Challenging the Authority of International Human Rights Law: Religion as a Malleable and Politicized Pretext for Governmental Noncompliance with Human Rights." Paper presented at 10th Annual Conference on The Individual vs. the State: Universalism in Law: Human Rights and the Rule of Law, Central European University, Budapest, 14–16 June 2002.

Mazrui, Ali A. *The African Condition: A Political Diagnosis.* London: Heinemann Educational, 1980.

———. *On Heroes and Uhuru-Worship: Essays on Independent Africa.* London: Longmans, 1967.

————. "The Social Origins of Ugandan Presidents: From King to Peasant Warrior." In *African Nationalism and Independence*, ed. Timothy K. Welliver. New York: Garland, 1993. 131–51.

————. *Towards a Pax Africana: A Study of Ideology and Ambition, Nature of Human Society Series*. London: Weidenfeld & Nicolson, 1967.

Mazrui, Ali A., and Australian Institute of International Affairs. *Africa, the West and the World; Politics in Modern Africa: Four Systems of Values*. Dyason Memorial Lectures, 1972. Melbourne: Australian Institute of International Affairs, 1972.

Mazrui, Ali A., and Alamin M. Mazrui. *The Power of Babel: Language & Governance in the African Experience*. Chicago: University of Chicago Press, 1998.

Mazrui, Ali A., and Hasu H. Patel. *Africa in World Affairs: The Next Thirty Years*. New York: Third Press, 1973.

Mboya, Tom. *The Challenge of Nationhood: A Collection of Speeches and Writings*. New York: Praeger, 1970.

McGaffey, David C. "Policy and Practice: Human Rights in the Shah's Iran." In *The Diplomacy of Human Rights*, ed. David D. Newsom. Lanham, Md.: University Press of America; Institute for the Study of Diplomacy, 1986. 69–79.

McGoldrick, Dominic. "The Origins, Drafting and Significance of the International Covenant on Civil and Political Rights." In *The Human Rights Committee: Its Role in the Development of the International Covenant on Civil and Political Rights*, ed. Dominic McGoldrick. Oxford: Clarendon, 1991. 3–43.

Meister, Irene W. "The Bandung Conference: An Appraisal." In *The Idea of Colonialism*, ed. Robert Strausz-Hup and Harry W. Hazard. New York: Praeger, 1958. 232–70.

Meredith, Martin. *The First Dance of Freedom: Black Africa in the Postwar Era*. London: Hamilton, 1984.

————. *The State of Africa: A History of Fifty Years of Independence*. New York; London: Free Press, 2005.

Mertus, Julie. *The United Nations and Human Rights: A Guide for a New Era*. Global Institutions Series. New York: Routledge, 2005.

Messer, Ellen. "Anthropology and Human Rights." *Annual Review of Anthropology* 22 (1993): 221–49.

Metz, Steven. "American Attitudes Toward Decolonisation in Africa." *Political Science Quarterly* 99, no. 3 (1984): 515–33.

Metzl, Jamie Frederic. *Western Responses to Human Rights Abuses in Cambodia, 1975–80*. New York: St. Martin's Press in association with St. Antony's College Oxford, 1996.

Meyer, Armin. *Quiet Diplomacy: From Cairo to Tokyo in the Twilight of Imperialism*. New York: iUniverse, 2003.

Middleton, Drew. "Thant Issues Plea on Race Conflict." *New York Times*, 23 April 1968, A15.

Miller, J. D. B. *The Politics of the Third World*. New York: Oxford University Press, 1966.

Milton-Edwards, Beverley. *Islamic Fundamentalism Since 1945*. New York: Routledge, 2005.

Mittelman, James H. "Collective Decolonisation and the U.N. Committee of 24." *Journal of Modern African Studies* 14, no. 1 (1976): 41–64.

Moaddel, Mansoor. *Islamic Modernism, Nationalism, and Fundamentalism: Episode and Discourse*. Chicago: University of Chicago Press, 2005.

Modell, Judith Schachter. *Ruth Benedict, Patterns of a Life*. Philadelphia: University of Pennsylvania Press, 1983.

Möller, Jakob Th. "Petitioning the United Nations." *Universal Human Rights* 1, no. 4 (1979): 57–72.

Moorhead, Caroline. "Prisoners of Conscience: Urbain Sossouhounto." *The Times*, 17 August 1981, 6.

Moraes, F. R. *Jawaharlal Nehru: A Biography*. New York: Macmillan, 1956.

Morphet, Sally. "Article 1 of the Human Rights Covenants: Its Development and Current Significance." In *Human Rights and Foreign Policy: Principles and Practice*, ed. Dilys M. Hill. Houndmills: Macmillan with Centre for International Policy Studies, University of Southampton, 1989.

Morsink, Johannes. *The Universal Declaration of Human Rights: Origins, Drafting and Intent*. Philadelphia: University of Pennsylvania Press, 1999.

———. "Women's Rights in the Universal Declaration." *Human Rights Quarterly* 13, no. 2 (1991): 229–56.

Mortimer, Robert A. *The Third World Coalition in International Politics*. 2nd ed. Boulder, Colo.: Westview Press, 1984.

Moskowitz, Moses. *Human Rights and World Order: The Struggle for Human Rights in the United Nations*. London: Stevens and Sons, 1959.

———. "Implementing Human Rights; Present Status and Future Prospects." In *Human Rights: Thirty Years After the Universal Declaration: Commemorative Volume on the Occasion of the Thirtieth Anniversary of the Universal Declaration of Human Rights*, ed. B. G. Ramcharan. The Hague: Nijhoff, 1979. 109–30.

———. *International Concern with Human Rights*. Dobbs Ferry, N.Y.: Oceana, 1974.

Moynihan, Daniel P. "The Politics of Human Rights." *Commentary* 64, no. 2 (1977): 19–26.

———. "The United States in Opposition." *Commentary* 59, no. 3 (1975): 31–44.

———. "Big Red Lie: It Was the Soviets, Not the Arabs, Who Came up with 'Zionism Is Racism.'" *Washington Post*, 29 September 1991, C7.

Moynihan, Daniel P., and Suzanne Weaver. *A Dangerous Place*. London: Secker & Warburg, 1979.

"Mr. Macmillan's Appeal to South Africans." *The Times*, 4 February 1960, 15.

Mulgan, R. G. "The Theory of Human Rights." In *Essays on Human Rights*, ed. Kenneth James Keith. Wellington: Sweet & Maxwell, 1968. 13–29.

Mullerson, Rein. "Universal Human Rights in a Multicultural World." In *The Dumbarton Oaks Conversations and the United Nations, 1944–1994*, ed. Angeliki E. Laiou and Ernest R. May. Washington, D.C.: Dumbarton Oaks Research Library and Collection; distributed by Harvard University Press, 1998. 111–29.

Mumtaz, Khawar, and Farida Shaheed. *Women of Pakistan: Two Steps Forward, One Step Back?* London; Atlantic Highlands, New Jersey: Zed Books, 1987.

Murray, Rachel. *Human Rights in Africa: From the OAU to the African Union*. Cambridge: Cambridge University Press, 2004.

Museveni, Yoweri T. "Fanon's Theory on Violence: Its Verification in Liberated Mozambique." In *Essays on the Liberation of Southern Africa*, ed. Nathan M. Shamuyarira. Dar es Salaam: Tanzania Publishing House, 1971. 1–24.

Mutua, Makau. *Human Rights: A Political and Cultural Critique*. Philadelphia: University of Pennsylvania Press, 2002.

Naas, Charles. "Further Comments on Iran." In *The Diplomacy of Human Rights*, ed. David D. Newsom. Lanham, Md.: University Press of America; Institute for the Study of Diplomacy, 1986. 81–83.

Naipaul, V. S. *Beyond Belief: Islamic Excursions Among the Converted Peoples.* New York: Random House, 1998.

Naraghi, Ehsan. *From Palace to Prison: Inside the Iranian Revolution.* London: I.B. Tauris, 1994.

Nashat, Guity. "Women in Pre-Revolutionary Iran: An Historical Overview." In *Women and Revolution in Iran*, ed. Guity Nashat. Boulder, Colo.: Westview Press, 1983. 5–35.

Nasser, Gamal Abdel. *Speeches and Press-Interviews.* Cairo, c. 1959.

———. Egypt's Liberation: The Philosophy of the Revolution. Washington, D.C.: Public Affairs Press, 1955.

Nasution, Adnan Buyung. *The Aspiration for Constitutional Government in Indonesia: A Socio-Legal Study of the Indonesian Konstituante 1956–1959.* Jakarta: Pustaka Sinar Harapan, 1992.

———. "Human Rights and the Konstituante Debates of 1956–59." In *Democracy in Indonesia: 1950s and 1990s*, ed. David Bourchier and John Legge. Clayton: Monash University, Centre for Southeast Asian Studies, 1994. 43–49.

Nehru, Jawaharlal. *Selected Works of Jawaharlal Nehru.* New Delhi: Jawaharlal Nehru Memorial Fund, distributed by Oxford University Press, 1984.

Newell, Richard S. *The Politics of Afghanistan.* Ithaca, N.Y.: Cornell University Press, 1972.

Normand, Roger, and Sarah Zaidi. *Human Rights at the UN: The Political History of Universal Justice.* Bloomington: University of Indiana Press, 2008.

Norris, William. "Officers Seize Power in Dahomey." *The Times*, 18 December 1967.

Nu, U. *U Nu, Saturday's Son.* New Haven, Conn.: Yale University Press, 1975.

Nwankwo, Arthur Agwuncha, and Samuel Udochukwu Ifejika. *The Making of a Nation: Biafra.* London: C. Hurst, 1969.

Nworah, Dike. "Nationalism Versus Coexistence: Neo-African Attitudes Toward Classical Neutralism." *Journal of Modern African Studies* 15, no. 2 (1977): 213–37.

Nyangoni, Wellington Winter. *Africa in the United Nations System.* East Brunswick, N.J.: Fairleigh Dickinson University Press; Associated University Presses, 1985.

Nyerere, Julius K. *Freedom and Socialism, Uhuru Na Ujamaa: A Selection from Writings and Speeches, 1965–1967.* Dar es Salaam: Oxford University Press, 1968.

O'Ballance, Edgar. *The Kurdish Struggle, 1920–1994.* Basingstoke: Macmillan, 1996.

O'Brien, Conor Cruise. *To Katanga and Back: A U.N. Case History.* London: Hutchinson, 1962.

"Officers in Mali Claim Seizure of Power." *The Times*, 20 November 1968, 5.

Ogbondah, Chris. *Military Regimes and the Press in Nigeria, 1966–1993: Human Rights and National Development.* Lanham, Md.: University Press of America, 1994.

Ojo, Olusola, Sesay, Amadu. "The O.A.U. and Human Rights: Prospects for the 1980s and Beyond." *Human Rights Quarterly* 8, no. 1 (1986): 89–103.

Okoli, Ekwueme. "Toward a Human Rights Framework in Nigeria." In *Toward a Human Rights Framework*, ed. Peter Schwab and Adamantia Pollis. New York: Praeger, 1982. 203–22.

Oladimeji, Aborisade, and Robert Mundt. *Politics in Nigeria.* New York: Longman, 1998.

Omara-Otunnu, Amii. *Politics and the Military in Uganda, 1890–1985.* Basingstoke: Macmillan, 1987.

Orizio, Riccardo. *Talk of the Devil.* London: Secker & Warburg, 2003.

Pahlavi, Ashraf. *Faces in a Mirror: Memoirs from Exile.* Englewood Cliffs, N.J.: Prentice-Hall, 1980.

———. "A Talk with Princess Ashraf of Iran." *UNESCO Courier* 21 1968 (April): 23–25.

Pahlavi, Farah. *An Enduring Love.* New York: Miramax, 2004.

Pahlavi, Mohammed Reza. *Mission for My Country.* London: Hutchinson, 1961.

———. *The White Revolution.* Tehran: Kayhan Press, 1964.

Paidar, Parvin. *Women and the Political Process in Twentieth-Century Iran.* Cambridge: Cambridge University Press, 1995.

Panikkar, Kavalam Madhava. *The Afro-Asian States and Their Problems.* London: Allen & Unwin, 1959.

Parker, Jason. "Cold War II: The Eisenhower Administration, the Bandung Conference, and the Reperiodization of the Postwar Era." *Diplomatic History* 30, no. 5 (2006): 867–92.

Patel, Rashida. *Socio-Economic Political Status and Women and Law in Pakistan.* Karachi: Faiza Publishers, 1991.

Pei, Minxin. "The Fall and Rise of Democracy in East Asia." In *Democracy in East Asia,* ed. Larry Jay Diamond and Marc F. Plattner. Baltimore: Johns Hopkins University Press, 1998. 57–78.

Pellet, Alain. "Individual Rights, Minority Rights, and Group Rights." In *The Dumbarton Oaks Conversations and the United Nations, 1944–1994,* ed. Angeliki E. Laiou and Ernest R. May. Washington, D.C.: Dumbarton Oaks Research Library and Collection; Distributed by Harvard University Press, 1998. 105–9.

Perry, Michael J. "Are Human Rights Universal? The Relativist Challenge and Related Matters." *Human Rights Quarterly* 19, no. 3 (1997): 461–509.

Plummer, Brenda Gayle. *Rising Wind: Black Americans and U.S. Foreign Affairs, 1935–1960.* Chapel Hill: University of North Carolina Press, 1996.

Pollis, Adamantia. "Cultural Relativism Revisited: Through a State Prism." *Human Rights Quarterly* 18, no. 2 (1996): 316–44.

———. "Liberal, Socialist, and Third World Perspectives of Human Rights." In *Toward a Human Rights Framework,* ed. Peter Schwab and Adamantia Pollis. New York: Praeger, 1982. 1–26.

———. "Towards a New Universalism; Reconstruction and Dialogue." *Netherlands Quarterly of Human Rights* 16, no. 1 (1998): 5–23.

Pollis, Adamantia, and Peter Schwab. *Human Rights: Cultural and Ideological Perspectives.* New York: Praeger, 1979.

———. *Human Rights: Cultural and Ideological Perspectives.* New York: Praeger, 1979.

———. "Human Rights: A Western Construct with Limited Applicability." In *Human Rights: Cultural and Ideological Perspectives,* ed. Adamantia Pollis and Peter Schwab. New York: Praeger, 1979. 1–18.

Pomerance, Michla. *Self-Determination in Law and Practice: The New Doctrine in the United Nations.* The Hague: Nijhoff, 1982.

Preis, Ann-Belinda S. "Human Rights as Cultural Practice: An Anthropological Critique." *Human Rights Quarterly* 18, no. 2 (1996): 286–315.

Pruden, Caroline. "Responding to the Underdeveloped World. Human Rights,

Multilateral Aid, and Racial Equality." In *Conditional Partners: Eisenhower, the United Nations, and the Search for a Permanent Peace*, ed. Caroline Pruden. Baton Rouge: Louisiana State University Press, 1998. 198–223.

———. "Walking the Tightrope. The Dilemma of Decolonisation." In *Conditional Partners: Eisenhower, the United Nations, and the Search for a Permanent Peace*, ed. Caroline Pruden. Baton Rouge: Louisiana State University Press, 1998. 173–97.

Quentin-Baxter, Robert Q. "International Protection of Human Rights." In *Essays on Human Rights*, ed. Kenneth James Keith,. Wellington: Sweet & Maxwell, 1968. 132–45.

———. "The United Nations Human Rights Commission and the Search of Measures of Implementation." *Victoria University of Wellington Law Review* 30 (1999): 567–76.

Radji, Parviz C. *In the Service of the Peacock Throne: The Diaries of the Shah's Last Ambassador to London*. London: H. Hamilton, 1983.

Raič, David. "The Emergence and Development of the Principle of Self-Determination: From the American and French Revolutions to the Era of Decolonisation." In *Statehood and the Law of Self-Determination*, ed. David Raič. The Hague: Kluwer Law International, 2002. 171–225.

———. "The Post-Colonial Era: Internal and External Self-Determination." In *Statehood and the Law of Self-Determination*, ed. David Raič. The Hague: Kluwer Law International, 2002. 226–307.

Ramcharan, B. G. "Implementing the International Covenants on Human Rights." In *Human Rights: Thirty Years After the Universal Declaration: Commemorative Volume on the Occasion of the Thirtieth Anniversary of the Universal Declaration of Human Rights*, ed. B. G. Ramcharan. The Hague: Nijhoff, 1979. 159–95.

Rasanayagam, Angelo. *Afghanistan: A Modern History: Monarchy, Despotism or Democracy?: The Problems of Governance in the Muslim Tradition*. London: I.B. Tauris, 2003.

Rassam, Amal. "Revolution within the Revolution? Women and the State in Iraq." In *Iraq, the Contemporary State*, ed. Tim Niblock. New York: St. Martin's, 1982. 88–99.

Reanda, Laura. "Human Rights and Women's Rights: The United Nations Approach." *Human Rights Quarterly* 3, no. 2 (1981): 11–31.

Rehman, Javaid. "Minority Rights and the Constitutional Dilemmas of Pakistan." *Netherlands Quarterly of Human Rights* 19, no. 4 (2001): 417–43.

Rejali, Darius M. *Torture & Modernity: Self, Society, and State in Modern Iran*. Institutional Structures of Feeling. Boulder, Colo.: Westview Press, 1994.

Renteln, Alison Dundes. "Relativism and the Search of Human Rights." *American Anthropologist* 90, no. 1 (1988): 56–72.

———. "The Unanswered Challenge of Relativism and the Consequences for Human Rights." *Human Rights Quarterly* 7, no. 4 (1985): 514–40.

Robertson, Geoffrey. *Crimes Against Humanity: The Struggle for Global Justice*. London: Allen Lane, 1999.

Romulo, Carlos Peña. *I Walked with Heroes*. New York: Holt, Rinehart and Winston, 1963.

———. *The Meaning of Bandung*. Chapel Hill: University of North Carolina Press, 1956.

Rosas, Allan. "Internal Self-Determination." In *Modern Law of Self-Determination*, ed. Christian Tomuschat. Dordrecht: Nijhoff, 1993. 225–52.

Rosenberg, David A. *Marcos and Martial Law in the Philippines.* Ithaca, N.Y.: Cornell University Press, 1979.

Rosenstock, Robert. "The Declaration of Principles of International Law Concerning Friendly Relations: A Survey." *American Journal of International Law* 65, no. 4 (1971): 713–15.

Rowe, Edward T. "The United States, the United Nations, and the Cold War." *International Organization* 25, no. 1 (1971): 59–78.

Sadjadi, Shahnaz, and Marianne Hedin-Pourghasemi. "Law and the Status of Women in Iran." *Columbia Human Rights Law Review* 8 (1976–1977): 141–64.

Said, Abdul Aziz. "Human Rights in Islamic Perspective." In *Human Rights: Cultural and Ideological Perspectives*, ed. Adamantia Pollis and Peter Schwab. New York: Praeger, 1979. 86–100.

Salmon, Jean. "Internal Aspects of the Right to Self-Determination: Towards a Democratic Legitimacy Principle?" In *Modern Law of Self-Determination*, ed. Christian Tomuschat. Boston: Nijhoff, 1993. 253–82.

Sami, Aziza. "Hot Line to Washington: Interview with Aziza Hussein on the 50th Anniversary of the July Revolution." *Al-Ahram Weekly*, 13 June 2002. http://weekly.ahram.org.eg/ 2002/590/special.htm, accessed 20 December 2005.

Sastroamidjojo, Ali, and C. L. M. Penders. *Milestones on My Journey: The Memoirs of Ali Sastroamijoyo, Indonesian Patriot and Political Leader.* St. Lucia: University of Queensland Press, 1979.

Saxon, Wolfgang. "Jamil M. Baroody, Saudi Arabia's U.N. Delegate, Dies." *New York Times*, 5 March 1979, A11.

Sullivan, Patricia. "Fereydoun Hoveyda; Iranian Delegate to United Nations During Shah's Rule." *New York Times*, 8 November 2006, 5.

Schwab, Peter. *Africa: A Continent Self-Destructs.* New York: Palgrave, 2001.

———. "The Response of the Left to Violence and Human Rights 'Abuses' in the Ethiopian Revolution." In *Toward a Human Rights Framework*, ed. Peter Schwab and Adamantia Pollis. New York: Praeger, 1982. 189–201.

Schwab, Peter, and Adamantia Pollis. *Toward a Human Rights Framework.* New York: Praeger, 1982.

Schwelb, Egon. "Civil and Political Rights: The International Measures of Implementation." *American Journal of International Law* 62, no. 4 (1968): 827–68.

———. "The International Convention on the Elimination of All Forms of Racial Discrimination." *International and Comparative Law Quarterly* 15, no. 4 (1966): 966–1068.

———. "International Conventions on Human Rights." *International and Comparative Law Quarterly* 9, no. 4 (1960): 654–75.

Searle, Patrick. "L'affaire Nasser (Review)." *International Affairs* 39, no. 1 (1963): 124–25.

Seebohm, Caroline. *No Regrets: The Life of Marietta Tree.* New York: Simon & Schuster, 1997.

Senghor, Léopold Sedar. *On African Socialism.* London: Pall Mall, 1964.

"The Shah Annuls Iran Elections." *The Times*, 2 September 1960, 8.

Shawcross, William. *The Shah's Last Ride: The Story of the Exile, Misadventures and Death of the Emperor.* London: Chatto & Windus, 1989.

———. *Deliver Us from Evil: Peacekeepers, Warlords, and a World of Endless Conflict.* New York: Simon & Schuster, 2000.

Shepherd, George W., Eileen McCarthy-Arnolds, David Penna, and Debra Joy

Cruz Sobrepeña. *Africa, Human Rights, and the Global System: The Political Economy of Human Rights in a Changing World.* Westport, Conn.: Greenwood Press, 1994.

Shestack, Jerome J. "The Philosophic Foundations of Human Rights." *Human Rights Quarterly* 20, no. 2 (1998): 201–34.

Shivji, Issa G. *The Concept of Human Rights in Africa.* London: Codesria Book Series, 1989.

Shue, Henry. *Basic Rights: Subsistence, Affluence, and U.S. Foreign Policy.* 2nd ed. Princeton, N.J.: Princeton University Press, 1996.

Simmonds, E. H. S. "The Evolution of Foreign Policy in Laos Since Independence." *Modern Asian Studies* 2, no. 1 (1968): 1–30.

Simpson, A. W. B. *Human Rights and the End of Empire: Britain and the Genesis of the European Convention.* Oxford: Oxford University Press, 2001.

Simpson, Bradley. *Economists with Guns: Authoritarian Development and U.S.-Indonesian Relations, 1960–1968.* Stanford, Calif.: Stanford University Press, 2008.

Sindi, Abudullah M. "King Faisal and Pan-Islamism." In *King Faisal and the Modernisation of Saudi Arabia*, ed. Willard A. Beling. London: Croom Helm, 1980.

"Sinyavsky's Defence Speech Quoted by Newspaper." *The Times*, 25 February 1966, 10.

Slyomovics, Susan. *The Performance of Human Rights in Morocco.* Philadelphia: University of Pennsylvania Press, 2005.

Smith, George Ivan. *Ghosts of Kampala.* London: Weidenfeld & Nicolson, 1980.

Smith, J. Clay. *Rebels in Law: Voices in History of Black Women Lawyers.* Ann Arbor: University of Michigan Press, 2000.

Smith, William E. "A Reporter at Large: Transition." *New Yorker*, 3 March 1986, 72–83.

Sohn, Louis B. "The Improvement of the UN Machinery on Human Rights." *International Studies Quarterly* 23, no. 2 (1979): 186–215.

———. "The New International Law: Protection of the Rights of Individuals Rather Than States." *American University Law Review* 32 (1982): 1–64.

———. *Rights in Conflict: The United Nations & South Africa.* Irvington, N.Y.: Transnational Publishers, 1994.

Soyinka, Wole. *The Open Sore of a Continent: A Personal Narrative of the Nigerian Crisis.* New York: Oxford University Press, 1996.

Spiro, Melford E. "Cultural Relativism and the Future of Anthropology." *Cultural Anthropology* 1, no. 3 (1986): 259–86.

Ssekandi, Francis M, and Cos Gitta. "Protection of Fundamental Rights in the Uganda Constitution." *Columbia Human Rights Law Review* 26 (1994–1995): 191–213.

Stamatopoulou, Elsa. "The Development of United Nations Mechanisms for the Protection and Promotion of Human Rights." *Washington and Lee Law Review* 55 (1998): 687–96.

Steiner, Henry J., and Philip Alston. *International Human Rights in Context: Law, Politics, Morals.* 2nd ed. Oxford: Oxford University Press, 2000.

———. *International Human Rights in Context: Law, Politics, Morals: Text and Materials.* Oxford: Oxford University Press, 1996.

Steward, Julian H. "Comments on the Statement on Human Rights." *American Anthropologist* 50, no. 2 (1948): 351–52.

Sukarno, Ahmed. *Marhaen and Proletarian: Speech Before the Indonesian Nationalist*

Party at the Party's Thirtieth Anniversary at Bandung, July 3 1957. Foreword by George Kahin. Ithaca, N.Y.: Modern Indonesia Project, Cornell University, 1960.

———. *Sukarno: An Autobiography.* Hong Kong: Gunung Agung, 1965.

Sullivan, Earl L. *Women in Egyptian Public Life.* Contemporary Issues in the Middle East. Syracuse, N.Y.: Syracuse University Press, 1986.

Sullivan, Patricia. "Fereydoun Hoveyda; Iranian Delegate to United Nations During Shah's Rule." *New York Times,* 8 November 2006, 5.

Sullivan, William H. "Some Comments from the Ambassador's Perspective." In *The Diplomacy of Human Rights,* ed. David D. Newsom. Lanham, Md.: University Press of America; Institute for the Study of Diplomacy, 1986.

Sundiata, Ibrahim K. "The Roots of African Despotism: The Question of Political Culture." In *African Nationalism and Independence,* ed. Timothy K. Welliver. New York: Garland, 1993. 35–57.

Suter, Keith D. *An International Law of Guerilla Warfare: The Global Politics of Law-Making.* Global Politics. London: F. Pinter, 1984.

Takeyh, Ray, and Nikolas K. Gvosdev. "Egypt: The Struggle for a Nation's Soul." In *The Receding Shadow of the Prophet: The Rise and Fall of Radical Political Islam,* ed. Ray Takeyh and Nikolas K Gvosdev. Westport, Conn.: Praeger, 2004.

Tanner, Henry. "In a Front-Line Village in Lebanon, Only the Baroody Family Stays on under Shell Bursts and Gunfire." *New York Times,* 3 October 1976, A11.

Tardu, M. E. "United Nations Response to Gross Violations of Human Rights: The 1503 Procedure." *Santa Clara Law Review* 20 (1980): 559–601.

Tardu, M. E., and Thomas E. McCarthy. *Human Rights: The International Petition System.* Dobbs Ferry, N.Y.: Oceana, 1980.

Tarling, Nicholas. "'Ah-Ah': Britain and the Bandung Conference of 1955." *Journal of Southeast Asian Studies* 23, no. 1 (1992): 74–111.

Taylor, Robert H., ed. *The Idea of Freedom in Asia and Africa,* The Making of Modern Freedom. Stanford, Calif.: Stanford University Press, 2002.

———. "Reverberations of Freedom in the Philippines and Vietnam." In *The Idea of Freedom in Asia and Africa,* ed. Robert H. Taylor. Stanford, Calif.: Stanford University Press, 2002. 143–213.

Teltsch, Kathleen. "Assembly Head Deplores Action." *New York Times,* 12 November 1975, A16.

———. "Private Appeals to the UN Barred: In Human Rights Commission, US, Britain, China, Soviet Block Small Nations' Move." *New York Times,* 9 June 1949, A8.

———. "U.N. Diplomats Asking Special Status on 'Gas'." *New York Times,* 25 February 1974, A14.

———. "U.N. Unit Said to Report Greeks Violate Human Rights." *New York Times,* 21 September 1972, A18.

Thapa, Deepak. "Nepal's Scholar-Statesman: Rishikesh Shaha (1925–2002)." *Himal South Asian,* January 2003.

Thompson, Bankole. *The Constitutional History and Law of Sierra Leone (1961–1995).* Lanham, Md.: University Press of America, 1997.

Thornberry, Patrick. "The Democratic or Internal Aspect of Self-Determination with Some Remarks on Federalism." In *Modern Law of Self-Determination,* ed. Christian Tomuschat. Dordrecht: Nijhoff, 1993. 101–38.

Tilley, John J. "Cultural Relativism." *Human Rights Quarterly* 22 (2000): 501–47.

Tinker, Catherine. "Human Rights for Women: The UN Convention on the

Elimination of All Forms of Discrimination against Women." *Human Rights Quarterly* 3, no. 2 (1981): 32–43.

Tolley, Howard. "The Concealed Crack in the Citadel: The United Nations Commission on Human Rights' Response to Confidential Communications." *Human Rights Quarterly* 6, no. 4 (1984): 420–62.

———. *The UN Commission on Human Rights*. Boulder, Colo.: Westview Press, 1987.

Tripp, Charles. *A History of Iraq*. Cambridge: Cambridge University Press, 2000.

Turits, Richard Lee. *Foundations of Despotism: Peasants, the Trujillo Regime, and Modernity in Dominican History*. Stanford, Calif.: Stanford University Press, 2003.

Umozurike, U. O. "The African Charter on Human and Peoples' Rights." *American Journal of International Law* 77, no. 4 (1983): 902–12.

———. *The African Charter on Human and Peoples' Rights*. The Hague: Nijhoff, 1997.

———. "The Domestic Jurisdiction Clause in the OAU Charter." *African Affairs* 78, no. 311 (1979): 197–209.

UNESCO. *Human Rights, Comments and Interpretations: A Symposium*. London: Allan Wingate, 1949.

United Nations. *The United Nations and Apartheid, 1948–1994*. New York: United Nations Department of Public Information, 1994.

United Nations Commission on Human Rights. *These Rights and Freedoms*. New York: United Nations Department of Public Information, 1950.

U.S. Department of State, House Committee on Foreign Affairs, Senate Committee on Foreign Relations. *Country Reports on Human Rights Practices, 1979*. Washington, D.C.: U.S. Government Printing Office, 1980.

U.S. Department of State and Department of State Historical Office. *Foreign Relations of the United States* (1951); vol. 2, *The United Nations: The Western Hemisphere* (1952–1954); vol. 7, *United Nations Affairs* (1958–1960). Washington, D.C.: U.S. Government Printing Office.

"Upper Volta Head in Full Control." *The Times*, 6 January 1966, 11.

Van Boven, Theo. "Chartering New Ground in Human Rights (1968)." In *Human Rights from Exclusion to Inclusion, Principles and Practice: An Anthology from the Work of Theo Van Boven*, ed. Fons Coomans, Cees Flinterman, Grunfeld Fred, Ingrid Westendorp, and Jan Willems. The Hague: Kluwer Law International, 2000. 3–16.

———. *People Matter: Views on International Human Rights Policy*. Amsterdam: Meulenhoff, 1982.

———. "United Nations Policies and Strategies: Global Perspectives?" In *Human Rights: Thirty Years After the Universal Declaration: Commemorative Volume on the Occasion of the Thirtieth Anniversary of the Universal Declaration of Human Rights*, ed. B. G. Ramcharan. The Hague: Nijhoff, 1979. 83–92.

Vidal-Naquet, Pierre. *Torture, Cancer of Democracy: France and Algeria, 1954–62*. Harmondsworth: Penguin, 1963.

Vincent, R. J. *Human Rights and International Relations*. Cambridge: Cambridge University Press, 1986.

———. "Human Rights in North-South Relations." In *Human Rights and International Relations*, ed. R. J. Vincent. Cambridge: Cambridge University Press, 1986. 76–91.

Von Eschen, Penny M. *Race Against Empire: Black Americans and Anticolonialism, 1937–1957*. Ithaca, N.Y.: Cornell University Press, 1997.

Wah Foon, Ho. "Mahathir Defiant Despite Criticism." *Straits Times*, 31 July 1997, 21.

Wai, Dunstan M. "Human Rights in Sub-Saharan Africa." In *Human Rights: Cultural and Ideological Perspectives*, ed. Adamantia Pollis and Peter Schwab. New York: Praeger, 1979. 115–44.

Wallerstein, Immanuel. *Africa: The Politics of Independence: An Interpretation of Modern African History*. New York: Random House, 1971.

——— *Africa: The Politics of Unity: An Analysis of a Contemporary Social Movement*. New York: Random House, 1967.

———. *European Universalism: The Rhetoric of Power*. New York: New Press, 2006.

———. "The Transformation of the Women's Movement in Pakistan." In *Contemporary Problems of Pakistan*, ed. J. Henry Korson. Lahore: Westview Press, 1993. 93–106.

Waltz, Susan Eileen. *Human Rights and Reform: Changing the Face of North African Politics*. Berkeley: University of California Press, 1995.

———. "Reclaiming and Rebuilding the History of the Universal Declaration of Human Rights." *Third World Quarterly* 23, no. 3 (2002): 437–48.

———. "Universal Human Rights: The Contribution of Muslim States." *Human Rights Quarterly* 26, no. 4 (2004): 799–844.

———. "Universalizing Human Rights: The Role of Small States in the Construction of the Universal Declaration of Human Rights." *Human Rights Quarterly* 23, no. 1 (2001): 44–72.

Washburn, Wilcomb E. "Cultural Relativism, Human Rights, and the AAA." *American Anthropologist* 89, no. 4 (1987): 939–43.

Waters, Christopher. "After Decolonisation: Australia and the Emergence of the Non-Aligned Movement in Asia, 1954–55." *Diplomacy & Statecraft* 12, no. 2 (2001): 153–74.

Weinstein, Warren. "Africa's Approach to Human Rights at the United Nations." *Issue: A Journal of Opinion* 6, no. 4 (1976): 14–21.

Weiss, Anita M. *Islamic Reassertion in Pakistan: The Application of Islamic Laws in a Modern State*. Contemporary Issues in the Middle East. Syracuse, N.Y.: Syracuse University Press, 1986.

———. "The Transformation of the Women's Movement in Pakistan." In *Contemporary Problems of Pakistan*, ed. J. Henry Korson. Boulder, Colo.: Westview Press, 1993. 93–106.

Weiss, Thomas George. *UN Voices: The Struggle for Development and Social Justice*, United Nations Intellectual History Project. Bloomington: Indiana University Press, 2005.

Welch, Claude E. "The African Commission on Human and Peoples' Rights: A Five-Year Report and Assessment." *Human Rights Quarterly* 14, no. 1 (1992): 43–61.

———. "Human Rights and African Women: A Comparison of Protection Under Two Major Treaties." *Human Rights Quarterly* 15, no. 3 (1993): 549–74.

———. "The O.A.U. and Human Rights: Towards a New Definition." *Journal of Modern African Studies* 19, no. 3 (1981): 401–20.

———. "The Organisation of African Unity and the Promotion of Human Rights." *Journal of Modern African Studies* 29, no. 4 (1991): 535–55.

Welch, Claude E., and Ronald I. Meltzer. *Human Rights and Development in Africa*. Albany: State University of New York Press, 1984.

Wiarda, Howard J., and Michael J. Kryzanek. *The Dominican Republic, a Caribbean*

Crucible. Nations of Contemporary Latin America. Boulder, Colo.: Westview Press, 1982.

Wilkins, Roy, and Tom Mathews. *Standing Fast: The Autobiography of Roy Wilkins.* New York: Da Capo Press, 1994.

Willetts, Peter. *The Non-Aligned Movement: The Origins of a Third World Alliance.* New York: F. Pinter, 1978.

Wilson, Dick. *Zhou: The Story of Zhou Enlai, 1898–1976.* London: Hutchinson, 1984.

Wilson, Richard. *Human Rights, Culture and Context: Anthropological Perspectives.* Anthropology, Culture and Society. London: Pluto Press, 1997.

Wiseberg, Laurie S. "Human Rights in Africa: Toward a Definition of the Problem of a Double Standard." *Issues: A Journal of Opinion* 10, no. 1–2 (1980): 66–76.

"World-Wide Pattern of Soldiers Taking over Power." *The Times,* 25 February 1966, 10.

Wright, Richard. *The Colour Curtain: A Report on the Bandung Conference.* London: Dobson, 1956.

Wrong, Michela. *In the Footsteps of Mr. Kurtz: Living on the Brink of Disaster in Mobutu's Congo.* New York: HarperCollins, 2001.

Young, Crawford. "African States and the Search for Freedom." In *The Idea of Freedom in Asia and Africa,* ed. Robert H. Taylor. Stanford, Calif.: Stanford University Press, 2002. 9–39.

Yusuf, Hamid. *Pakistan in Search of Democracy, 1947–77.* Lahore: Afrasia Publications, 1980.

Zonis, Marvin. *Majestic Failure: The Fall of the Shah.* Chicago: University of Chicago Press, 1991.

Zook, Darren C. "Decolonizing Law: Identity Politics, Human Rights, and the United Nations." *Harvard Human Rights Journal* 19 (2006).

Zhou Enlai. *China and the Asian-African Conference.* Peking: Foreign Languages Press, 1955.

Zia-ul-Haq, Mohammad. Introduction of Islamic Laws: Address to the Nation. Islamabad: Ministry of Information and Broadcasting Directorate of Films and Publications, Government of Pakistan, 1979.

———. President Addresses Non-Aligned Summit: Address . . . to the Sixth Summit Conference of the Non-Aligned Countries, Havana, 6 September 1979. Islamabad: Ministry of Information and Broadcasting, 1979.

———. President Addresses Shariah Seminar: Inaugural Address . . . At the International Seminar on Application of Shariah, Islamabad, October 9, 1979. Islamabad: Ministry of Information and Broadcasting, 1979.

———. President Ends Political Uncertainty: Address to the Nation: Rawalpindi, October 16, 1979. Islamabad: Directorate of Films and Publications Ministry of Information and Broadcasting, 1979.

———. The President on Pakistan's Ideological Basis: Address At the Inauguration of Shariat Faculty of the Quaid-I-Azam University, Islamabad, October 8, 1979. Islamabad: Ministry of Information and Broadcasting, 1979.

———. President Reviews National Issues: Address to the Nation: August 30, 1979. Islamabad: Ministry of Information and Broadcasting, 1979.

Zuijdwijk, T. J. M. *Petitioning the United Nations: A Study in Human Rights.* New York: St. Martin's, 1982.

Index

Acknowledgments

I would like to thank Dr. Robert Horvath (La Trobe University) and Associate Professor David Philips (University of Melbourne), for guiding my work on this topic since it commenced in March 2003. The training and experience they generously provided was pivotal to the completion of this project. Sadly, David passed away before the work was finished.

The patience and care of the staff at the University of Pennsylvania Press was central to the evolution and production of this book, and in particular, the faith of Peter Agree.

I am also most grateful for the commentary and careful examination of various iterations of this work from Professor Glenda Sluga (University of Sydney), Professor A. W. Brian Simpson (University of Michigan), Professor Susan Waltz (University of Michigan), and Professor Reza Afshari (Pace University). In future, I hope to pursue their many excellent suggestions more fully in a new project. In addition to the invariably helpful and generous advice from these scholars, I was also assisted by extensive comments from Professor Michla Pomerance (The Hebrew University of Jerusalem), on the question of self-determination, explored most fully in Chapter 2.

Several former members of the UN human rights program lent their experience and insight to my research, offering indispensable personal reflections on the events discussed, and well-timed encouragement. Theo Van Boven, former director of the UN Human Rights Division, Ambassador John Carey, U.S. representative to both the Commission on Human Rights and the Sub-Commission on the Prevention of Discrimination, and Fereydoun Hoveyda, Iranian ambassador to the General Assembly and a pupil of René Cassin, greatly enhanced my understanding of the politics of the UN in the late 1960s and 1970s, with knowledge that the documentary record failed to capture.

A number of other academic experts assisted me developing the topic into a sustained study, suggesting many useful areas of research and intellectual inquiry, chief among them were Professor Roger Clark (Rutgers University), Professor Antonia Finnane (University of Melbourne), Dr.

Christopher Waters (Deakin University), Dr. Richard Pennell (University of Melbourne), Professor Richard Wilson (Director of the Human Rights Institute, University of Connecticut), Professor Penelope Andrews (CUNY), Neici Zeller (University of Illinois, Chicago), Associate Professor Silvio Torres-Saillant (Syracuse University), Professor Peter Sluglett (University of Utah), Dr. Charles Tripp (University of London), Dr. Tareq Ismael (University of Calgary), and Professor Amal Rassam (CUNY).

Many of the archival materials on which this study depends were much more readily accessed due to the courteous and professional service of the staff at the National Archives and Records Administration (College Park), the National Archives of Australia (Canberra), the United Nations Archive (New York), and the Library of Congress (Washington DC). Dr. Habib Malik kindly assisted me in locating the Personal Papers of Charles Malik.

I am most grateful to the Norman Macgeorge Bequest, which funded my research trip to the United Nations Archives, and to the University of Melbourne Scholarships Office, which provided financial assistance for my work at the US National Archives and the Library of Congress. During my time at the UN, Monika Tvkacova (United Nations Archives), and Benjamin Playle (Australian Mission to the United Nations) were most helpful in obtaining UN records and other archival materials.

Immense practical assistance was provided by the staff of the School of Historical Studies, and the Library Services of the University of Melbourne. The work of Erica Mehrtens, Jo Helsby, Ron Baird, Ashleigh Rees, and Talith Jennison made the everyday aspects of the research and writing much more manageable.

Finally, the completion of this manuscript would have been impossible without the support and encouragement of my family, Andy, Steve, and Isabelle, and the counsel and friendship of colleagues at the University of Melbourne, Dr. Timothy Jones, Dr. Barbara Keys, Dr. Sean Scalmer, Dr. Bryony Coleman, Professor Vera Mackie, Dr. Kate McGregor, Dr. Noah Riseman, and Dr. Charles Coppel. I would also like to thank my good friends, Kirk Docker, Angie Hesson, Elise Aplin, Alison Smith, Tony Brain, and Nicholas Luxton for their great enthusiasm, advice, and practical help.

An earlier version of Chapter 1 appeared in Roland Burke, "The Compelling Dialogue of Freedom: Human Rights at the Bandung Conference," *Human Rights Quarterly* 28, no. 4 (2006): 947-965, © 2006 The Johns Hopkins University Press. Reprinted with permission of Johns Hopkins University Press.

CPSIA information can be obtained at www.ICGtesting.com
Printed in the USA
BVOW080432040213

312240BV00002B/4/P